ANGLO-AMERICAN CORPORATE TAXATION

The UK and the USA have historically represented opposite ends of the spectrum in their approaches to taxing corporate income. Under the British approach, corporate and shareholder income taxes have been integrated under an imputation system, with tax paid at the corporate level imputed to shareholders through a full or partial credit against dividends received. Under the American approach, by contrast, corporate and shareholder income taxes have remained separate under what is called a 'classical' system in which shareholders receive little or no relief from a second layer of taxes on dividends.

Steven A. Bank explores the evolution of the corporate income tax systems in each country during the nineteenth and twentieth centuries to understand the common legal, economic, political, and cultural forces that produced such divergent approaches and explains why convergence may be likely in the future as each country grapples with corporate taxation in an era of globalization.

STEVEN A. BANK is a professor of law at the University of California, Los Angeles School of Law, where he uses history and finance to explore the taxation of business entities in the United States and other countries.

CAMBRIDGE TAX LAW SERIES

Tax law is a growing area of interest, as it is included as a subdivision in many areas of study and is a key consideration in business needs throughout the world. Books in the Cambridge Tax Law series expose and shed light on the theories underpinning taxation systems, so that the questions to be asked when addressing an issue become clear. Written by leading scholars and illustrated by case law and legislation, they form an important resource for information on tax law while avoiding the minutiae of day-to-day detail addressed by practitioner books.

The books will be of interest for those studying law, business, economics, accounting and finance courses in the UK, but also in mainland Europe, the USA, and ex-Commonwealth countries with a similar taxation system to the UK.

Series Editor

Professor John Tiley, *Queens' College, Director of the Centre for Tax Law.*

Well known internationally in both academic and practitioner circles, Professor Tiley brings to the series his wealth of experience in tax law study, practice and writing. He was made a CBE in 2003 for services to tax law.

ANGLO-AMERICAN CORPORATE TAXATION

Tracing the Common Roots of Divergent Approaches

STEVEN A. BANK

CAMBRIDGE UNIVERSITY PRESS

CAMBRIDGE UNIVERSITY PRESS
Cambridge, New York, Melbourne, Madrid, Cape Town,
Singapore, São Paulo, Delhi, Tokyo, Mexico City

Cambridge University Press
The Edinburgh Building, Cambridge CB2 8RU, UK

Published in the United States of America by Cambridge University Press, New York

www.cambridge.org
Information on this title: www.cambridge.org/9780521887762

First published 2011

Printed in the United Kingdom at the University Press, Cambridge

A catalog record for this publication is available from the British Library

Library of Congress Cataloging in Publication data
Bank, Steven A., 1969–
Anglo-American corporate taxation : tracing the common roots of divergent
approaches / Steven A. Bank.
p.   cm. – (Cambridge tax law series)
Includes index.
ISBN 978-0-521-88776-2
1. Corporations – Taxation – Law and legislation – Great Britain – History.
2. Income tax – Law and legislation – Great Britain – History.
3. Corporations – Taxation – Law and legislation – United States – History.
4. Income tax – Law and legislation – United States – History.
I. Title. II. Series.
KD5504.B36   2011
343.4105′267–dc23
2011019853

ISBN 978-0-521-88776-2 Hardback

CONTENTS

Introduction

Over the last century, countries have typically followed either the United States model or the United Kingdom model in taxing corporate income. In the USA, corporations are subject to tax as separate entities under what is called the classical system. Income is taxed first to the corporation when earned and a second time to the shareholders when distributed as a dividend. This double taxation was mitigated to some extent in the USA by a 2003 reduction in the rate applied to the shareholder-level tax on certain dividend payments, but it left the basic double tax system intact. The UK system of corporate taxation has traditionally stood in sharp contrast to the US approach by integrating the corporate income tax with the taxation of shareholders. Although this integration could be effected through a variety of means, including a corporate deduction for dividends paid or a shareholder exemption for dividends received, the UK has historically integrated the corporate and individual income taxes through an imputation approach in which shareholders are provided a credit designed to offset at least a portion of the tax paid on that income at the company level. The amount of that credit has declined in recent years, but the UK has retained at least a hybrid approach to corporate income taxation.

This sharp divide between the US and UK approaches has not always existed. When income taxation was employed during the nineteenth century, both countries taxed corporate income in a system that was integrated with the individual income tax. It was only around World War I that the nations began to diverge as the USA moved to a classical system while the UK retained a largely integrated approach. Moreover, there have been several instances during the last century when the countries moved closer together, including most notably during the last decade or so. This book seeks to explore the history of British and American corporate income taxation in search of the factors that may help explain why they diverged and converged over the years and what this portends for the future of corporate income taxation in the two countries and around the globe.

1

The United States and the United Kingdom have always provided a strong basis for comparative study in the legal context. This is primarily because the two countries share a background in the common law method of jurisprudence. Moreover, as a former British colony, the USA inherited or adopted many of the laws and legal practices of the United Kingdom. For example, in Maryland the English common law retained precedential value after America became independent.[1] Because of these similarities, comparing the development of the law in the two jurisdictions is often considered instructive for understanding the circumstances under which they have diverged in their approaches.

In the tax arena, the basis for comparison between the USA and the UK is not as obvious. On the one hand, since tax is primarily a legislative and administrative, rather than judicial, undertaking, the shared common law background is less relevant.[2] Moreover, because the UK first adopted an income tax in 1799, there was little colonial experience to draw upon in the construction of an income tax system.[3] On the other hand, each country at least experimented with an income tax during the nineteenth century and this became the centerpiece of each country's revenue systems during the twentieth century. Under Victor Thuronyi's modern classification of nations, the two countries would be considered members of distinct families of income tax laws and therefore appropriate objects of comparative study.[4] The USA and the UK also have industrialized economies and well-developed capital markets, with frequent market interaction between businesses in both jurisdictions that trace to the founding of America, suggesting that a comparison of business taxation employed by each nation is particularly appropriate. Finally, the fact that the countries began with similar systems of business

---

[1] See, e.g., *A Declaration of Rights, and Constitution and Form of Government agreed to by the Delegates of Maryland*, November 3, 1776 at III:

> 'That the inhabitants of Maryland are entitled to the common law of England, and the trial by jury, according to that law, and to the benefit of such of the English statutes as existed at the time of the first emigration, and which, by experience, have been found applicable to their local and other circumstances, and of such others as have been since made in England, or Great Britain, and have been introduced, used and practiced by the courts of law or equity ...'

[2] William B. Barker, "A Comparative Approach to Income Tax Law in the United Kingdom and the United States," *Catholic University Law Review* 46 (1997): 7, 8.

[3] Ibid.

[4] Victor Thuronyi, "Introduction," in *Tax Law Design and Drafting* (Victor Thuronyi, ed.) (Washington, DC: International Monetary Fund, 2000): xxiv.

taxation and then those systems diverged (and converged) over the years, suggests both an inter-jurisdictional and a historical comparison may yield distinctive insights.

Thus, while the typical colonial grounds for a comparative US–UK study are less relevant, tax is still well suited to comparative analysis. Indeed, the early drafters of US tax legislation frequently looked to the United Kingdom as a model or source of inspiration or contrast.[5] Similarly, post-World War II reformers in the UK have on several occasions looked to the operation of the US tax for guidance in modernizing the British version, most notably in 1965 when the UK adopted an American-style classical corporate income tax.

Despite the interconnectedness of the USA and the UK and the economic and business similarities, few scholars have examined the similarities and differences between the American and British income taxes in any systematic way. Edwin Seligman, one of the most prominent public finance economists of his day, compared income tax systems in a variety of countries, including the USA and the UK, in his seminal work *The Income Tax*.[6] This book, however, was originally published before the modern income tax was adopted in America and even the second edition in 1914 only covered the very first post-Sixteenth Amendment statute. Moreover, Seligman's work was more broadly focused and was not concerned with a direct comparison between the two countries, let alone a comparison of the treatment of corporate income in the USA and the UK.

Harrison Spaulding published one of the earliest comparative studies of the modern US and UK tax systems in 1927.[7] Spaulding, a Canadian lawyer who received a Ph.D. from the London School of Economics, described his study as "badly needed," noting that although each country principally relied on an income tax as its main source of revenue, their respective understandings of income and the administration of an income tax differed greatly.[8] From his 1920s-era perspective, one of the principal differences involved the pace of change in the two systems:

---

[5] See, e.g., André Bernard, *Income Tax in Great Britain, Including a Description of Other Inland Revenue Taxes*, prepared for the Joint Committee on Internal Revenue Taxation (Washington, DC, 1928); Roswell Magill, L.H. Parker, and Eldon P. King, *A Summary of the British Tax System – With Special Reference to its Administration*, prepared for the use of the Joint Committee on Internal Revenue Taxation (Washington, DC, 1934).

[6] Edwin R. A. Seligman, *The Income Tax: History, Theory and Practice of Income Taxation* (New York: Macmillan Company, 1911).

[7] Harrison B. Spaulding, *The Income Tax in Great Britain and the United States* (London: P. S. King & Son, Ltd., 1927).

[8] Ibid. at 5–6.

"If the British are slow to change the income tax, the Americans are sometimes apt to make important changes without sufficient deliberation."[9] While this may have paid insufficient deference to the dramatically shorter period of existence for the income tax in the United States and the upheaval occasioned by World War I – indeed, the British income tax might be similarly described from the perspective of the early nineteenth century right after the Napoleonic Wars – it did not miss the mark too greatly for the taxation of corporate income.

Spaulding briefly speculated on the possible explanations for why America took a different path in taxing corporate income, conceding that the reason for the divergence is "not entirely clear."[10] He identified at least three possible "contributing factors" that could account for the more entity-focused tax system in the USA. The first was a decidedly formal legal explanation. According to Spaulding, entity theory doctrine was "carried much farther than in Great Britain," leading Americans to "see a corporation as a thing different from other taxpaying persons, and . . . as a thing peculiarly suitable for specially heavy taxation."[11] The second was a reflection of the American experience with special corporate taxes on the state and local level, where corporations were subject to special franchise taxes, capital stock taxes, and other levies. Ostensibly, such taxes were the price businesses paid for the privilege of operating in the corporate form. Spaulding theorized that these taxes helped to familiarize the general public with the concept of entity-level taxation, even though the rationale for such taxation was different on the federal level.[12] Finally, the third explanation offered by Spaulding was that corporate shareholders in the USA were perceived to be wealthier and less deserving than those in British corporations. According to Spaulding, "[p]ersons living on small incomes derived from dividends are relatively fewer in the United States than in Great Britain, and, in any event, people in the United States who live on investment income without work are not regarded with much favour."[13] Based on the popular view that the corporate tax burden fell on shareholders, the public thus favored entity-level taxation in the USA as an indirect aid to progressivity.

One could quibble with each of Spaulding's explanations. For instance, the first two were over-generalized in their descriptions of the treatment of corporations in doctrine and theory. There were many examples of an aggregate approach to corporations and corporate taxation in the USA throughout the nineteenth and early twentieth

---

[9] Ibid. at 296.   [10] Ibid. at 94.   [11] Ibid. at 92.   [12] Ibid. at 92–93.   [13] Ibid. at 94.

centuries, both at the state level and at the federal level in the early income tax. The third of Spaulding's explanations may have been accurate as an historical statement about the wealth of corporate shareholders in the USA, but it was a reality that was quickly changing as stock ownership spread. Moreover, all of these explanations were made from the perspective of explaining the divergence in the USA and did little to help explain why the UK viewed the situation differently. Most importantly, though, is the fact that Spaulding's explanations were static. Intervening events belie some of these interpretations, including events that occurred in the few years before his account was published.

A few years after Spaulding's book appeared, Roswell Magill, an economics professor from Columbia who was then serving as special assistant to the Secretary of the Treasury, led the completion of a comparative study on the USA and the UK.[14] This study, which was prepared for the Joint Committee on Taxation, was initially designed to focus on the administration of the British tax. It soon broadened, though, to encompass all relevant points of comparison between the two systems. Despite frequently interspersing US comparisons with the description of the British system, there was little attempt to highlight the difference between the two countries' approaches with respect to taxing corporate income. The study did note, however, that the "British have encountered the same trouble from the avoidance of surtaxes by incorporation that we have encountered in the United States," on account of the fact that in the UK only the income tax was paid on the shareholder's behalf at the company level while the surtax was only paid when income was distributed.[15] So, in effect, this study was quicker to note the similarities between the two systems than to try to explain their differences, and in any case this was more an examination of the British system than a comparison of the two.

Perhaps the most serious attempts to compare the US and British approaches to corporate taxation came out during and immediately after World War II, when the USA and the UK were both in the midst of thinking about significant corporate tax reform.[16] In 1943, George May,

---

[14] Magill, Parker, and King, *A Summary of the British Tax System.* [15] Ibid. at 25.
[16] For a general discussion of this period of corporate tax reform in the USA, see Steven A. Bank, "The Rise and Fall of Post-World War II Corporate Tax Reform," *Journal of Law & Contemporary Problems* 73 (2010): 207. For an example of the comparative push occurring at the same time, see e.g., [unsigned] "Some Techniques of Taxation in the United Kingdom," *Yale Law Journal* 52 (1942–43): 400 ("Today, when the tax structure of the United States is in violent flux, the tax system employed in the United Kingdom offers a valuable source of information and experience.")

an accountant with Price Waterhouse, wrote a brief article for the *Harvard Business Review* comparing the US and British systems of taxing corporate income.[17] May attributed the difference in approaches primarily to the fact that the UK income tax preceded the development of the business corporation while the modern US income tax was enacted not only after the business corporation had begun to solidify its place in the economy, but during a period when corporations had "become important and were unfavorably regarded."[18] As a consequence, May maintained, "it is not surprising that our law fell into two sections: one levying taxes on individuals, and the other, levying taxes on corporations."[19]

This notion that corporate animus was responsible for the development of the classical corporate tax in the USA is plausible. Indeed, it has achieved some supporters in modern tax scholarship.[20] Nevertheless, it does not quite fit the story's chronology.[21] While it was certainly popular at the turn of the last century to advocate the regulation of business corporations, the original formation of what would be considered the classical corporate tax in the USA arguably occurred during World War I when the corporate and individual rates separated. This was at a time when Congress was trying to balance the staggering need for revenue with a desire to protect corporate retained earnings from the rise in individual surtax rates. Moreover, even if the US Congress was motivated by the dangers of corporate growth in pushing for a separate corporate tax, it is not clear that May's explanation holds for the UK as well. The business corporation may not have been prevalent at the turn of the nineteenth century in the UK, but the British decision to focus on the source of income rather than the identity of the recipient was likely

---

[17] George O. May, "Corporate Structures and Federal Income Taxation," *Harvard Business Review* 22 (1943): 10. Another article came out a few months earlier comparing British and American approaches to taxation, but it only devoted a few paragraphs to the comparison of corporate taxation as one of the examples it used to dispute the commonly held belief that the British paid more in taxes during the war than Americans: H. Arnold Strangman, "British and American Taxes," *Taxes* 21 (1943): 207, 208.

[18] May, ibid., at 11.   [19] Ibid.

[20] See, e.g., Reuven Avi-Yonah, "Corporations, Society, and the State: A Defense of the Corporate Tax," *Virginia Law Review* (2004): 1193; Marjorie E. Kornhauser, "Corporate Regulation and the Origins of the Corporate Income Tax," *Indiana Law Journal* (1990): 53, 136.

[21] See Steven A. Bank, "Entity Theory as Myth in the US Corporate Excise Tax of 1909," in *Studies in the History of Tax Law* 2 (John Tiley, ed.) (Oxford: Hart Publishing, 2007): 393.

fueled by the broader moves toward a scheduler system of taxation, which helped preserve individual privacy, and toward a withholding system, which allowed individual taxes to be collected by a third party, rather than by the absence of income-producing entities. In any event, May offered what was more of a brief hypothesis in search of validation than a true explanation.

In the UK, a decade after May's article, Geoffrey Hornsey, a lecturer in law at the University of Leeds, offered a similar comparison of the US and UK corporate tax systems, along with the French system.[22] This article offered little in the way of explanation for the differences among the three countries, other than to recount different legal decisions that affected the tax treatment of dividends and of the corporate entity itself. Hornsey conceded that "[i]t would be difficult, even if one felt tempted to try, to extract any broad principle from the necessarily abbreviated study of a topic which has so many facets," but concluded that "[t]he one striking fact which does emerge is the universality of the problems involved and the similarity of the solutions achieved."[23] Nevertheless, Hornsey provides some hint of the problem, and a possible means of reconciling the differences between the USA and the UK in their approaches to taxing the corporation, when he noted that it would be easier to advocate a uniform approach to corporate taxation "if only the relationships between companies and their shareholders were everywhere uniform."[24]

Since the early 1950s, there has been little attempt to explain the divergence of the American and British corporate tax systems. Peter Harris, an expert on taxation on the Cambridge Faculty of Law, has written two major works that consider the question of corporate taxation more closely, but neither focuses on the explanations for the differences in the US and UK approaches to corporate taxation. In his exhaustingly detailed study of corporate taxation,[25] Harris principally examined the different forms of corporate/shareholder imputation methods in use around the world. He briefly discussed the ways in which the US system departed from the British system in the early twentieth century, but this was more of a description than an explanation. According to Harris,

---

[22] Geoffrey Hornsey, "Corporate Taxation – A Comparative Study," *Modern Law Review* 16 (1953): 26.

[23] Ibid. at 33.   [24] Ibid. at 26.

[25] Peter A. Harris, *Corporate/Shareholder Income Taxation and Allocating Rights Between Countries* (Amsterdam: IBFD Publications, 1996).

"[a]lthough providing full dividend relief, the 1913 US income tax differed from that of the UK's in some important respects," noting that the British tax was refundable if the shareholder owed no tax while the USA only offered an exemption from further tax on the dividend.[26] Harris also considered the question of corporate taxation in his history of income taxation in common law jurisdictions.[27] One of his principal inquiries was "why are corporations treated as separate taxpayers from their shareholders?"[28] Given the focus on very early history, though, stopping in 1820, this had very little relevance for any modern comparison of corporate tax systems.

Several additional comparative tax history studies involving the United States have been undertaken in recent years,[29] but none has focused on comparing the US and the UK systems generally or on the taxation of corporate income in particular. Most recently, sociologists Kimberly Morgan and Monica Prasad compared the origins of the US and French tax systems, but they focused almost exclusively on the choice between income and consumption taxes and did not consider the structural differences in business taxation.[30] Similarly, Alexander Nützenadel and Christoph Strupp edited a volume that collected articles primarily on the history of taxation in Germany or the USA, but the emphasis was on tax and state-building rather than on the details of either system.[31] Political scientist Sven Steinmo compared the American, British, and Swedish tax systems in 1993, with the political and institutional bases for the level of progressivity in each system serving as his departure point.[32] Although he briefly discussed the taxation of

---

[26] Ibid. at 81–2.
[27] Peter Harris, *Income Tax in Common Law Jurisdictions: From the Origins to 1820* (Cambridge University Press, 2006).
[28] Ibid. at 5.
[29] The historical comparison of non-US tax systems has been more common. See, e.g., Richard Bonnedy, ed., *The Rise of the Fiscal State in Europe, c1200–1815* (Oxford University Press, 1999); Peter Mathias and Patrick K. O'Brien, "Taxation in Britain and France, 1715–1810: A Comparison of the Social and Economic Incidence of Taxes Collected for the Central Governments," *Journal of European Economic History* 5 (1976): 601.
[30] Kimberly J. Morgan and Monica Prasad, "The Origins of Tax Systems: A French-American Comparison," *American Journal of Sociology* 114 (2009): 1350.
[31] Alexander Nützenadel and Christoph Strupp, eds., *Taxation, State, and Civil Society in Germany and the United States from the 18th to the 20th Century* (Baden-Baden, Germany: Nomos, 2007).
[32] Sven Steinmo, *Taxation & Democracy: Swedish, British, and American Approaches to Financing the Modern State* (New Haven: Yale University Press, 1993).

corporate income in each jurisdiction, Steinmo offered little comparative analysis on the different methods of taxing corporations.

This is not to suggest that modern tax scholars have refrained from cross-country comparisons. Indeed, quite the contrary. A number of comparative tax studies have been published in recent years,[33] spurring several commentators to call for a fundamental examination of the methodology of comparative tax study.[34] This renewed interest in comparative tax study, however, has neither been historical nor focused on the USA or the UK. While several articles have attempted to bridge the gap by comparing one or more aspects of the US and UK income tax systems,[35] there have been very few comparative tax histories. As Assaf Likhovski, one of the few authors to broach this subject, wrote, "comparative methodology has had little effect on the legal history of taxation or in tax law scholarship."[36]

One of the unique difficulties in writing a comparative legal history is that it has to proceed along two axes. The first axis is comparative, which involves describing the legal systems in existence in both countries and examining the points of similarity and difference, while the second axis is historical, which involves tracing the development of those legal systems

---

[33] See, e.g., *Comparative Income Taxation: A Structural Analysis*, 3d edn. (Hugh J. Ault and Brian J. Arnold, eds.) (New York: Aspen Publishers, 2010); Victor Thuronyi, *Comparative Tax Law* (The Hague, The Netherlands: Kluwer Law International, 2003); *Tax Law Design and Drafting*; William Barker, "Expanding the Study of Comparative Tax Law to Promote Democratic Policy: The Example of the Move to Capital Gains Taxation in Post-Apartheid South Africa," *Penn State Law Review* 109 (2005): 703; Anthony C. Infanti, "Spontaneous Tax Coordination: On Adopting a Comparative Approach to Reforming the US International Tax Regime," *Vanderbilt Journal of Transnational Law* 35 (2002): 1105.

[34] Omri Y. Marian, "The Discursive Failure in Comparative Tax Law," *American Journal of Comparative Law* 58 (2010): 415; Carlo Garbarino, "An Evolutionary and Structural Approach to Comparative Taxation: Methods and Agenda for Research," *American Journal of Comparative Law* 57 (2009): 677; Michael A. Livingston, "Law, Culture, and Anthropology: On the Hopes and Limits of Comparative Taxation," *Canadian Journal of Law & Jurisprudence* 18 (2005): 119.

[35] See, e.g., William G. Gale, "What Can America Learn from the British Tax System?" *National Tax Journal* 50 (1997): 753; Joseph Guardino, "Comparative Tax Systems – United States v. Great Britain," *International Tax Journal* 21 (1995): 31; Bernhard Grossfeld and James D. Bryce, "A Brief Comparative History of the Origins of the Income Tax in Great Britain, Germany and the United States," *American Journal of Tax Policy* 2 (1983): 211.

[36] Assaf Likhovski, "A Map of Society: Defining Income in British, British-Colonial and American Tax Legislation," *British Tax Review* (2005): 158, 159 n 4.

throughout some period of time. Accomplishing both of these tasks simultaneously is problematic. It is not easy to make comparative insights without first setting forth a full picture of the two systems, but it is even more challenging to make those comparative insights over the history of the two jurisdictions. A purely chronological approach simplifies things greatly, but potentially at the cost of identifying themes and common issues that extend over multiple historical periods. By contrast, a purely thematic approach provides the maximum flexibility for drawing comparative inferences, but can leave the reader confused because of a lack of understanding about the legal system and its sequential development.

This book tackles this two-axes problem by using a hybrid approach involving both chronological and thematic approaches. Part I of the book is chronological, setting forth the background for the development of the corporate income tax in the two countries over the last two hundred years. Chapter 1 describes the origins of corporate taxation in the two countries, first in the UK in 1799 and later in the USA during the Civil War in the 1860s. Chapter 2 and Chapter 3 then proceed to chronicle the evolution of each system over the nineteenth and twentieth centuries. The key insight from this part of the book is that both countries developed corporate taxation using an integrated system in which corporate income was generally subject to one layer of tax, but the USA diverged from the UK around World War I by moving to a classical corporate income tax.

Part II, unlike Part I, is thematic, exploring several possible explanations for the divergence, including profits, power over the corporation, and politics. Chapter 4 discusses how the growth of corporate profits forced both systems of income taxation to focus on the corporation in the nineteenth century and why this focus diverged and converged in the twentieth century. Throughout much of the nineteenth century, the business corporation was more closely related to the British East India Company in its behavior and governance than to the railroad corporations that would begin to dominate certain sectors of the American economy at the end of the century. For these early corporations, there was an expectation that all profits would be distributed each year as dividends and any additional capital needs would be satisfied through the debt or equity markets. Thus, it is not surprising that the corporation would be viewed as a convenient vehicle for taxation at the source when the first Anglo-American income taxes appeared in the UK and the USA in the nineteenth century. Both countries' systems reflected the desire to use corporate income taxation as an aid in the administration of the individual income tax by collecting shareholder income at the source. Enacted during times of crisis – the Napoleonic Wars in the UK and the Civil War in the USA – the corporate income taxes were considered a less invasive and less costly means of collecting the income tax. This attitude continued in the USA even when the dividends tax of the Civil War was abandoned in favor of a direct tax on corporation income at the end of the century. In fact, William L. Wilson, chairman of the US House Ways and Means Committee, originally proposed limiting income taxation to corporations before expanding the proposal to a general income tax in 1894. The excise taxes enacted in 1898 and 1909 were similarly designed to reach corporate profits as a proxy for the income tax that had been declared unconstitutional in 1895.

In the USA, however, corporations began to retain an increasing percentage of earnings as a hedge against panics, large-scale capital requirements, and fickle markets. This "American theory" of finance, as it came to be known,[37] was originally prompted by the needs of railroads at the end of the nineteenth century. It soon spread to other industries, though. With earnings retained and the individual income tax subject to the high surtax rates imposed during World War I, the former method of integrating the two taxes through an exemption from the standard rate of tax was no longer a viable proxy for a tax on shareholder income. Thus, unlike the UK, the USA began to separate the corporate income tax rates from the individual income tax rates throughout the 1920s and 1930s.

Notwithstanding such differences in evolution of the underlying corporate tax systems, the UK and the USA both resorted to tax overlay provisions to grapple with the problem of ensuring that corporate profits were adequately taxed. In the USA, for example, this partially explains the enactment of an excess profits tax during World War I, the personal holding company and undistributed profits taxes of the New Deal, and the Windfall Profits Taxes of the 1970s. Similarly, in the UK, the Corporation Profit Tax enacted in 1920 and the post-World War II differential profits tax had similar aims of ensuring that corporations contributed their fair share of profits to financing post war recovery.

Chapter 5 discusses the different attitudes toward the location of power in the British and American corporation and the influence this

---

[37] Benjamin Graham and David L. Dodd, *Security Analysis: Principles and Technique* (2d. edn., New York: McGraw-Hill Book Co., 1940): 379.

has had on the respective development of corporate tax systems. During much of the nineteenth century, when the nature of the corporation in the USA and the UK was similar, there was little difference in their taxation. In the USA, however, the separation of ownership and control and the change in corporate finance to favor retained earnings appeared to create a powerful new class – the corporate manager. As the demographic of US shareholders changed, becoming widely dispersed and less confined to the super-rich, popular attention focused on this new repository of corporate power and the increasing wealth at its disposal. In the UK, by contrast, the separation of ownership and control did not take place until later. Even though markets were active and ownership was spreading in the 1950s and 1960s, family control still dominated in many large corporations and industries. Moreover, even apart from the relative timing of the separation of ownership and control, there is a long tradition of shareholder power in the UK, traced back into the nineteenth century when the Company Code's default bylaws first granted shareholders a veto right over management-sponsored dividend proposals. As a consequence of this delayed separation of ownership and control and the corporate finance norm against retaining large percentages of corporate profits, the popular focus in the UK has been directed at wealthy shareholders and the extent to which dividends further enrich these groups at the expense of other segments of the economy and society. While these differences are, of course, too generalized, they do reflect broad trends in popular attitudes.

This general difference in attitudes toward the *locus* of corporate power appears to have had an effect on the development of corporate tax systems in the USA and the UK. In the USA, for example, while the corporate tax has often shielded managers from high individual income tax rates, there has been a persistent concern about the risk that managers will abuse their ability to control large sums of corporate wealth. This was especially evident in the first part of the twentieth century, which led to numerous tax provisions designed to penalize excessive retained earnings and encourage dividends, highlighted by the undistributed profits tax enacted by President Roosevelt in 1936. Such a concern has not been limited to the first half of the twentieth century, though. President Bush's recent move to cut the rate of tax on dividends was designed in part to respond to corporate scandals based on managerial abuses. In the UK, however, concern about corporate power appears to have been directed less at managers and more at wealthy shareholders who drain the corporate coffers, often at the perceived expense of labor and wages. Thus, while the system generally is designed to permit distributions to shareholders, tax legislation has often been adopted to penalize dividends when concern becomes acute about the risk of excessive distributions. Here, the differential profits tax is the most prominent example. Contemporary observers pointed out that it was the polar opposite of the US undistributed profits tax. Even beyond this example, however, the UK's adoption of a classical corporate double tax in 1965 had similar aims of restraining dividends. During a period of rampant inflation and the resulting wage and dividend controls, the corporate tax system was seen as an instrument for reining in wealthy shareholders and keeping the wealth invested in the economy and in production.

There are a couple possible explanations for divergent attitudes toward corporate power. One is that a divergence in the treatment of corporations under the law that either derived from or fostered such a difference in attitudes dictated a difference in tax treatment of corporations. Thus, for example, if corporations were considered aggregations of individual shareholders under British law, but as real entities in the USA, that would help explain why the UK naturally taxed corporations under an integrated system designed to reach shareholders while the USA taxed corporations separately from the shareholders under a classical corporate double tax scheme. The problem with this entity theory-based explanation is that there are numerous instances in which the UK treated corporations as separate entities and the USA treated corporations as aggregations of individual shareholders. Another possible explanation is that cultural differences account for the divergence in treatment. Many comparative studies of taxation have relied upon cultural explanations to discuss divergence in law.[38] Although such cultural explanations are appealing, it is difficult to attribute legislative decisions over short periods to broad cultural trends, at least where such cultural differences are confined to attitude and intellectual theory rather than actual differences in organization or form. This chapter suggests that functional explanations are more plausible in the context of the divergence and growing convergence of the corporate income tax, but concedes that culture may help explain the underlying developments in the nature and operation of the corporation in the two countries that led to the original divergence of the two systems.

---

[38] See., e.g., Livingston, "Law, Culture, and Anthropology": 118; Ajay Mehrotra, "The Public Control of Corporate Power: Revisiting the 1909 US Corporate Tax from a Comparative Perspective," *Theoretical Inquiries in Law* 11 (2010): 497; Morgan and Prasad, "The Origins of Tax Systems": 1350.

Chapter 6 discusses the extent to which politics and ideology have played a significant role in the evolution of the corporate tax systems, particularly in the last fifty years. While the first two themes reflect differences in the development of corporate structure and behavior, they cannot completely explain the evolution of the two systems. This is especially true given that both corporate tax systems have undergone significant changes, and in the case of the UK, multiple changes in both directions, at times when corporate structure and behavior should have been converging.

The influence of politics and ideology may supply the missing ingredient. For example, in the UK, the country has veered toward double taxation when Labour is in power and away when the Conservatives are in power, although even Conservatives allowed the differential profits tax to survive for a number of years before pushing its repeal. Similarly, in the USA, the move to reduce double taxation has been more recently a Republican issue, although in the 1970s it was an idea pushed by Democrats. In both countries, trade groups and unions have attempted to exert influence, although often to differing ends. For industry trade groups, the incentive in the USA has been to preserve managerial control over corporate earnings. This includes contesting not only the undistributed profits tax, but also most serious attempts to integrate the corporate and shareholder income taxes in the last fifty years. In the UK, while industry trade groups had similar concerns, they also voiced concern about any limits on dividends. The Federation of British Industries specifically opposed the differential profits tax in 1951, arguing that "every time there is an additional profits tax on distributed profits there appears to be the inference that the payment of dividends is a bad and improper thing; that, from the point of view of British Industry, we regard as unsound."[39] By contrast, while labor unions in the USA have not been major players in the debate over corporate tax reform, UK trade unions have frequently tied dividend taxation to the question of wage controls and wage reforms, arguing that any attempt to reduce wages should be accompanied by an equal sacrifice from shareholders with respect to dividends.

One possible additional explanation for the divergence in the British and American corporate income tax is that the policymakers in the two

---

[39] Minutes of Evidence taken before the Royal Commission on the Taxation of Profits and Income 84, para. 808 (November 1, 1951) (testimony of S. P. Chambers, C. D. Hellyar, and A. G. Davies on behalf of the Federation of British Industries).

countries had differing opinions about the incidence of the corporate income tax. This possibility is not explicitly discussed in this book in great detail, but bears some discussion here. Economists and lawyers have long grappled with the question of where the burden of the corporate income tax should fall as between shareholders, employees, consumers, or suppliers.[40] In the nineteenth, and even well into the twentieth century, this question was about whether corporations in certain quasi-public industries such as railroads could legally pass the cost of the tax along to their customers in the form of higher prices. In more modern terms, the question is more economic than legal, in the sense that the ability of corporate managers to pass along the cost of the corporate tax to any particular group is in part a function of the ability of that group to avoid the cost.

If policymakers in the two countries held different views about the incidence of the corporate income tax, it is plausible that this could have helped to influence the divergence of the corporate income taxes in the two countries. Thus, if, for example, policymakers in the UK thought the corporate tax was borne solely by capital, while in the USA they thought it was entirely shifted to labor or consumers, that might help explain why the UK would refrain from taxing shareholders twice, while the USA would tax shareholders to make sure they paid at least once. Moreover, one can imagine various groups with differing views on the subject being influenced to take corresponding positions on the appropriate corporate tax. For instance, if unions thought that the corporate tax was borne by employees in the form of lower wages or fewer hires, this could have explained a focus on shareholder-level taxation rather than entity-level taxation.

Notwithstanding such conjectures, there is little evidence that there were radically different conceptions of incidence in the two countries that affected the direction of the respective corporate tax schemes. During much of the period in which the corporate income tax diverged in the two countries, economists on both sides of the Atlantic agreed that capital bore the lion's share of the burden in a closed economy model. For example, John Connolly, the general counsel of the Minnesota

---

[40] See, e.g., John G. Cragg, Arnold C. Harberger, and Peter Mieszkowski, "Empirical Evidence on the Incidence of the Corporation Income Tax," *Journal of Political Economy* 75 (1967): 811; William A. Klein, "The Incidence of the Corporation Income Tax: A Lawyer's View of a Problem in Economics," *Wisconsin Law Review* (1965): 576, 581–7; Alan J. Auerbach, "Who Bears the Corporate Tax? A Review of What We Know," *Tax Policy and the Economy* 20 (2006): 1.

Mining and Manufacturing Company, the forerunner to 3M, noted that "[i]n the early twenties economists and a British Royal Commission made an announcement to the effect that corporate taxes could not be and were not passed on."[41] In the 1927 report of the Royal Commission on National Debt and Taxation that Connolly referred to, the Commission concluded that "the incidence, with unimportant exceptions, is upon the payer of the tax or, in the case of income taxed at the source, the recipient of the income; it is not shifted on to any other person."[42] This apparently remained the view in both countries in 1946, with Connolly reporting that "[m]ost economists are staunch supporters of the theory that corporate taxes are not shifted or passed on."[43] Professor Arnold Harberger provided evidence for this view in the landmark 1962 article in which he concluded that capital bore the burden of corporate income taxation in a closed economy.[44]

When this model came under attack because of the increasing mobility of capital in a globalizing world, the popular view shifted in favor of the less mobile labor as the most likely object of the corporate income tax. Indeed, Harberger actually embraced this view himself in later years.[45] Others have since embraced this view, using cross-country data on wages and corporate taxes.[46] By 1994, for example, in a survey of American and Canadian economists, 75 percent responded affirmatively to the question "[a]re corporate income taxes largely passed on to workers and consumers?"[47] Similarly, a 1997 survey of economists at leading universities found that the average estimate of the share of the

[41] See John L. Connolly, "Should Corporations be Taxed as Such?" in *How Should Corporations be Taxed?* (New York: Tax Institute, Inc., 1947): 38, 39; Report of the Royal Commission on the Income Tax, Cmd. 615 (1920): 39–40.

[42] Report of the Committee on National Debt and Taxation, Cmd. 2800 (1927): 119.

[43] Connolly added, though, that "I wonder if the same conclusion would be reached today if such a study were made." Connolly, "Should Corporations be Taxed as Such?" at 39.

[44] Arnold C. Harberger, "The Incidence of the Corporation Income Tax," *Journal of Political Economy* 70 (1962): 215.

[45] Arnold C. Harberger, "The ABCs of Corporate Tax Incidence: Insights into the Open Economy Case," in *Tax Policy and Economic Growth* (Washington, D.C.: American Council for Capital Formation, 1995).

[46] William M. Gentry, "A Review of the Evidence on the Incidence of the Corporate Income Tax," Department of Treasury, Office of Tax Analysis Paper No. 101 (December 2007): 34; Jane G. Gravelle and Thomas L. Hungerford, "Corporate Tax reform: Issues for Congress," Congressional Research Service Report for Congress (April 6, 2010): 14–22 (describing studies).

[47] Joel Slemrod, "Professional Opinions About Tax Policy: 1994 and 1934," in *Tax Policy in the Real World* (Joel Slemrod, ed.) (Cambridge University Press, 1999): 435, 445.

burden borne by capital was 40 percent.[48] Nevertheless, there are those who still conclude that capital bears the lion's share of the burden,[49] reinforcing the notion that it would be difficult for policymakers in either country to have developed well founded views on incidence that guided recent corporate tax reform efforts. Thus, incidence is not separately discussed in the chapters in Part II, although it is implicit in the assumptions policymakers and opposition groups are using in framing their arguments for or against a shareholder or entity focus.

Finally, Part III is forward-looking, exploring the recent history of the corporate income tax systems in the two countries and the possible influences that may lead to a convergence or divergence over the next several decades. Chapter 7 discusses how all three of the themes outlined in Part II are still present in the debate over corporate tax reform that has taken place in the UK and the USA over the last thirty years. This chapter then connects these developments with the growth in the influence of the European Union, the European Court of Justice, and other international trade organizations. Treaty obligations underlie all of these developments and bilateral tax treaties are briefly explored as well, although neither this chapter nor the book as a whole focuses on the history of tax treaties. Finally, even beyond such treaty-based external influences, the book examines the effect that the competitive pressure of corporate tax reform in other countries has had on the UK and US experience, suggesting that the combined effect of all of these external influences may make the internal factors that differentiated British and American corporate income taxation in the twentieth century much less important to the direction of corporate tax reform in the UK, the USA, and around the world in the twenty-first century.

This project has had a long gestation period, emerging originally as the natural extension of a study on the origins of the classical corporate income tax. Several of the chapters draw substantially upon work completed earlier, including articles published in the *William and Mary Law Review*, the *Tax Law Review*, the *Journal of Contemporary Law & Policy*, and especially the *Journal of Corporation Law*, from which much of Chapter 4's discussion of the importance of dividend policy in the

---

[48] Victor Fuchs, Alan Krueger, and James Poterba, "Why Do Economists Disagree About Policy? The Role of Beliefs about Parameters and Values," National Bureau of Economic Research Working Paper No. 6151 (1997).

[49] See Jane G. Gravelle and Kent A. Smetters, "Does the Open Economy Assumption Really Mean that Labor Bears the Burden on a Capital Income Tax," *Advances in Economic Analysis and Policy* 6 (2006), Article 3; Auerbach, "Who Bears the Corporate Tax?", at 33.

divergence of the British and American corporate tax systems is drawn. Part of the unique contribution of this book is to expand that central insight, both by discussing additional influences that were important in the historical evolution of corporate income taxation in the two countries and by considering how those factors may play a role in the future development of Anglo-American corporate income taxation.

A number of people provided useful suggestions on my earlier work and earlier versions of several of the chapters in this book, including Reuven Avi-Yonah, Jordan Barry, Karen Burke, Brian Cheffins, Martin Daunton, Boyd Dyer, Victor Fleischer, Peter Harris, Bill Klein, Bert Lazerow, Assaf Likhovski, Christopher Nicholls, Peter Oh, David Oliver, Frank Partnoy, Ed Rock, Kirk Stark, Lynn Stout, Eric Talley, John Tiley, Fred Tung, Manuel Utset, and Mark Weinstein. The project was also enriched by productive discussions in workshops and lectures held at the University of Cambridge, where the author was a Herbert Smith visitor, the University of San Diego, the University of Utah, and Tel Aviv University, and in conferences and symposia such as the UCLA/USC Corporate Law Roundtable, the Tax History Conference at Cambridge, and the annual meeting of the Law and Society Association. In addition, several student research assistants contributed to this project, including Rob Abiri, Drew Capurro, Shane Noworatzky, Yuriy Silchuk, Jacob Veltman, and Camille Woolley.

A brief history of early Anglo-American corporate income taxation

Both the United Kingdom and the United States first used an income tax during the nineteenth century, with the UK's adoption of such a tax occurring just before the turn of the century. Eventually, this development forced the two nations to face the question of how to deal with the nascent corporate entity in the context of their early forays into income taxation. Although they relied on different methods, they were substantially aligned in approach. Thus, during the nineteenth century, the UK and the USA can be characterized as having an integrated corporate and individual income tax system.

1.1   The United Kingdom

1.1.1   1799–1802

The income tax was first adopted in the United Kingdom in 1799, during the Napoleonic Wars, under the leadership of the long-serving Prime Minister, William Pitt the Younger. Faced with the need for more revenue to wage the fight against France, Parliament had adopted what was called the "Triple Assessment" the year before as a form of quasi-income tax. Under this law, duties were imposed based upon the amount of assessed taxes the individual had paid the prior year on items such as carriages, horses, and other forms of property, with an exemption for those individuals having incomes below £60 a year.[1] Because of its lack of success in raising the necessary funds, the Triple Assessment was abandoned after only a year. Its successor, the income tax (adopted in 1799), was imposed at a 10 percent rate on incomes of £200 and up with

---

[1] Harrison B. Spaulding, *The Income Tax in Great Britain and the United States* (London: P. S. King & Son, Ltd., 1927), p. 16.

exemptions similar to those in place under the Triple Assessment and a graduated rate on incomes between £60 and £200.[2]

From the perspective of at least some observers, this original income tax had been designed for use only during war. Arthur Hope-Jones, in his 1939 book on this early income tax, describes it as the "War Income Tax of 1799 to 1816," although this may describe its period rather than its motivation.[3] A mid-nineteenth century commentator is more explicit in characterizing it as a product of the war:

> The expenses of the nation were enormous; the amount of debt was then represented as intolerable; and it was said that all sources of ordinary taxation were dried up. It was therefore, the utter hopelessness of successfully meeting the claims occasioned by the war, which induced the laying a tax upon incomes; a tax, in its origin, and always afterwards . . . emphatically designated and considered a *war tax*.[4]

Pitt, himself, characterized the tax in this way. In his Budget speech for 1801, Pitt stated "I did first propose it with a view that it should be a war tax which, in time of peace, should repay the excess of the public debt beyond a given amount. If I was to push it so as to make it a perpetual tax, I feel that I should be destroying the object for which I introduced it."[5] A 1928 study of the British tax system prepared for the US Joint Committee on Internal Revenue Taxation thus concluded that "the tax was purely a war measure and shortly after the signing of the Treaty of Amiens in May, 1802, it was repealed."[6]

There had been very little mention of corporations under the Triple Assessment. This was not because corporations did not exist, nor because it was unheard-of to subject them to any form of tax. As early as 1450, corporations were specifically mentioned as potentially liable for a tax on the "yearly value" of property they owned.[7] Similar laws in 1489 and 1515 mentioned corporations among the possible subjects of

---

[2] Peter Harris, *Income Tax in Common Law Jurisdictions: From the Origins to 1820* (Cambridge University Press, 2006), p. 406.
[3] Arthur Hope-Jones, *Income Tax in the Napoleonic Wars* (University of Cambridge Press, 1939), p. 2.
[4] William Tayler, *The History of the Taxation of England: With an Account of the Rise and Progress of the National Debt* (London: Hope & Co., 1853), p. 52.
[5] Albert Farnsworth, *Addington, Author of the Modern Income Tax* (London: Stevens & Sons, Ltd., 1951), p. 24 (*quoting* Pitt's *Speeches* 4 (1806), pp. 162–3).
[6] André Bernard, *Income Tax in Great Britain, Including a description of Other Inland Revenue Taxes, prepared for the Joint Committee on Internal Revenue Taxation* (Washington, DC, 1928), p. 5.
[7] Spaulding, *The Income Tax in Great Britain and the United States*, p. 49.

taxation.[8] While the passage of the Bubble Act in 1720 following a period of overspeculation and crash had inhibited the growth of business corporations in England during the eighteenth century, the rate of incorporations had begun to pick back up by the end of the century.[9] This was especially true in the canal industry, with eighty-one charters being granted to canal operators between 1791 and 1794,[10] but soon after the turn of the century it became evident that "companies might be extended to every branch of trade and manufacture."[11]

Rather than being a sign that corporations were not considered taxable, the absence of references to corporations under the Triple Assessment tax was simply because corporations were not treated differently from individuals under the levy. A "Committee, Steward, or Agent" was entitled to claim a reduction in the assessment on the grounds of income by making a declaration on behalf of the "Body Corporate or Politick," but otherwise corporations were just another object of taxation.[12]

When the first income tax was adopted in 1799, corporations were once again treated the same as other taxable actors. "Residents" subject to the tax included "every body, politic or corporate, company, fraternity or society of persons, whether corporate or not corporate, in Great Britain."[13] There was one exception to this lockstep treatment of corporations and individuals. Under Pitt's scheme, the income of any "Corporations, Fraternity, or Society of persons established for charitable purposes only" was exempt from taxation.[14]

There was no intention to subject corporate income to two layers of taxation under the 1799 tax. Pitt integrated the corporate and shareholder income taxes through a dividend deduction method. Thus, "income distributed in dividends" was "not to be charged [to the corporation] ... provided proprietors of such dividends pay in respect thereof."[15] The

---

[8] Ibid., pp. 55, 59.

[9] Bishop Hunt, "The Joint-stock Company in England, 1800–1825," *Journal of Political Economy* 43 (1935): 1.

[10] Bishop Hunt, *The Development of the Business Corporation in England, 1800–1867* (Cambridge, Mass.: Harvard University Press, 1936), p. 10.

[11] Hunt, "The Joint-stock Company," 3.

[12] Spaulding, *The Income Tax in Great Britain and the United States*, p. 403.

[13] Income Tax Act, 10 Geo. III c. 13, sec. 8 (1799). Stephen Dowell, *A History of Taxation and Taxes in England From the Earliest Times to the Year 1885*, vol. III (London: Longmans, Green, and Co., 1888), p. 92.

[14] Martin Daunton, *Trusting Leviathan: The Politics of Taxation in Britain, 1799–1914* (Cambridge University Press, 2001), p. 211.

[15] Income Tax Act, 10 Geo. III ch. 13, sec. 88 (1799).

requirement that the shareholders pay tax on dividends applied regardless of whether the dividends actually been paid by the time the tax statement was due: "If any ... dividends ... shall not have been, or shall not be received by him or her previous to such statement or assessment, it shall be lawful nevertheless to charge such person for the same, as if the same had been actually then received."[16] This meant that the shareholder could not avoid liability for tax on a dividend payment that had already been deducted by the corporation, ensuring that at least one layer of tax would be imposed.

1.1.2   1803–1815

The income levy was hastily reintroduced in 1803 when the war resumed.[17] Lord Henry Addington, who replaced Pitt as prime minister after the latter's resignation and who is generally considered the author of the 1803 income tax, faced considerable opposition in proposing its reintroduction. In 1802 William Mainwaring of Middlesex had praised the repeal of the income tax in the House of Commons, noting that the tax was "so oppressive and odious as to excite the horror and indignation of every class of people."[18] Love Parry Jones had gone further, predicting that "the nation had so unequivocally expressed their indignation at the degrading and oppressive nature of the tax, that he was sure no minister would ever dare to reinflict it on the country."[19]

In part because of such opposition to Pitt's income tax, the 1803 Act was not a mere reenactment of the 1799 version. Indeed, Addington attempted to highlight distinctions by calling it "a tax upon property" and emphasizing his proposal that it "should cease within six months after the restoration of peace."[20] Nevertheless, most saw through the income tax's thinly veiled disguise. Alderman Harvey Christian Combe of London "considered this tax as merely an income tax," noting that he opposed the proposal because his constituents "considered it a measure so unjust in its principle, and partial in its operation, that no modification of it could remove their objections."[21] Addington, therefore, had his work cut out in selling the tax.

---

[16] Ibid.
[17] Income Tax Act, 10 Geo. III c. 122, sec. 127 (1803); Meade Emory, "The Early English Income Tax: a Heritage for the Contemporary," *American Journal of Legal History* 9 (1965): 291 n. 14.
[18] Parl. Deb., vol. 36, ser. 3, col. 462, 5 April 1802.   [19] Ibid.
[20] Parl. Deb., vol. 36, ser. 3, col. 1596, 13 June 1803.
[21] Parl. Deb., vol. 36, ser. 3, col. 1662, 5 July 1803.

There had been two primary objections to Pitt's income tax, both of which were at least partially addressed when the tax was revived in 1803. The first was that it invaded privacy. According to Addington, "one of the greatest inconveniences which could be attributed to the late Income Tax was, the necessity and hardship it imposed on individuals, in making a full disclosure of the amount of their fortunes."[22] As one nineteenth-century observer later reported, "The obligation to make such a [general] return, involving, as it did, a disclosure of the taxpayer's circumstances in life, had been regarded as the chief objection to the tax."[23] Consequently, there was reportedly much rejoicing in the apparent care taken to destroy the records of the 1799 income tax once that law was repealed, although it later turned out that copies had indeed been saved.[24]

This concern about disclosure extended to businesses, which were more worried about the prying eyes of their competitors than about privacy in the individual sense. Even under the 1799 tax, merchants had successfully lobbied for some protections. The act provided for a special Commercial Commission, with commissioners appointed by the Lord Mayor, the Bank of England, and the East India Company, to hear matters regarding the amount of income from trade.[25] The Commission was charged with receiving "sealed" statements, which were not available for review by the Crown.[26] Despite such protections, businessmen argued "that it has the tendency to reveal the circumstances of persons in business."[27] There was some skepticism about such claims, with *The Times* suggesting they were "to a great degree imaginary."[28] *The Times* later noted that "we never heard of an instance, in which, during the operation of the former tax, this was attended with the smallest prejudice to any individual," but it acknowledged that the argument was "urged with some vehemence."[29] Similarly, Addington understood that perception was important in the business community: "In a commercial country," he explained, "it was unquestionably most desirable that no disclosure of circumstances should be made, further than was absolutely necessary to secure the payment of the tax."[30]

---

[22] Farnsworth, *Addington*, p. 52 (quoting Addington, [Speech delivered to Parliament], *Times* (London), June 14, 1803, p. 13).

[23] Dowell, *History of Taxation and Taxes*, p. 99.

[24] See William Phillips, "A New Light on Addington's Income Tax," *British Tax Review* (1967): 271–2.

[25] Emory, "The Early English Income Tax," 303.   [26] Farnsworth, *Addington*, p. 21.

[27] "Editorial," *The Times* (London), 28 June 1803, p. C4.

[28] "Editorial," *The Times* (London), 19 October 1803, p. B1.

[29] "Editorial," *The Times* (London), 28 June 1803, p. C4.

[30] Farnsworth, *Addington*, p. 60 (quoting Addington).

To remedy the perceived threats to privacy for both individuals and businesses, Addington introduced a schedular system. This eliminated the need to report a person's income on one return by replacing it with a set of schedules for different types of income, each schedule being filed in a different office. Schedule A was for income from land and buildings, Schedule B was for income from the occupation of land, such as the amounts earned by tenant farmers, profits from public securities were reported on Schedule C, and Schedule D covered profits from commercial and industrial ventures as well as incomes from vocational or professional services. Schedule D also contained a default clause for income from any other sources. In this connection, *The Times* reported that "measures will be taken for conducting this part of the business with the utmost secrecy and delicacy possible, so that no person whatever need entertain any apprehension of his circumstances being made public."[31]

The second objection to Pitt's version of the income tax had been that it was susceptible to evasion. There had been "shameful evasion" under the Triple Assessment according to Pitt, but his income tax fared little better.[32] Estimated to produce revenue of approximately £10 million, the actual yield was only £5.8 million.[33] Addington's response was to rely more heavily upon stoppage-at-source methods of collection.[34] The final schedule of the five he devised – Schedule E – was a withholding tax for all income received in "public office or employment," which was defined broadly to include income from any activity in the public interest.

In another change from the 1799 version, the company-level tax acted much like Schedule E as a withholding provision for the individual income tax.[35] According to an excerpt from Addington's *Private Memoir on Finance* from June 1803, his vision was to collect the tax at source: "Dividends in the Funds and in Corporation Stocks to be also charged at 1/– in the pound [5 percent], and to be deducted at the Bank or Office where the same shall be payable."[36] Abandoning the dividend

---

[31] "Editorial," *The Times* (London), 28 June 1803, p. C4.
[32] Emory, "The Early English Income Tax," 297 (quoting Pitt's *Speeches* 4 (1806), p. 429).
[33] Emory, "The Early English Income Tax," 301.
[34] As Phillips emphatically maintained, Addington did not invent or introduce deduction at the source, but rather popularized it. Phillips, "A New Light," 276.
[35] See Peter A. Harris, *Corporate/Shareholder Income Taxation and Allocating Taxing Rights Between Countries: A Comparison of Imputation Systems* (Amsterdam: IBFD Publications, 1996), p. 76.
[36] Farnsworth, *Addington*, p. 119 (quoting from Addington).

deduction method, the new act integrated the corporate and individual income taxes under what effectively served as an imputation system. Corporations were subject to a tax on the "amount of the annual profits, and gains" of the company "before any dividend shall have been" paid, effectively amounting to a tax on the entire corporate income, rather than on the income other than that set aside for payment of a dividend, as under a dividend deduction scheme.[37] Corporations were then entitled to deduct from the dividends and retain for themselves an amount sufficient to cover the corporate-level tax, defined as "a proportionate deduction in respect of the duty so charged."[38] While the process was not well specified in the statutes, Peter Harris noted that after the corporation had paid the corporate-level tax and been compensated by withholding the proper amount from the dividends, "[s]hareholders received a dividend tax credit for tax so deducted resulting in a form of imputation system."[39]

The reliance on stoppage at source for the taxation of corporate dividends is sometimes considered Lord Addington's "most brilliant" reform,[40] not only because it both reduced the risk of evasion and lessened the invasion of privacy associated with other collection techniques, but also because it was such an enduring innovation. It was understood at the time to be a useful device for collection of the tax on dividends. *The Times* explained after the passage of the Act, "the most convenient mode of payment for money in the funds will be ... to pay 5 per cent on the dividends as they arise into the Bank, and to take a receipt, specifying the stock on account of which the payment is made; which receipt must be sent to the Office of the Commissioners for the City of London."[41] As Farnsworth pointed out, though, the amazing point was that Addington devised this simple scheme in an era when "the modern limited liability company was not known."[42]

According to Hope-Jones, corporations may have also served to facilitate collection at source more directly: "Large corporations, such as the Bank of England, the East India Company, the Royal Exchange and London Insurance Companies may have assisted" in the collection of

---

[37] Income Tax Act 1803, 43 Geo. III c. 122, sec. 127.   [38] Ibid.
[39] Harris, *Corporate/Shareholder Income Taxation*, p. 769.
[40] Seán Réamonn, *The Philosophy of the Corporate Tax* (Dublin: Institute of Public Administration, 1970), p. 29.
[41] "Editorial," *The Times* (London), 19 October 1803, p. B1.
[42] Farnsworth, *Addington*, p. 119.

the income tax by withholding from employee salaries "before the employees were paid."[43] The combination of these measures helped yield the same amount in 1803 as in 1801, at a tax rate that was 50 percent lower than the one in place two years earlier.[44]

Notwithstanding the fact that the schedular system and the increasing use of withholding in the amendments subsequently enacted in 1806 managed to reduce concerns about privacy and evasion, there was substantial sentiment to repeal the tax after the war ended. According to Stephen Dowell, "the total repeal of the tax formed the subject of innumerable petitions to the House of Commons."[45] The City of London developed a petition in December of 1814 and other towns followed suit so that when Parliament reconvened in February of 1815, the Chancellor of the Exchequer, Nicholas Vansittart, received great acclaim when he announced that he would not seek the renewal of the tax.[46] William Tayler later recalled in his 1853 treatise the "satisfaction which only a people overburdened with taxation can know" that people experienced upon learning that the tax would be allowed to expire.[47] While Vansittart backtracked on his promise even after the war had finally concluded with the Battle of Waterloo, "agitation throughout the country was fomented by the opposition in every conceivable way" and eventually the tax was continued only through the signing of a peace treaty "and" in the words of Parliament, "no longer."[48]

1.1.3   1842–1861

In the decades following the conclusion of the war, there was frequent agitation in favor of reviving an income tax. One commentator observed that "no sooner was the income tax repealed than writers began to repent of its abolition, suspect the motives which caused it, and advocate its revival."[49] In 1833, Benjamin Sayer, who had been an official under the

---

[43] Hope-Jones, *Income Tax in the Napoleonic Wars*, p. 22.

[44] Ibid., p. 72.

[45] Stephen Dowell, *A History of Taxation and Taxes in England, From the Civil War to the Present Day*, vol. II (London: Longmans, Green, and Co., 1884), p. 253.

[46] Edwin R. A. Seligman, *The Income Tax: A Study of the History, Theory, and Practice of Income Taxation at Home and Abroad* (New York: The MacMillan Co., 1911), p. 106.

[47] Tayler, *The History of the Taxation of England*, p. 63.

[48] Seligman, *The Income Tax*, pp. 111–13.

[49] Fakhri Shehab, *Progressive Taxation: A Study in the Development of the Progressive Principle in the British Income Tax* (Oxford: Clarendon Press, 1953), p. 72.

original income tax, published a monograph arguing that an income tax was preferable to the indirect taxes then in use.[50] In 1837 Sayer's book was liberally cited by J. S. Buckingham when he unsuccessfully introduced a motion in Parliament to direct a committee to take up the question of reviving the income tax.[51] This led Buckingham himself to write his own essay, entitled "The Superiority of an Income and Property Tax to every Other Source of Revenue."[52] Much like Sayer's earlier volume, though, this failed to remove the political taint from the tax.

Within five years, the deteriorating financial situation led politicians to take another look at the income tax. The Panic of 1837 had produced five consecutive years of budget deficits in amounts averaging £1.5 million per year, primarily due to shortfalls in expected revenue.[53] Attempts to improve the situation by adjusting Customs duties both upward and downward had been unsuccessful.[54] In his Budget speech of March 11, 1842, Sir Robert Peel, the Chancellor of the Exchequer, noted that the growing deficit could not be contained through expenditure cuts. He also stated "I cannot consent to increase the taxation upon articles of subsistence consumed by the great body of the labouring portion of the community."[55] Rather, he proposed "for a time to be limited, the income of this country shall be called upon to contribute a certain sum for the purpose of remedying this mighty and growing evil."[56] In support of reviving the income tax Peel referenced not only the deficit, but also business conditions, suggesting that the additional revenue would enable him "with confidence and satisfaction to propose great commercial reforms, which will afford a hope of reviving commerce and such an improvement in the manufacturing interests as will

---

[50] Ibid., p. 124 (citing Benjamin Sayer, *An Attempt to Shew the Justice and Expediency of Substituting an Income or Property Tax for the Present Taxes, or a Part of Them; as Affording the Most Equitable, the Least Injurious, and (Under the Modified Procedure Suggested Therein) the Least Obnoxious Mode of Taxation; Also, the Most Fair, Advantageous, and Effectual Plans of Reducing the National Debt* (London: Hatchard and Son, 1833)).

[51] Shehab, *Progressive Taxation*, p. 126.

[52] Ibid., p. 127 (citing *The Parliamentary Review* 5 (1934): 363).

[53] Stafford Northcote, *Twenty Years of Financial Policy: A Summary of the Chief Financial Measures Passed Between 1842 and 1861, with a Table of Budgets* (London: Saunders, Otley, and Co., 1862), p. 5.

[54] Shehab, *Progressive Taxation*, p. 129.

[55] "Financial Statement of Sir Robert Peel, in the House of Commons, Friday, March 11, 1842," in William Painter (ed.), *Speeches in Parliament*, 3d edn. (London: William Edward Painter, 1842), p. 9.

[56] Ibid., p. 13.

react on every other interest in the country."[57] Such reforms included reductions in tariff rates on various items, including both imported supplies and exported goods.[58] While Peel's income tax proposal was "violently opposed both in and out of Parliament,"[59] it was ultimately adopted in the Income Tax Act of 1842, albeit for an initial term of only three years.[60]

While nominally an entirely new statute, the Act was essentially a "reprint" of the 1803 Act with respect to its treatment of corporate income, with only the section numbers changing.[61] As under the 1803 Act, companies were subject to a tax on all profits and gains prior to the payment of any dividend.[62] Shareholders were not specifically exempted from taxation of dividends, but the practice once again was "to regard the dividends paid to shareholders as distributions of profits which had already paid tax in the hands of the company, and the shareholders (like partners) as immune from further taxation in respect of the sums so distributed to them."[63] Peel estimated, on the basis of dividends from railways, canals, and similar sources and from profits in the mines and iron works industry, that the tax on companies would bring in almost £8.5 million, less the applicable exemption of £150 per individual.[64]

What was perhaps unique about the 1842 income tax (compared with its earlier incarnation) was that it outgrew the budgetary crisis to become a permanent fixture of the British revenue system. An initial renewal of the tax for a second three-year term was designed to address increased expenditures and further cuts to Customs duties, while a subsequent renewal in the late 1840s was necessary because of decreased revenues in the wake of poor harvests and failures in the railroad industry.[65] Growing controversy over the lingering income tax led to the creation of a government Select Committee in 1851, chaired by Joseph Hume, to investigate whether the income tax should be repealed or whether some

---

[57] Ibid., pp. 13–14.
[58] Northcote, *Twenty Years of Financial Policy*, p. 20; John Noble, *Fiscal Legislation, 1842–1865: A Review of the Financial Changes of That Period, and Their Effects Upon Revenue, Trade, Manufactures, and Employment* (London: Longmans, Green, Reader & Dyer, 1867), p. 13.
[59] Noble, *Fiscal Legislation*, p. 14.   [60] Income Tax Act 1842, 5 & 6 Vict. c. 35, sec. 54.
[61] Income Tax Codification Committee Report, Cmd 5131 (1936), p. 9.
[62] Income Tax Act 1842, 5 & 6 Vict. c. 35, sec. 54.
[63] Income Tax Codification Committee Report, Cmd 5131 (1936), p. 61.
[64] "Financial Statement of Sir Robert Peel," p. 16.
[65] Shehab, *Progressive Taxation*, pp. 98–9; Northcote, *Twenty Years of Financial Policy*, p. 64.

revised version of it should be adopted permanently.[66] Hume's committee conducted hearings with extensive witness testimony that extended into the next session of Parliament, all resulting in the production of two reports.[67] Failing to arrive at any consensus among the witnesses or on the committee itself, they submitted the minutes of evidence with no further recommendation.[68] In the meantime, the income tax, which had only been extended for one year while Hume's committee studied it, had expired. Nevertheless, William Gladstone, who became Chancellor of the Exchequer in 1852, reluctantly saved the income tax from repeal on a number of occasions, pushing its extension to help pay for the Crimean War.[69] At its height in 1857, the income tax brought in more than £16 million, constituting almost a quarter of total revenues from taxation.[70] By 1861, despite violent objection from some quarters,[71] Seligman reports that there "came to an end, for a time at least, all thought of abandoning the income tax."[72]

1.1.4   1861–1900

During the latter half of the nineteenth century, the income tax only solidified its place in the revenue scheme. John G. Hubbard, the one-time Governor of the Bank of England and a Conservative Member of Parliament, lamented this development: "Detested, denounced, and doomed again and again to extinction, it has crept on by stages of three years – of seven years, but mostly by yearly renewals, and its continuance now stands more firmly rooted than ever as a permanent instrument of revenue."[73] Hubbard moved for the creation of a Select

---

[66] Shehab, *Progressive Taxation*, p. 99.

[67] First Report from the Select Committee on the Income and Property Tax, HC354 (1852); Second Report from the Select Committee on the Income and Property Tax, HC510 (1852).

[68] Shehab, *Progressive Taxation*, p. 111.

[69] Northcote, *Twenty Years of Financial Policy*, pp. 194, 250; Seligman, *The Income Tax*, p. 166.

[70] Leone Levi, "On the Reconstruction of the Income and Property Tax," *Journal of the Statistical Society of London* 37 (1874): 175, tbl. 1.

[71] According to one observer, Gladstone reported that he received a letter shortly before his delivery of the Budget speech in 1860 "complaining of the monstrous injustice and iniquity of the Income Tax, and proposing that, in consideration thereof, the Chancellor of the Exchequer should be publicly hanged." R. Dudley Baxter, *The Taxation of the United Kingdom* (London: Macmillan and Co., 1869), pp. 92–3.

[72] Seligman, *The Income Tax*, p. 166.

[73] John G. Hubbard, "Forty Years of Income Tax," *The National and English Review* (1884): 772.

Committee on Income and Property Tax in 1861, but this focused more on reforming the tax than on doing away with it altogether.[74]

There was little change in the integrated approach to taxing corporate and individual income during the second half of the nineteenth century,[75] but a proposal was raised for the taxation of charitable corporations, which suggests some nuance in the UK's attitude toward corporate taxation. As far back as 1845 Peel had suggested that charities merited a separate tax because they were often corrupt, serving the needs of a small group rather than the larger society.[76] It was not until 1863, though, that the idea reemerged and focused on corporations. In his Financial Statement and in a subsequently introduced bill, Gladstone proposed a corporation tax on so-called endowed charities, while leaving exempt charities that received their support from voluntary contributions rather than endowment income.[77] According to Gladstone, voluntary charities operated through contributions of after-tax income, and thus at a disadvantage compared to endowed charities.[78]

Although "the proposed corporation tax met strong resistance," leading Gladstone to withdraw it, he revived it when he returned to power and it was enacted in 1885.[79] Under this later version, a 5 percent tax was imposed on endowed charities in lieu of succession duties imposed in probate.[80] Because of exemptions for religious, charitable, educational, and other similar purposes, however, the tax only applied to endowments such as City livery companies, Inns of Court, and the City of London.[81] Thus, to the extent that it operated as a corporation tax in any real sense, it was so limited in scope that it effectively was a tax targeted on particular activities rather than a tax on the corporate form itself.

1.2   United States

Although the income tax was not adopted in the USA until midway through the nineteenth century during the Civil War, and then only

---

[74] Report from the Select Committee on Income and Property Tax, HC503 (1861); Shehab, *Progressive Taxation*, p. 139.

[75] Indeed, there were few changes made to the income tax of any kind, save for a reduction in the overall rate. Seligman, *The Income Tax*, p. 167.

[76] Daunton, *Trusting Leviathan*, p. 211.

[77] David Owen, *English Philanthropy, 1660–1960* (Cambridge, Mass.: Belknap Press, 1964), p. 331.

[78] Daunton, *Trusting Leviathan*, p. 213.   [79] Ibid., p. 213.

[80] Ibid., p. 213; Avner Offer, *Property and Politics, 1879–1914: Landownership, Law, Ideology, and Urban Development in England* (Cambridge University Press, 1981), p. 94.

[81] Offer, *Property and Politics*, p. 94.

temporarily, the approach it did use was roughly similar to the integrated treatment in place in the UK. A later attempt to implement an income tax at the end of the century was ultimately thwarted in the courts, but this too pursued an integrated approach, albeit through different means. The result was that, while the two countries were not identical in their treatment of corporate income during the nineteenth century, they were generally aligned.

1.2.1   Civil War and Reconstruction

In the face of mounting debt and a pressing need for funds to help finance the war effort,[82] a federal income tax was first collected in 1862.[83] The Union had actually adopted an income tax the previous year, but Salmon Chase, Lincoln's Treasury Secretary at the beginning of the Civil War, made no effort to assess or collect any taxes under the Act and thus rendered it a dead letter.[84] Chase, who had originally proposed to ease the debt through more traditional means such as issuing Treasury notes, increasing tariffs, increasing reliance on excise taxes, imposing license fees, and selling public lands,[85] also failed to nominate anyone to serve as commissioner of taxes, apparently hoping that the war would be short-lived and the need for additional revenue would recede.[86] When that hope proved too optimistic and Congressional leaders sought to dramatically expand the base of taxation, the income levy became inevitable. As adopted in July, the 1862 Act imposed a tax of 3 percent on all income between $600 and $10,000 and a 5 percent tax on incomes in excess of $10,000.[87]

The 1862 Act did not specifically mention income from corporate or partnership profits, but it did impose a form of withholding tax on certain businesses. A tax of 3 percent was levied on all dividends issued and interest paid by railroads and a similar tax was assessed on all

---

[82]   See John Witte, *The Politics and Development of the Federal Income Tax* (Madison, Wis.: University of Wisconsin Press, 1985), pp. 67–8.

[83]   Act of August 5, 1861, ch. 45, 12 Stat. 309 (1861).

[84]   See Steven A. Bank, "Origins of a Flat Tax," *Denver University Law Review* 73 (1995): 345.

[85]   Steven A. Bank, Kirk J. Stark, and Joseph J. Thorndike, *War and Taxes* (Washington, DC: Urban Institute Press, 2008), p. 35.

[86]   "Report of the Secretary of the Treasury," Senate Executive and Misc. Doc. No. 2, 1st Sess. 37th Cong. 7–8 (1861); Harry Smith, *The United States Federal Internal Tax History from 1861 to 1871* (Boston: Houghton Mifflin Company, 1914), pp. 24–5; Sidney Ratner, *Taxation and Democracy in America* (New York: Octagon Books, 1980), p. 70.

[87]   Act of July 1, 1862, ch. 119, § 90, 12 Stat. 473 (1862).

dividends issued and on all sums added to surplus by banks, trust companies, savings institutions, and insurance companies.[88] Despite the inclusion of these provisions under a separate section, they were generally regarded as a part of the income tax.[89]

This tax on dividends was carefully constructed to avoid imposing double taxation on business income. There was already significant concern about double taxation in other contexts. As Representative Justin Morrill noted when introducing the bill on behalf of the Ways and Means Committee, one of the aspects of the income tax that made it "the least defensible" of all taxes was that "nearly all persons will have been already once taxed upon the sources from which their income has been derived."[90] Representative Thomas Edwards, in protesting an inheritance tax because it would burden property that had been taxed during the owner's life, echoed these concerns when he declared "I do not think that the Government should derive double taxation from the same property for the same period of time. That is a proposition, the correctness of which I think every member will concede."[91] Others agreed with this statement, calling double taxation "not just" and proposing amendments to avoid this result wherever appropriate.[92]

Thus, the Union Congress enacted a variety of measures to minimize the risk of double taxation for businesses. Most significantly, shareholders and bondholders were permitted to exclude from income the receipt of dividends and interest from corporations already taxed under the Act.[93] This, of course, was not a perfect solution. Unlike the income tax itself, the rate was not graduated and there was no exemption for

[88]   Ibid., ch. 119, §§ 81, 82, 12 Stat. 469–70 (1862).

[89]   Joseph A. Hill, "The Civil War Income Tax," *Quarterly Journal of Economics* 8 (1894): 427. Sections 89–93 were listed under the heading "Income Duty," while the dividend and interest taxes were included under the headings "Railroad Bonds" and "Banks, Trust Companies, Savings Institutions, and Insurance Companies." See Act of July 1, 1862, 12 Stat. 469–75 (1862).

[90]   Cong. Globe, 37th Cong., 2d Sess. 1196 (1862).   [91]   Ibid., 1534.

[92]   Ibid., 1527 (statement of Rep. Sherman) (proposing to exempt mortgages from tax because of concerns about double taxation). See also ibid., 1486 (statement of Rep. Eliot) (proposing amendment to relieve savings banks from tax on dividends arising from earnings received on bank stock holdings); ibid., 1545 (statement of Rep. Stevens) (protesting property tax on stocks and bonds as a double tax when combined with an income tax); ibid., 2555 (statement of Sen. McDougall) (objecting to tax on insurance companies would be doubled because of the reinsurance industry); ibid., 2573 (proposed integration scheme offered by Sen. Howe).

[93]   Act of July 1, 1862, ch. 119, § 91, 12 Stat. at 473–4 (1862).

shareholders with incomes below $600. According to at least one explanation, this was because "it seemed impracticable to Congress to permit" anything other than a tax "assessed in a lump sum on all money paid out as interest or dividends."[94] Nevertheless, it produced some inequities. Individuals with incomes in excess of $10,000 would be taxed at 3 percent on dividends or interest from railroads and other such corporations, but at 5 percent on all other income. Conversely, individuals not subject to the income tax because their income was less than $600 would still pay at a 3 percent rate on dividends and interest from specified businesses because the withholding tax was not relieved for dividends and interest paid to lower income taxpayers.[95] While the latter problem was controversial,[96] albeit rare in occurrence given the low proportion of income tax revenues attributable to the dividend provisions,[97] the former problem was partially alleviated by administrative practice. George S. Boutwell, the first Commissioner of Internal Revenue, issued a regulation instructing the assessors of the income tax to assess an additional 2 percent tax on individuals with income in excess of $10,000 who received dividends and interest from taxable corporations.[98]

The 1862 Act did appear to impose a separate tax upon certain corporations in the form of a gross receipts tax. Under Section 80 of the Act, businesses operating railroads, steamboats, and ferry-boats were required to pay a 3 percent tax on the gross amount of their receipts.[99] The provision, however, applied regardless of whether the business was incorporated.[100] It also explicitly permitted the affected company to pass on the amount of the tax to their customers in the form of higher fares.[101]

---

[94] Smith, *The United States Federal Internal Tax History*, p. 55.

[95] Hill, "The Civil War Income Tax," 427–8.

[96] See Harold Langenderfer, *The Federal Income Tax, 1861–1872* (New York: Arno Press, 1980), pp. 508–9.

[97] See Robert Stanley, *Dimensions of Law in the Service of Order: Origins of the Federal Income Tax 1861–1913* (New York: Oxford University Press, 1993), p. 279, n. 74.

[98] George Boutwell, *A Manual of the Direct and Excise Tax System of the United States* (Boston: Little, Brown, 1863), p. 197; Smith, *The United States Federal Internal Tax History*, p. 55. This addressed the inequality of taxing 5% taxpayers at a 3% rate on corporate income, but it did not address the reverse problem of taxing 0% taxpayers at a 3% rate. See Ratner, *Taxation and Democracy in America*, p. 75.

[99] Act of July 1, 1862, ch. 119, § 80, 12 Stat. 468–9 (1862).   [100] Ibid.

[101] Ibid. ("*Provided*, That all such persons, companies, and corporations shall have the right to add the duty or tax imposed hereby to their rates of fare.")

Thus, it was arguably more like a sales tax than a tax on the business itself, although only if the business chose to pass on the tax. Even if it paid the tax without raising rates, however, this was still more like a proxy tax because shareholders were entitled to exempt from income the receipt of dividends from corporations subject to the gross receipts tax.[102]

Between 1862 and 1864, the country's financial position worsened and the public debt grew to over $1 billion.[103] Revenue from the 1862 Act had been disappointingly low;[104] thus, Congress focused more of its efforts on the income tax in hopes of bolstering its financial condition.[105] Under the 1864 Act,[106] Congress increased the individual income tax rate to 5 percent on incomes between $600 and $5,000, 7.5 percent on incomes between $5,000 and $10,000, and 10 percent on incomes in excess of $10,000, although before the 1864 Act went into effect Congress eliminated the 7.5 percent bracket and imposed a 10 percent tax on all incomes in excess of $5,000 in an effort to further increase revenues.[107]

Unlike the income tax provisions in the 1862 Act, which did not mention income from corporate or partnership profits, the 1864 Act specifically provided that income from each type of entity would be taxed the same. Section 117 of the Act stated that "the gains and profits of all companies, whether incorporated or partnership, other than the companies specified in this section, shall be included in estimating the annual gains, profits, or income of any person entitled to the same, whether divided or otherwise."[108] The Commissioner interpreted this latter phrase to permit the taxation of shareholders on the undivided profits

---

[102] Ibid., § 91, 12 Stat. at 473–4.
[103] Ratner, *Taxation and Democracy in America*, p. 80; Langenderfer, *The Federal Income Tax*, pp. 451–2.
[104] Ratner, *Taxation and Democracy in America*, p. 82.
[105] See Hill, "The Civil War Income Tax," 423 ("This act [the 1864 Act] was the most important revenue measure of the war, and was expected to produce revenue of about $250,000,000.")
[106] Act of June 30, 1864, ch. 173, §§ 116–23, 13 Stat. 281–5 (1864).
[107] Ibid.; Act of March 3, 1865, ch. 78, 13 Stat. 469 (1865); Hill, "The Civil War Income Tax," 425. Apparently, the need arose because new estimates suggested that the receipts from the 1864 Act would fall far short of the predictions when the bill was introduced. See Stanley, *Dimensions of Law*, p. 35.
[108] Act of June 30, 1864, ch. 173, § 117, 13 Stat. 281 (1864): 282.

of a corporation,[109] but soon after the 1864 Act was adopted this reading of the statute was challenged in court. Eventually, the Supreme Court considered the issue in *The Collector* v. *Hubbard*.[110] The Court agreed, albeit in dicta, that the "whether divided or otherwise" meant that a corporation's undistributed profits were generally taxed as income to its shareholders as if they had been received by the shareholder as a dividend or liquidating distribution.[111] Thus, regardless of a business's form of organization, its owners were taxed on a conduit basis.

Congress's decision to refrain from levying a separate entity-level tax on corporations and to instead tax both corporate and partnership income to their owners on a pass-through basis was not simply a product of the contemporary understanding of the corporation. In the Confederacy, for example, corporations were subject to an entity-level tax on annual earnings set apart for dividends and reserves, while dividends were exempt from individual income in the hands of stockholders to avoid double taxation.[112] Moreover, the view of corporations in the courts would have permitted an entity-level tax. In an 1865 case challenging the ability of a state to tax the shareholders of a bank that had all of its assets invested in tax-exempt US securities, the Supreme Court concluded that while "the individual members of the corporation are no doubt interested in one sense in the property of the corporation . . . in no legal sense are the individual members the owners."[113]

---

[109] See United States Internal Revenue Service, *Digest of Decisions and Regulations Made by the Commissioner of Internal Revenue Under Various Acts of Congress Relating to Internal Revenue, and Abstracts of Judicial Decisions, and Opinions of Attorneys-General, as to Internal-Revenue Cases. From December 24, 1864, to June 13, 1898.* (Washington, DC: Government Printing Office, 1906), pp. 16, 36, 37, 39, and 40. Although the principal challenges surrounding this provision applied to corporate profits, the provision actually applied to the undistributed profits of both corporations and partnerships. It appears that some limited partnerships operated under a corporate model and agreed not to allow funds to be distributed prior to the liquidation of the partnership. See Smith, *The United States Federal Internal Tax History*, p. 57. When faced with such a situation, the Commissioner ruled that each partner was required to report his or her share of profits as income as if a distribution had been made.

[110] *The Collector* v. *Hubbard*, 79 US 1 (1870).

[111] Ibid. at 16–18 (1870) (dicta). The Court struck down the challenge on the grounds that it was barred on jurisdictional grounds: ibid. at 14–15.

[112] Seligman, *The Income Tax*, p. 487. When dividends and reserves exceeded 10 percent of the paid-in capital stock, the Confederacy imposed a 12.5 percent tax on such amounts and when the dividends and reserves exceeded 20 percent of the paid-in capital stock the tax rate increased to 16.66 percent.

[113] *Van Allen* v. *The Assessors*, 70 US 573 (1865).

Congress deviated from the pure conduit approach with respect to an expanded group of the "taxable" businesses assessed under the 1862 Act. These included banks, trust companies, savings institutions, and insurance, railroad, canal, turnpike, canal navigation, and slackwater companies.[114] Such businesses were subject to a tax of 5 percent on all dividends as well as "all undistributed sums, or sums made or added during the year to their surplus or contingent funds."[115] While it is likely that most such businesses were conducted in corporate form, the critical distinction between these taxable businesses and other businesses was the specified industry rather than the form of organization. Additionally, businesses in the transportation fields mentioned above were subject to a tax of 5 percent on interest paid pursuant to bonded indebtedness.[116] One commentator has speculated that the reason banks and savings institutions were excluded from this list was concerns about vertical equity, since railroads and other transportation companies issued bonds in large denominations, while banks had many depositors with incomes below the $600 exemption.[117]

Despite the increased pressure to raise revenue, Congress sought to avoid imposing double taxation. As with the 1862 Act, several measures were enacted with this goal in mind. At the company level, taxable businesses were permitted to deduct amounts previously taxed, such as undistributed sums, from the tax due on the dividend.[118] At the investor level, investors were permitted to exclude dividends and interest received from taxable businesses.[119] Despite these efforts, the 1864 Act did not completely integrate the business/investor income taxes with respect to these taxable businesses. Most seriously, the 1864 Act imposed a flat, 5 percent, entity-level withholding tax on dividends and interest from taxable businesses while imposing a graduated tax with an exemption for incomes under $600 and a top marginal rate of 10 percent on income from other sources. This meant that shareholders who would not otherwise have been subject to tax under the individual income tax would pay tax on their corporate investments, while shareholders subject to the top marginal rates would pay at a lower rate on their dividends. Under the original scheme, however, at least the progressive marginal rate aspect of

---

[114] Act of June 30, 1864, ch. 173, §§ 120–22, 13 Stat. 283–5 (1864).
[115] Ibid., § 120, 13 Stat. 283 (1864).   [116] Ibid., § 122, 13 Stat. 284 (1864).
[117] See Scott A. Taylor, "Corporate Integration in the Federal Income Tax: Lesson from the Past and a Proposal for the Future," *Virginia Tax Review* 10 (1990): p. 261, n. 131.
[118] Act of June 30, 1864, ch. 173, § 121, 13 Stat. 284 (1864).
[119] Ibid., § 117, 13 Stat. 281 (1864).

this problem would not have been as significant. In the bill introduced by the House Ways and Means Committee, the income tax portion of the 1864 Act proposed a flat 5 percent tax on all income, including income from dividends and interest.[120] Graduated rates were later added to the individual income tax sections during the debates in Congress, but no similar change was made to the taxation of the specified businesses on their dividends and interest.[121] While some have suggested that this failure to adjust the business rates may have been merely an oversight,[122] more likely it was due to what one commentator described as "the problem of administration" involved with levying a graduated tax at the business level.[123] As Seligman explained, "[t]he graduated principle of the income tax could, however, obviously not be applied to the dividends and interest tax, and it was for this reason that the proportional rate of five per cent was imposed."[124]

The 1864 Act, as amended, remained in effect until the end of Reconstruction in 1872. Some thought the income tax should be retained as part of a general overhaul of the federal revenue system. Senator John Sherman declared that "the modification or repeal of the income tax should be postponed until, by a general revision of our whole revenue system, we can determine what taxes bear most heavily upon the people, and distribute the reduction so as to give them the greatest relief."[125] David Wells, the Commissioner of Internal Revenue, also stated in his annual report of December 1869 that he was in favor of continuing the income tax.[126] The general sentiment, however, was that the income tax was an emergency measure that should exist only so long as the lingering financial effects of the war continued to be felt.[127] Each of the acts passed from 1864 through 1867 thus contained a provision stipulating that the income tax would remain in effect until 1870 and no longer.[128] After receiving a short reprieve, the income tax ultimately expired after

---

[120] Seligman, *The Income Tax*, p. 440.
[121] Ibid., p. 441; Taylor, "Corporate Integration," p. 264.
[122] See Taylor, "Corporate Integration," p. 264.
[123] Langenderfer, *The Federal Income Tax*, p. 475.
[124] See Seligman, *The Income Tax*, p. 444.
[125] See, e.g., John Sherman, *Selected Speeches and Reports on Finance and Taxation, from 1859 to 1878* (New York: D. Appleton and Co., 1879), p. 319.
[126] See Seligman, *The Income Tax*, p. 456.
[127] Ibid., pp. 7–8; Ratner, *Taxation and Democracy in America*, pp. 121–7; Stanley, *Dimensions of Law*, p. 45.
[128] See Roy G. Blakey and Gladys Blakey, *The Federal Income Tax* (London: Longmans, Green and Co., 1940), p. 7.

1872.[129] Financial prosperity and the declining national debt combined to drain the income tax of its original wartime imperative.[130]

1.2.2   1894

Although political support for an income tax continued after the end of Reconstruction, with an income tax bill introduced in Congress virtually every year from 1873 until the early 1890s,[131] it was not successfully revived until after the Panic of 1893.[132] The high rates instituted by the McKinley tariff in 1890 had already focused attention on the inequity of the current revenue system.[133] Coupled with the unrest occasioned by the Panic's economic dislocation,[134] the time was ripe for another attempt at an income tax. In early 1894, Democrats attached an income tax amendment to the Wilson tariff bill in the House.[135] After much political wrangling over the tariff provisions, including an attempt to separate the income tax provision from the larger tariff bill,[136] the 1894 Act passed over the objection and without the signature of President Grover Cleveland.[137]

[129] See Ratner, *Taxation and Democracy in America*, pp. 126–7; Jeffrey Kwall, "The Uncertain Case against the Double Taxation of Corporate Income," *North Carolina Law Review* 68 (1990): 618, n. 23.

[130] See Stanley, *Dimensions of Law*, p. 54.

[131] See Bennett Baack and Edward John Ray, "Special Interests and the Adoption of the Income Tax in the United States," *The Journal of Economic History* 45 (1985): 608; Witte, *The Politics and Development of the Federal Income Tax*, p. 70. Fourteen different income tax bills were introduced into Congress between 1873 and 1879. Lawrence Friedman, *A History of American Law*, 2d edn. (New York: Simon & Schuster, 1985), p. 565. Representative Benton McMillin of Tennessee introduced bills to reinstitute an income tax virtually every year from 1879 through the early 1890s. Ratner, *Taxation and Democracy in America*, p. 172.

[132] Witte, *The Politics and Development of the Federal Income Tax*, p. 70.

[133] Ibid., p. 70; Baack and Ray, "Special Interests," 609.

[134] Witte, *The Politics and Development of the Federal Income Tax*, p. 70; Ratner, *Taxation and Democracy in America*, p. 170.

[135] *Cong. Rec.* vol. 26, p. 1594 (1894) (statement of Rep. Benton McMillin (D-Tenn.)); Baack and Ray, "Special Interests," 609; George Tunell, "The Legislative History of the Second Income-tax Law," *The Journal of Political Economy* 3 (1895): 311.

[136] Ratner, *Taxation and Democracy in America*, p. 173; Stanley, *Dimensions of Law*, p. 113.

[137] See Tariff Act of 1894, ch. 349, 28 Stat. 509 (1894). See Tayler, *The History of Taxation of England*, p. 268; Kossuth Kennan, *Income Taxation: Methods and Results in Various Countries* (Milwaukee, Wis.: Burdick and Allen, 1910), p. 259. Cleveland's objections arose primarily from disagreements over the Democrats' compromise on tariff relief. See Blakey and Blakey, *The Federal Income Tax*, p. 17.

Under the income tax provisions of the 1894 Act, Congress abandoned the graduated tax employed during the Civil War and Reconstruction in favor of a flat rate. All incomes in excess of $4,000 were taxed at a rate of 2 percent per year.[138] As the high exemption suggests, however, the tax was still primarily aimed at the wealthiest segment of society.[139] Most notably, however, Congress for the first time specifically levied an income tax on the corporation.

Initially the House had passed a bill with a provision that was fairly similar to the dividend tax employed during the Civil War and Reconstruction. Following the model of the 1864 Act, a 2 percent tax was imposed on the "dividends" and "undistributed sums or sums made or added during the year to [the] surplus or contingent funds" of certain banks and insurance companies.[140] The primary innovation was that this tax applied to all corporations or limited liability business enterprises rather than merely industries in which corporations were prevalent. Specifically, the House Bill provided that the tax would apply to

> all dividends, annuities, or interest paid by corporations or associations organized for profit by virtue of the laws of the United States or of any State or Territory, by means of which the liability of the individual stockholders is in anywise limited, in cash, scrip, or otherwise, and the net income of all such corporations in excess of such dividends, annuities, and interest, or from any other sources whatever.[141]

As with the 1864 Act, all entities taxable under this provision of the House bill were required to deduct and withhold from any dividends paid the amount necessary to pay the 2 percent tax.[142]

---

[138] Tariff Act of 1894, ch. 349, § 27, 28 Stat. 553 (1894).
[139] See Taylor, "Corporate Integration," p. 268; Stanley, *Dimensions of Law*, p. 132.
[140] Section 59 of the House bill provided, in relevant part,

> [t]hat there shall be levied and collected a tax of 2 per cent on all dividends in scrip or money thereafter declared due, wherever and whenever the same be declared payable to stockholders, policy holders, or depositors or parties whatsoever, including nonresidents, whether citizens or aliens, as part of the earnings, income or gains of any bank, trust company, savings institution, and of any fire, marine, life, inland insurance company, either stock or mutual, under whatever name or style known or called in the United States or Territories, whether specially incorporated or existing under general laws, and on all undistributed sums, or sums made or added during the year to their surplus or contingent funds.

Cong. Rec. vol. 26, p. 6831 (1894).
[141] Ibid.   [142] Ibid.

In the Senate, the corporate tax provision was significantly altered, at least on its face, from the House bill and the earlier 1864 version. Rather than imposing a tax on dividends and undistributed profits, the Senate Finance Committee introduced a bill that imposed a tax directly on the net income of corporations. Moreover, the Senate bill specifically identified a set of tax-exempt corporations, including states and municipalities as well as corporations organized for charitable, religious, or educational purposes.[143] This might have been designed to assure the constitutionality of the provision, although it was more likely designed to make it more politically appealing for those concerned about a general corporation tax.[144] Ultimately, the Senate version of the corporate income tax provision prevailed. Under Section 32 of the 1894 Act, a 2 percent tax was imposed on all "corporations, companies, or associations doing business for profit in the United States, no matter how created and organized, but not including partnerships."[145]

At the federal level the simultaneous income taxation of individuals and corporations was unprecedented, but there was no evidence that Congress intended to subject corporate income to double taxation. At the state level the sentiment against double taxation was just as strong as it had been during the Civil War and Reconstruction. Entire pamphlets were dedicated to the subject and the rhetoric of such pamphlets was highly charged. One pamphleteer wrote that "those features of our tax laws which involve double taxation ... violate the principles at the foundation of all systems of taxation; namely, justice or equality,

---

[143] Ibid. This was not necessary in the 1864 Act because its income tax provisions specified the industries to which the tax would apply. See Tayler, *The History of the Taxation of England*, p. 271.

[144] *Cong. Rec.* vol. 26, p. 6621 (1894) (statement of Sen. Hill questioning the constitutionality or prudence of taxing certain public or quasi-public corporations).

[145] Tariff Act of 1894, ch. 349, § 32, 28 Stat. 556 (1894). In full, the statute provided as follows:

> That there shall be assessed, levied, and collected, except as herein otherwise provided, a tax of two per centum annually on the net profits or income above actual operating and business expenses, including expenses for materials purchased for manufacture or bought for resale, losses, and interest on bonded indebtedness of all banks, banking institutions, trust companies, savings institutions, fire, marine, life, and other insurance companies, railroads, canal, turnpike, canal navigation, slack water, telephone, telegraph, express, electric light, gas, water, street railway companies, and all other corporations, companies, or associations doing business for profit in the United States, no matter how created and organized, but not including partnerships.

certainty, efficiency, and economy."[146] Another demanded that "[t]he folly, injustice, and demoralization which go with our present attempts at double taxation are first to be assailed."[147] Other sources, while treating the subject more even-handedly, were similarly consumed with double taxation.[148]

Double taxation concerns dominated consideration of the corporate income tax provisions of the 1894 Act. One Senator asked pointedly, "if I understand the bill, as it stands now there is to be double taxation; first, the dividends are taxed as the income of corporations, and then they are taxed when they reach the stockholders."[149] Members of Congress were quick to point out that the corporate income tax was deliberately structured so that it would complement rather than overlap the individual income tax.[150] Section 28 of the Act excluded from income dividends received from entities already taxed under the Act.[151] As under the 1864 Act, however, this was only a partial solution because, unlike individuals, entities could not exempt the first $4,000 of income from tax.[152] Thus, for shareholders with incomes below the exemption level, the tax on corporate income imposed an indirect tax where none should have been imposed at all. For all intents and purposes, however, the corporate income tax was integrated with the individual income tax.

This new corporate-level income tax was not implemented, however, because of a challenge to the constitutionality of the 1894 Act. Soon after the Act took effect on January 1, 1985, two shareholder suits were filed in federal court in New York to prevent their respective corporations from paying the tax.[153] Eventually, the court in *Pollock* v. *Farmers' Loan & Trust Co.* declared the income tax unconstitutional as an unapportioned

---

[146] George G. Crocker, *An Exposition of the Double Taxation of Personal Property in Massachusetts* (self-published, 1885), p. 3.

[147] Josiah P. Quincy, *Double Taxation in Massachusetts: Its Injustice as Between Towns and as Between Citizens; Its Abolition: the First Step Towards an Equitable Assessment of Wealth* (Boston: Houghton, Mifflin, 1889), p. 4.

[148] See Francis Walker, *Double Taxation in the United States* (New York: Columbia College, 1895), p. 9; Edwin Seligman, "The Taxation of Corporations III," *Political Science Quarterly* 5 (1890): 636.

[149] *Cong. Rec.* vol. 26, p. 6876 (1894) (statement of Sen. Dolph, R-Or).

[150] Ibid. (statement of Sen. Hill).   [151] Tariff Act of 1894, ch. 349, § 28, 28 Stat. 554 (1894).

[152] See Taylor, "Corporate Integration," p. 269.

[153] The cases were consolidated before the Supreme Court under the name *Pollock* v. *Farmers' Loan & Trust Co.*, 157 US 429 (1895). As originally filed, the other case was *Hyde* v. *Continental Trust Co.* See Witte, *The Politics and Development of the Federal Income Tax*, p. 73, n. 14.

direct tax.[154] Arguably, it could have concluded that the corporate income tax provision was permissible, while still striking down the individual income tax.[155] On rehearing, however, the court emphasized that, while certain similar provisions – such as "excise taxes on business, privileges, employments, and vocations" – might be permissible, the income measure was void *in toto*.[156]

1.2.3   1898

During the Spanish-American War in 1898, Congress once again considered the possibility of a tax on corporations. With the expected rise in government expenses from the onset of the war, Congress had to seek alternative revenue sources.[157] Thus, in May of 1898, a war revenue bill was introduced with one of its major innovations being the utilization of an excise tax on the gross receipts of corporations.[158] The thinking was that this would be consistent with the strictures laid down in *Pollock* and therefore survive judicial scrutiny, while still allowing the government to levy a tax that reached corporate income.

There was significant debate as to why the bill targeted corporations rather than taxing all businesses in a particular industry, regardless of

---

[154] *Pollock v. Farmers' Loan & Trust Co.*, 157 US 429 at 572. Article I of the Constitution provides, "No Capitation, or other direct, Tax shall be laid, unless in Proportion to the Census or Enumeration herein before directed to be taken:" US Const. Art. 1, § 9. The rule of apportionment, a compromise born in part out of the divide between small and large states and in part out of the question of how to count slaves, requires that direct taxes such as poll or property taxes be apportioned between the states according to each state's population: Seligman, *The Income Tax*, p. 594. In this manner, large and powerful states are prevented from causing the national government to impose all the taxes on citizens of the smaller states. See generally, Erik Jensen, "The Apportionment of 'Direct Taxes': are Consumption Taxes Constitutional?" *Columbia Law Review* 97 (1997): 2380–89.

[155] See Taylor, "Corporate Integration," pp. 271–2.

[156] *Pollock v. Farmers' Loan & Trust Co.*, 158 US 601 at 635–7 (1895).

[157] See Steven Weisman, *The Great Tax Wars: Lincoln to Wilson: The Fierce Battles Over Money and Power That Transformed the Nation* (New York: Simon & Schuster, 2002), p. 177; "Finances in War time," *Washington Post*, April 6, 1898, p. 3A; "The financial situation," *The Commercial and Financial Chronicle* 66 (1898): 728.

[158] "This week in Congress; The War Revenue Bill may be completed, passed, and signed before Saturday," *New York Times*, May 23, 1898, p. 4. The corporate excise tax was first considered in an amendment to the bill in the Senate. See "Taxes to Wage a War," *Washington Post*, May 17, 1898, p. 4A (noting that it was "inserted without the co-operation of the Republican members of the Finance Committee"). The other major innovation was the adoption of a federal inheritance tax. See Act of June 13, 1898, ch. 448, §§ 27, 29, 30 Stat. 464 (1898).

their form. While the sponsors may have made this distinction because of constitutional and practical concerns,[159] it nevertheless was criticized because of the disparate treatment of similarly situated businesses.[160] Republican Senator Henry Cabot Lodge from Massachusetts characterized the failure to tax corporations and partnerships equally as "the extreme injustice of the bill."[161] Senator John Spooner, a Republican from Wisconsin, added that "[i]t amounts to a bonus to the individual or the private partnership."[162]

Ultimately, in the War Revenue Act of 1898,[163] Congress rejected the proposed tax in favor of a tax defined by line of business – sugar and oil. While this was both broader and narrower than the original corporate excise tax, it was commonly understood that the object of the tax was two concerns – the Standard Oil Company and the American Sugar Refining Company.[164] The main impetus for the move to an industry-based tax appeared to be federalism.[165] This was both the practical concern at depriving the states of a revenue source and the constitutional concern

---

[159] *Cong. Rec.* vol. 26, p. 5138 (1894) (statement of Sen. Platt (R-Conn.): "You cannot tax the property of a corporation because it is personal property, and because the Supreme Court has said in the income-tax decision that a tax upon personal property is a direct tax. Therefore, they attempt to get away from the inhibition by saying that they put a tax on corporations."); ibid., p. 5101 (statement of Sen. Turley (D-Tenn.) noting that the significantly undertaxed property in the country is held in corporations).

[160] Ibid., p. 5090 (statement of Sen. Spooner (R-Wisc.): "I know a city in my State, in which one side of a street there is a corporation engaged in the business of manufacturing furniture, and on the other side of the street is a partnership engaged in the business of manufacturing furniture. I think the business is precisely the same. Under this bill, as I understand it, the firm would not be taxed."); ibid., p. 5099 (statement of Sen. Lodge (R-Mass.): "Does not the Senator see that the partnerships, which in the shoe and leather industry are quite as numerous, and I think more numerous, than corporations, would not have to pay anything, and therefore they would not add it and they would cut the business right out from under these other people.").

[161] Ibid., p. 5098 (statement of Sen. Lodge).

[162] Ibid., p. 5099 (statement of Sen. Spooner).

[163] Act of June 13, 1898, ch. 448, 30 Stat. 448.

[164] See "Voted to tax trusts" *Washington Post*, June 2, 1898, p. 4A. As first proposed, the tax would have been levied on other industries as well, including transportation and public utility corporations. *The Commercial and Financial Chronicle* was indignant at the singling out of these industries, calling it "an odd proposal. It would seem difficult to say on just what principle the selections for taxation named in the proposed amendment were made. The selections appear eminently inequitable." "The financial situation", 1019.

[165] *Cong. Rec.* vol. 31, p. 5106 (1898) (statement of Sen. Spooner: "The question is, whether Congress can any more tax the franchise, the right to be, of the corporation than the State can tax a Federal corporation?").

about interfering with states' rights given the fact that states were the primary chartering authorities for corporations.[166] Significantly, some argued as well that taxing corporate gross receipts would be double taxation in light of the state taxation of the corporate stock and the practical, if not legal, equivalence between the shareholder and the corporation.[167] Finally, there was also some disagreement about whether this would aid or exacerbate the shifting incidence problem,[168] but in the end the revised bill passed with a minimum of debate.

Although Congress opted not to tax corporations in 1898, the sugar and petroleum excise taxes set the stage for a later expansion of the concept. In *Spreckels Sugar Refining Company* v. *McClain*,[169] the court rejected a constitutional challenge to the use of excise taxes in lieu of an income levy. Justice Harlan, writing for the court, resolved the question

---

[166] Ibid., p. 5098 (statement of Sen. Lodge, saying that the national government "has left to the States as one of their principal sources of taxation the aggregate capital engaged in banks and corporations, and I think to take that from the States or largely reduce it will have the precise effect which it is said we desire to avoid; that is, it will force the State taxation on the class of people least able to bear a heavy direct tax."); ibid., p. 5138 (statement of Sen. Platt: "The power to tax implies the power to destroy. If the Congress of the United States can impose a tax upon the corporation itself as a corporation, it can destroy it; it can destroy what the State alone can create and what the State has a right to create and a right to maintain; and that is as applicable to one kind of corporation as to another.").

[167] Ibid., p. 5103 (statement of Sen. Allen: "A certificate of stock represents the interest of a stockholder in the aggregate property. If you tax that aggregate property to its full limit, making the taxes imposed on it equal to those imposed on other property, then taxing the stock would be simply double taxation on the property."). The response was that there was no legal restriction, although this didn't address the underlying policy claim. Ibid., p. 5103 (statements of Sens Turley and Lindsay).

[168] Ibid., p. 5396 (statement of Sen. Platt: "It is picking out from all the interests of the country two classes of business where it is absolutely certain that the corporations will not pay the tax, but that it will be paid by the consumer . . . the persons engaged in the business will be very careful in raising the price of oil and sugar to raise it a little more than the tax, so that the consumer will pay not only the tax, but the additional profit to these two companies.") with Edwin Seligman, *The Shifting and Incidence of Taxation*, 2d edn. (New York: Macmillan Co., 1899), pp. 286–8 (noting that in the case of a monopoly a tax on gross receipts is not always shifted to the consumer). In the immediate aftermath of the tax, the results were mixed as to whether the tax was actually shifted. See Max West, "The Income Tax and the National Revenues," *The Journal of Political Economy* 8 (1900): 449 n. 2 ("It seems quite impossible to say whether or to what extent this tax actually has been shifted to the consumers. Since it was imposed the general tendency of prices has been upward in petroleum, but downward in sugar; but in neither case was there any increase in price at the time the act was passed or for some weeks thereafter.")

[169] *Spreckels Sugar Refining Co.* v. *McClain*, 192 US 397 (1904).

fairly summarily: "Clearly the tax is not imposed upon gross annual receipts as property, but only in respect of the carrying on or doing the business of refining sugar. It cannot be otherwise regarded because of the fact that the amount of the tax is measured by the amount of the gross annual receipts."[170] This had little precedential value for the collection of the since-repealed sugar and petroleum taxes, but it eventually provided cover for President William Howard Taft when he introduced a corporate excise tax in 1909.

1.3 Conclusion

Although the USA and the UK were formally quite different in their tax treatment of corporations by the end of the century – since the Americans did not tax corporations on account of their corporate status at all at that point – they were in fact quite similar in their approaches to corporate taxation. Neither considered double taxation acceptable, nor did they subscribe to a classical approach to corporate taxation in which the tax at the entity level was viewed as separate and distinct from any shareholder-level tax. Rather, both viewed the corporation as a means for reaching shareholder income. This convergence on the aim of corporate taxation, if not the means of achieving that aim, would begin to unravel early in the twentieth century.

---

[170] Ibid. at 411.

PART I

Twentieth century and the divergence in systems

2

The United Kingdom

Although the United Kingdom formally maintained its shareholder imputation approach through much of the twentieth century, a variety of new challenges – wars, depressions, and emerging political and economic forces – led it to try alternative methods of corporate taxation. During large swaths of the century, the UK deviated from its pure imputation system, either by adopting an additional entity-level tax as an overlay on the shareholder imputation system or by adopting an entirely new system of entity-focused taxation. In large part, the UK was motivated to adopt these fairly radical innovations during periods in which it sought to dampen the amount of dividends and increase the tendency of corporations to plow back earnings into the business.

2.1   1900–18

The major innovation in the British income tax system between 1842 and 1918 was the introduction of the principle of graduation in 1909.[1] Graduated rates had been introduced indirectly starting in 1853 with the use of abatements, but this was found to be impractical for reaching higher incomes without completely exempting lower incomes.[2] For most of this earlier period, all attempts to explicitly introduce progressivity beyond an exemption or abatement amount were rejected. Seligman reported that during the nineteenth century "the principle of progressive or graduated taxation ... had been uniformly reprobated not only by all English statesmen, but by the great mass of important British thinkers."[3]

By 1906, with the election of the Liberal Party, the principle of graduation grew in popularity. Herbert Asquith, the Chancellor of the Exchequer, maintained in his Budget Statement delivered in April

---

[1] See Report of the Royal Commission on the Income Tax, Cmd 615 (1920), p. 28.   [2] Ibid.
[3] Edwin R. A. Seligman, *The Income Tax: A Study of the History, Theory, and Practice of Income Taxation at Home and Abroad* (New York: The MacMillan Co., 1911), p. 180.

of 1906 that "[t]here are two familiar, and in point of justice and economic principle, valid objections to the incidence of the tax. They are, as everyone knows, first that above the limits of exemption and abatement it is levied at a uniform rate; and secondly, that no distinction is made between precarious and permanent income. It appears to me that the time has come for a searching and authoritative enquiry."[4]

This led Parliament to appoint a Select Committee, chaired by Sir Charles Dilke, "to inquire into and report upon the practicability of graduating the income tax, and of differentiating, for the purpose of the tax, between permanent and precarious incomes."[5] Two years earlier, a Departmental Committee had been established, originally with the intent that it would investigate whether the income tax should be revised to reflect the principles of differentiation and graduation; but the committee was ultimately charged with other matters, including the question of fraud and evasion and the appropriate means to penalize these.[6] Advocates of progressivity, however, pressed for a more focused study, which resulted in the creation of the Select Committee.[7] While the Committee's charge ostensibly left open the question of whether to adopt progressivity at all, it had become a foregone conclusion by this point. Thus, efforts were primarily focused on the method of implementation.

The Select Committee considered three possible methods of introducing graduation to the income tax. The method that would have involved the least structural change to the existing system, and which was ultimately recommended in its report, was to extend the system of abatements by charging lower rates on smaller incomes and then proportionately higher rates on larger incomes. Since this would still be collected through stoppage at source, the method would necessitate large refunds when the tax actually due proved less than that imputed by reference to an amount received through an individual source. This was considered to be both an administrative burden and a potential source of great irritation for those subject to taxpayers large withholdings.

The solution to the problem of large refunds and the most radical method of implementing the progressivity principle considered by the

---

[4] Sir Herbert Asquith, "Budget statement" in *The Parliamentary Debates* (4th series, 1906), p. 300.
[5] Report from the Select Committee on Income Tax, Cd 365 (1906), p. iii.
[6] It delivered its report in 1905. Report of the Departmental Committee on the Income Tax, Cds 2375 and 2376 (1905); Seligman, *The Income Tax*, p. 185.
[7] Fakhri Shehab, *Progressive Taxation: A Study in the Development of the Progressive Principle in the British Income Tax* (Oxford: Clarendon Press, 1953), p. 222.

Committee was using the "lump sum" approach, which involved "collecting the whole of the tax directly from each person, upon his declaration."[8] This would allow the rate to rise or fall depending upon the amount declared. The problem with this method is that it would have necessitated abandoning the stoppage-at-source scheme employed throughout the British schedular system, including most notably in the collection of tax on corporate income from dividends. As Seligman reported, "[t]o such a course the committee were unalterably opposed."[9]

A compromise method of graduating the tax was to impose a "supertax." As the Select Committee Report explained, "this is a combination of the method of a direct personal tax with that of taxation at the source."[10] The primary concern with this method was that, while individuals with incomes below £700 a year were already required to file something akin to the modern income tax return, "it does not follow that other people with much larger and more complicated incomes would be equally willing to declare their actual income, when the object for which that declaration was required was that an additional tax should be levied upon them."[11] The Committee considered a super-tax on larger incomes to be "practicable," but acknowledged that it had potential disadvantages.[12]

The Select Committee also considered whether it should differentiate between "permanent," or unearned, and "precarious," or earned income, with the former subject to a higher rate of taxation. While acknowledging that the line between the two types of income was not entirely clear, it did identify "the profits of public companies" as one type of income typically regarded as unearned in the hands of shareholders because this derived from investment rather than an individual's own activities.[13] According to the Select Committee Report, "[t]he mere supervision of invested capital should not be sufficient to entitle the income to be regarded as earned."[14] The Report further distinguished between the income from small businesses and the income from highly profitable, complex businesses, noting that

> [t]he more extensive and remunerative the business is, the larger, as a rule, is the part which capital plays in it, and the more practicable and equitable it will be to regard the profit derived from it as an income derived from an investment which is personally supervised as distinguished from an income earned by personal effort.[15]

---

[8] Shehab, *Progressive Taxation*, p. 222.   [9] Seligman, *The Income Tax*, p. 197.
[10] Report from the Select Committee on Income Tax, Cd 365 (1906), p. iv.
[11] Ibid.   [12] Ibid, p. v.   [13] Ibid, p. vi.   [14] Ibid.   [15] Ibid, p. vii.

This meant that corporate income, and in particular income from publicly-traded companies, would be subject to higher taxes than most partnership income.

Parliament acted first upon the recommendation for differentiation. Under the Finance Act of 1907, taxpayers were taxed at a lower rate on earned income below £2,000 p.a.[16] Most notably, the definition of earned income strictly distinguished between income earned individually or through a partnership, and income earned through a corporation. As Seligman observed, "as soon as a private business becomes a corporation, the profits change from earned to unearned income," whereas if "the recipient is actively engaged therein and is not protected by limited liability, then such income is earned."[17] Thus, for the first time the corporation was treated differently for purposes of the income tax.

Implementing the Select Committee's recommendation regarding the principle of graduated rates was delayed because of the complexities of introducing it alongside differentiation, but it was eventually introduced by Chancellor of the Exchequer David Lloyd George in the Finance Act of 1910.[18] Under this act, individuals with incomes of £5,000 p.a. or more were subject to a super-tax of 2.5 percent, or sixpence for every pound, on the amount in excess of £3,000, in addition to the regular income tax of just under 6 percent.[19] This super-tax, however, was not applicable to corporations under the withholding-at-source scheme. Corporations paid tax at the standard rate and shareholders received a credit against the standard rate for tax paid at the corporate level on dividends. Dividends, however, were still subject to the super-tax in the hands of shareholders when applicable.

Theoretically, the introduction to the British income tax of a progressive super-tax (which was eventually replaced by a surtax[20]) created the conditions for an eventual move to a classical corporate income tax. When income was only subject to a flat rate, a shareholder imputation system assured its subjection to that rate when earned at the corporate

---

[16] Finance Act 1907, 7 Edw. VII c. 13, ss. 18–28; Seligman, *The Income Tax*, pp. 203–4.
[17] Seligman, *The Income Tax*, p. 205.
[18] Finance Act of 1910, 10 Edw. VII and 1 Geo. V c. 8, s. 66.
[19] Report of the Royal Commission on the Income Tax, Cmd 615 (1920), p. 123. The actual percentage for the standard rate on the income tax was 14d or 5.83 percent.
[20] See Roswell Magill, L. Parker, and Eldon King, *A Summary of the British Tax System, With Special Reference to Its Administration* (Washington, DC: US Government, 1934), pp. 24–5 (prepared for the Joint Committee on Internal Revenue Taxation pursuant to §1203(b)(6), Revenue Act of 1926).

level. Under these circumstances, the decision to distribute profits as dividends was of little consequence to the government. Now that some shareholders were subject to a progressive rate, though, a decision not to distribute profits as a dividend could deprive the government of super-tax revenues. This suggested an entity-focus rather than a focus on the shareholder exclusively, but it did not lead to structural reform.

The super-tax remained when the Income Tax Act of 1842 was consolidated with all succeeding modifications of the system in the Income Tax Act of 1918.[21] The principal provision governing the taxation of corporate income was contained in General Rule 20. Under this provision, the 1842 version of the corporate income tax scheme was adopted with only mild changes in phrasing.[22] Thus, the shareholder imputation system survived the consolidation. Corporations were subjected to tax on their income, but to compensate them for paying this tax, they were entitled to deduct from any dividends an amount equal to the proportionate share of the tax paid at the corporate level. Shareholders then received a credit to reflect the fact that tax had already been paid at the corporate level on any dividend income, although the credit did not extend to relieve the application of the super-tax.

One interpretation of General Rule 20 was that the corporation served as a mere agent of the shareholders, with the income tax being imposed on the dividend rather than on the entity itself. The implication was that a corporation was not merely permitted to deduct tax from the dividend payment, but was required to do so. The House of Lords, though, in a 1934 case,[23] rejected this notion. According to Lord Wright, "[t]he company is not bound but only authorized to deduct tax in paying dividends; whether it deducts or not is left to its discretion because the profits once having been taxed in the company's hands, do not bear further tax (apart from surtax) in the shareholders' hands."[24]

Some shareholders also tried to avoid the super-tax by arguing that General Rule 20 removed dividend income from the taxable income of

---

[21] Income Tax Act 1918, 8 and 9 Geo. V c. 40.
[22] Income Tax Act 1918, 8 and 9 Geo. V c. 40, at general Rule 20:

> The profits and gains to be charged on any body of persons shall be computed in accordance with the provisions of this Act on the full amount of the same before any dividend thereof is made in respect of any share, right, or title thereto, and the body of persons paying such dividend shall be entitled to deduct the tax appropriate thereto.

[23] *Neumann* v. *Commissioners of Inland Revenue*, 18 Tax Cas. 332, AC 215, 236 (1934).
[24] Ibid.

the shareholder altogether. This may have been caused in part by the practice of issuing dividends "free of tax." Under this method as described in a 1920 Royal Commission report, a £10 dividend, less £3 deducted for the corporation's income tax would be issued as a £7 dividend "free of tax." According to the report, "[i]t has also been urged that the system leads to confusion in the taxpayer's mind, because it is frequently difficult to convince him that in making a return of his total income (e.g., for Super-tax purposes) the amount he must show as his income from a 'free of tax' dividend is more than the actual net amount he has received."[25] The courts rejected such arguments, however, holding that the super-tax was due on dividends regardless of whether they were issued free of tax.[26]

2.2   1920–24: Corporation Profits Tax

Although the treatment of corporate income under the system of differentiation and graduation suggested a separate entity focus, the first UK tax to explicitly target the corporation *qua* corporation was the Corporation Profits Tax in 1920.[27] Parliament had enacted an Excess Profits Duty at the onset of World War I in 1915,[28] but this levy was applicable to the profits of all business.[29] When the war ended, however, and the government sought to extend its claim on the lingering stream of war profits to help pay off its war debt and finance the recovery,[30] it limited its focus to corporations. The tax operated as an additional 5 percent tax on corporate income in excess of £500, with rates up to 10 percent on amounts remaining after paying interest and preferred dividends, even though it was styled as a separate form of tax.[31] Predictions

---

[25] Report of the Royal Commission on the Income Tax, Cmd 615 (1920), p. 39.

[26] See, e.g., *Brooke v. Commissioners of Inland Revenue*, 1 KB 257, 7 Tax Cas. 261 (1918); *Whitney v. Commissioners of Inland Revenue*, AC 37, 10 Tax Cas. 88 (1926).

[27] Finance Act 1920, 10 and 11 Geo. V c. 18, s. 52.

[28] Finance (No. 2) Act 1915, 5 and 6 Geo. V c. 89, ss. 38–45.

[29] See Harrison Spaulding, *The Income Tax in Great Britain and the United States* (London: P. S. King & Son, Ltd., 1927), p. 78 (the rate rose from 15 percent in 1915 to 80 percent in 1918).

[30] Josiah C. Stamp, "The Special Taxation of Business Profits in relation to the Present Position of National Finance," *The Economic Journal* 29 (1919): 407. In addition to the long-term debt, the country faced a large short-term debt that reached as high as £1.57 million in June of 1919, "which caused the Treasury more alarm than the long-term debt." Martin J. Daunton, "How to Pay for the War: State, Society and Taxation in Britain, 1917–24," *The English Historical Review* 111 (1996): 882, 903.

[31] Spaulding, *The Income Tax in Great Britain*, p. 87.

placed revenues from the tax as high as £30 million by the second year of operation.[32] This tax appeared to be a shift to the American system because it treated the corporation as a separate taxable entity.[33]

One of the reasons the corporation profits tax appeared to be a fundamental shift in approach is that it was justified on grounds similar to those raised for the development of a separate corporate tax. Supporters argued that it served as a remedy for the inequity between corporations and partnerships in the application of the super-tax.[34] Corporate income was subject to the standard rate when earned and, when distributed, to the super-tax. Partnership income was subject to both the standard rate and the super-tax when earned, regardless of when the money was distributed. The corporation profits tax, therefore, was necessary as a proxy for the application of the super-tax to retained earnings.

Despite the apparent paradigm shift, the corporation profits tax did not signify as great a departure from the pass-through nature of the shareholder imputation system as one might assume. During the debates over its adoption, Colonel Josiah Wedgwood explained that "[t]he Corporation tax is an additional income tax, which amounts to 2s. in the pound on the ordinary holders of stocks and shares."[35] Perhaps to underscore the view that the tax did not represent a paradigm shift, the Inland Revenue report recommending a corporation profits tax did so under the explicit assumption that the government would soon revert to the former system of taxing corporations.[36] This is consistent with a more contextual and contingent explanation for the adoption of the profits tax.

The corporation profits tax was largely considered a temporary response to pressure to end the excess profits duty.[37] Although Josiah Stamp, a member of the Royal Commission on the Income Tax in 1920 and later the Committee on Debt and Taxation in 1924, argued that this entity-based approach should be made permanent, that was a non-starter. The Treasury and the Inland Revenue believed that a temporary

---

[32] "Taxes throttling industry – A £910,000,000 Budget – Chambers of Commerce proposal," *The Times* (London), December 2, 1920, p. 9.

[33] Martin J. Daunton, *Just Taxes: The Politics of Taxation in Britain, 1914–1979* (Cambridge University Press, 2002), p. 89.

[34] Ibid., p. 91; Rufus S. Tucker, "The British Finance Act, 1920," *Quarterly Journal of Economics* 35 (1920): 167, 170.

[35] *Hansard*, HC, vol. 128, col. 5, 1920.

[36] Daunton, *Just Taxes*, p. 91. This, however, was not immediately obvious to all contemporary observers, with one Harvard professor describing the corporation profits tax as "presumably permanent." Tucker, "The British Finance Act, 1920," 167, 169.

[37] Daunton, *Just Taxes*, pp. 89–92.

profits tax was a way to accommodate a diverse set of interests. According to Martin Daunton "[t]he continuation of some form of profits tax offered a way of containing the pressure of Labour for a capital levy, of the middle class for a curtailment of profiteering, and of industry for the reform of the EPD."[38] Business leaders argued that the tax should not be applied only to corporations, but they agreed that it was preferable to the excess profits duty. The National Union of Manufacturers approved of the new tax at a conference in the spring of 1920 and, in passing a resolution condemning the excess profits duty, noted that "the corporation profits tax offers a more equitable basis for producing the revenue required."[39] "The EPD and corporation profits tax," Daunton concluded, "were therefore short-term expedients to cover the immediate postwar crisis."[40]

As soon as the economy recovered sufficiently to produce a surplus, businesses' opposition to the tax resumed in full force. The Federation of British Industries reported to the Chancellor of the Exchequer in 1923 that "a large majority of members attending the special taxation meetings held last autumn [decided] that the abolition of the corporation profits tax should be placed in the forefront of the Federation's taxation policy."[41] Later that same year, in light of the surplus, the Chancellor unexpectedly proposed in his Budget that the rate be cut in half – to 2.5 percent.[42] While the yield of the corporation profits tax had never been as high as expected, this proposal was met with great approval in the business community, leading to "appreciable rises" in the stock prices of "a number of the leading commercial and industrial shares."[43] The tax was repealed altogether the following year and the country resumed the single layer of corporate tax under the shareholder imputation system.[44]

---

[38] Ibid., p. 91; Daunton, "How to Pay for the War," 882, 901.

[39] "Excess Profits a 'lottery' – manufacturers and the Corporation Tax," *The Times* (London), May 8, 1920, p. 11.

[40] Daunton, *Just Taxes*, at p. 92.

[41] "Lighter burden of taxes – Appeal by FBI to government – Cooperators' quota," *The Times* (London), January 31, 1923, p. 7.

[42] Basil E. V. Sabine, *A History of Income Tax* (London: George Allen & Unwin Ltd., 1966), p. 165.

[43] "City notes – Budget reception – Effect on markets," *The Times* (London), April 18, 1923, p. 18; Sabine, *A History of Income Tax*, p. 164.

[44] Daunton, *Just Taxes*, p. 93. See Finance Act 1924, 14 and 15 Geo. V c. 21, s. 34; Peter Harris, *Corporate/Shareholder Income Taxation and Allocating Taxing Rights Between Countries: A Comparison of Imputation Systems* (Amsterdam: IBFD Publications, 1996), p. 89.

2.3   1924–37

After the repeal of the corporation profits tax, the British reverted to
their prewar scheme. Nevertheless, questions continued to arise regarding the unequal treatment of companies and other, non-corporate,
businesses as a result of the super-tax. The Labour Party, in satisfying
an election year pledge, had established a commission under the direction of Lord Colwyn to study the question of how to address the growing
debt. While primarily occupied with the effect of taxation on savings and
the debt, it also became a forum for discussion of the inequality of
company taxation.[45] In 1927, the commission's findings, formally
released as the Report of the Committee on National Debt and
Taxation, acknowledged the issue of corporate taxation in examining
the effect of taxation on a company's reserves:

> When the standard rate of Income Tax was 6s. in the pound, in 1920–21
> and 1921–22, £50,000 allocated to reserve by a public company would
> have borne £15,000 tax. The same sum kept in the business by an
> individual trader (unmarried) with a total chargeable income of £150
> would, as part of that income, have borne Income Tax and Super-tax
> amounting to £30,000.[46]

The Colwyn Commission dismissed this equity concern, however, suggesting that there was a real difference between corporations and individuals or partnerships:

> Judged by the above comparison, the company appears to be fortunate.
> But a comparison between the public company and the big individual
> trader is in many respects a comparison between unlikes and must not be
> pressed too far. For the company, as such, is a collective body, which
> cannot enjoy the privilege of personal wealth, and its shareholders may
> be rich or poor.[47]

This implied that the lines between corporations and businesses operating in non-corporate form might be growing stronger.

Although there were some signs that the shareholder imputation
system was weakening after the repeal of the corporation profits tax,

---

[45] Daunton, *Just Taxes*, p. 73; Willson Coates, "Report of the Committee on National
Debt and Taxation," *Journal of the Royal Statistical Society* 90 (1927): 353; J. Maynard
Keynes, "The Colwyn Report on National Debt and Taxation," *The Economic Journal*
37 (1927): 198.

[46] Report of the Committee on National Debt and Taxation, Cmd 2800 (1927), p. 148.

[47] Ibid.

these were more akin to minor adjustments than the separation of the corporate and individual income taxes that was simultaneously occurring in the USA. For example, in 1927 Parliament clarified one potential ambiguity in the withholding-at-source scheme by providing that the corporation's right to deduct from a dividend was based on the corporate tax rate in the year of distribution rather than the rate actually imposed on the distributed profits.[48] Thus, if a corporation paid income tax on its profits at one rate and then distributed those profits in a subsequent year in which a higher rate was in effect, it would withhold from the dividend an amount based on the higher rate even though it had actually paid at the lower rate.[49] While this meant that the deduction was not strictly tied to the amount of tax actually paid, it only enacted what was already imposed in practice on the grounds of administrative simplicity.[50]

2.4   1937–58

Parliament continued the shareholder imputation system for taxing corporate income throughout the 1930s, but concerns about the high cost of rearmament led to a search for alternative sources of revenue. In 1937, this resulted in a return to profits taxation in the form of a "National Defence Contribution."[51] Part of the ostensible justification for proposing this particular tax stemmed from the massive five-year rearmament campaign initiated to keep pace with the Germans.[52] As *The Times* explained, "[t]his revival of the excess profits duty is, of course, in fulfillment of the Government's undertaking that profiteering shall not be allowed in connection with the rearmament programme."[53] Neville Chamberlain expanded on this sentiment, noting that "it does not seem

---

[48] Finance Act 1937, 1 Edw. VIII and 1 Geo. VI c. 54, ss. 19–25.
[49] See 1936 Income Tax Codification Committee Report, Cmd 5131 (1936), p. 64. While this meant that the corporation could actually profit from the deal by withholding more from the dividend than was necessary to compensate it for the tax paid on the underlying profits, the converse was also true and corporations would not be made whole if the tax rate dropped between the year tax was paid on the profits and the year in which those profits were distributed as dividends. See H. Arnold Strangman, "British and American Taxes," *Taxes* 21 (1943): 208.
[50] Strangman, "British and American Taxes," 208.
[51] Finance Act 1937, 1 Edw. VIII and 1 Geo. VI c. 54, ss. 19–25.
[52] Albert Farnsworth, "Some Reflections upon the Finance Act, 1937," *Modern Law Review* 1 (1938): 290–91; Robert Shay, Jr., "Chamberlain's Folly: the National Defence Contribution of 1937," *Albion* 7 (1975): 317.
[53] "The new excess profits tax," *The Times* (London), April 21, 1937, p. 22.

to me to be unreasonable to ask that this growth in business profits should be made the occasion of some special and temporary contribution on the part of those concerns which have benefited, towards the cost of National Defence."[54] Notwithstanding such statements, it was neither clear that profits had indeed risen as a result of rearmament nor that the tax was limited to those firms engaging in profiteering.[55]

Unlike the corporation profits tax of the 1920s, the national defence contribution applied to virtually all businesses.[56] Nevertheless, as originally proposed, the tax treated public corporations differently from private companies. Under the invested capital portion of the levy, public corporations were limited to a return on capital of 6 percent while private companies were permitted as much as an 8 percent return before being subject to the tax.[57] Corporations were subject to the tax at a 5 percent rate, while individuals and partnerships were levied at 4 percent.[58] From the perspective of contemporary commentators, the tax was "merely another version of C.P.T. [corporation profits tax], a tax on the total profits of firms, both incorporated and not incorporated."[59]

In part because the national defence contribution, as amended, amounted to little more than a general tax on the profits of all businesses, Parliament re-enacted the World War I-era Excess Profits Tax in 1939.[60] Rather than supplanting the national defence contribution, the excess profits tax supplemented it, with the former levying a tax on profits and the latter targeting increases in profits as compared with the pre-war base. Although, as enacted, the excess profits tax was scheduled to apply at a 60 percent rate on all amounts in excess of the base, it was soon increased to a 100 percent rate, even where the corporation's profits could not be attributed to the war effort.[61] According to a memorandum privately circulated by the Chancellor of the Exchequer in support of the 100 percent rate, part of the justification was that "controlled

---

[54] *Hansard*, HC, vol. 322, ser. 5, col. 1617, 1937 (statement of Mr. Chamberlain).

[55] Farnsworth, "Some Reflections," 291.

[56] It did not apply to public utilities on the grounds that their profits were already subject to regulation. John Hicks, Ursula Hicks, and Laszlo Rostas, *The Taxation of War Wealth* (Oxford: Clarendon Press, 1942), p. 90.

[57] Daunton, *Just Taxes*, p. 172.

[58] H. Arnold Strangman, "Great Britain's National Defence Contribution," *Taxes* 15 (1937): 694.

[59] J. Hicks, U. Hicks, and L. Rostas, *The Taxation of War Wealth*, p. 90.

[60] Finance (No. 2) Act 1939, Part III; "Business notes," *The Economist*, March 9, 1946, p. 385.

[61] J. Hicks, U. Hicks, and L. Rostas, *The Taxation of War Wealth*, pp. 100–101.

undertakings," or those determined to be necessary for war production, were already subject to such a rate and the difficulty of drawing a line between types of industries led the Chancellor to advocate "on grounds of equity" the application of the same rate to both.[62] In 1942 the national defense contribution was extended "until such date as Parliament might determine."[63]

The combined effect of the two measures was to subject corporate income to a form of de facto double taxation.[64] This was because neither the national defence contribution nor the excess profits tax could be deducted from dividends paid to shareholders. Therefore, although profits were taxed only once under the regular income tax, they were subject to a second layer of tax at the entity level under the two profits taxes.

In 1937 business reaction to the proposal for a national defence contribution had reflected a concern about government interference with retained earnings that echoed similar concerns expressed in the United States. According to one commentator,

> [u]nderlying these specific complaints, all of which had merit, was a more fundamental concern about the precedent of the Government assuming power to compel business to relinquish part of its profits. Businessmen viewed their profits as their personal property, and regarded any attempt by government to dictate how they were to dispose of them as a violation of their rights.[65]

Although both the national defence contribution and the excess profits tax could be dismissed as war-related, only the latter was repealed after the war. The former was instead converted to a permanent tax on corporate profits, applicable exclusively to corporations, in 1947.[66] The decision to limit the new version of profits tax to corporations was justified in part because individuals and partners were already subject to the individual surtax and in part because non-corporations had only accounted for a small percentage of the revenues from the prior version of the profits tax.[67] This new profits tax was a sharp departure from the

---

[62] Memorandum by the Chancellor of the Exchequer to the War Cabinet, "Excess Profits Tax," National Archives, May 28, 1940, CAB/66/8/6.

[63] Daunton, *Just Taxes*, p. 173.

[64] Spaulding, *The Income Tax in Great Britain and the United States*, p. 89.

[65] Shay, "Chamberlain's Folly," 325.

[66] Finance Act 1946, 9 and 10 Geo. VI c. 64, ss. 36 and 44; Finance Act 1947, 10 and 11 Geo. VI c. 35, s. 31.

[67] See *Hansard*, HC, vol. 436, ser. 5, col. 85, 1947 (statement of Mr. Dalton).

shareholder-focused model of corporate taxation, in part because of its unique structure.

Under the measure, Chancellor of the Exchequer Hugh Dalton sought to modify the concept of a profits tax so as to levy a heavier burden on distributed than on retained earnings.[68] In introducing this tax, Dalton explained

> I cannot pretend to be satisfied with the large increases in distributed profits and the higher dividends which have been paid out in so very many cases in the last 12 months. Too much, in my judgment, has been distributed, and too little ploughed back into the business. These increased dividends are the clearest case, anywhere in our national economy, of an inflationary element.[69]

This reflected the concern that dividends had become the object of "widespread prejudice" since the end of the war.[70] There were two complaints about the high level of dividends. First, critics charged that dividends contributed to postwar inflation by increasing consumer spending.[71] Second, and perhaps more importantly, dividends were viewed as an obstacle to the capital investment necessary to rebuild postwar Britain. In a speech to Parliament in 1945, Hugh Dalton, the Chancellor of the Exchequer, pleaded with business to cut back on their dividends:

> The reduction of the standard rate ... benefits companies as well as individuals, but I hope that the resulting increase in net profits of companies will be spent on new and up-to-date plant and will not go straight into the shareholders' pockets. We cannot afford that right now. In the national interest, capital development must stand in front of high dividends, particularly in the critical next years when we have to convert and modernise at high speed so large a part of our industrial outfit, much of which is badly outmoded.[72]

---

[68] *Hansard*, HC, vol. 436, ser. 5, col. 84, 1947.   [69] Ibid.

[70] "Business notes," *The Economist*, March 9, 1946, p. 385. See Daunton, *Just Taxes*, p. 199 (noting that the prejudice against dividends, but not against reinvestment of company profits in the business, was part of a Labour "belief that wealth became more reprehensible as it was further removed from its active creation.").

[71] See, e.g., "Taxes and incentives," *The Economist*, April 6, 1946, p. 546; *Hansard*, HC, vol. 436, ser. 5, col. 1122, 1947 (statement of Major Bruce: "After having pronounced this grave homily on the danger to the nation, they would proceed to add to the inflationary position by declaring an increased dividend for distribution among their shareholders.").

[72] *Hansard*, HC, vol. 414, ser. 5, cols. 1896–7, 1945 (statement of Mr. Dalton).

Businesses, however, had apparently failed to heed his warnings and invest profits in the business. Dalton reported that industry's response to his invitation to engage in voluntary dividend restraint "has been patchy. Many of the most efficient and up-to-date concerns have responded very well; but others have shown a tendency to chuck money about among the shareholders, rather than to strengthen their reserves and improve their equipment."[73]

To address this perceived imbalance in favor of dividends, Dalton proposed to tax undistributed profits at the prevailing rate of 5 percent, but subject distributed profits to a higher rate of 12.5 percent.[74] Soon after its passage, those rates were raised to 10 percent on undistributed profits and 25 percent on distributed profits because of what Dalton called "a continuing and persistent inclination on the part of many concerns to declare increased dividends."[75] The doubling of the rates was said to constitute a "psychologically much greater" inducement to retain earnings, "whatever may be the mathematics of the matter."[76] As profits increased and the rate of dividends did not appear to decline, the

---

[73] *Hansard*, HC, vol. 421, ser. 5, col. 1833, 1946 (statement of Mr. Dalton). Dalton's claim that business had failed to stem the increase in dividends was not uncontroversial. One member cited articles in *The Economist* and *The Times* that reported annual figures suggesting that dividend payout ratio and retained earnings percentage numbers were flat. See *Hansard*, HC, vol. 436, ser. 5, cols. 1117–18, 1947 (statement of Mr. Assheton, citing a report in *The Economist* that companies paid 53.5 percent of profits as dividends in 1945 and 53.2 percent in 1946, and a report in *The Times* that companies put 24.7 percent of profits into free reserves in 1945 and 25.6 percent in 1946). Others rejected such figures, reporting anecdotal evidence that many large companies had increased their dividend. See *Hansard*, HC, vol. 436, ser. 5, col. 1121, 1947 (statement of Mr. Bruce: "All I can say is that, of the large number of companies whose results I was examining in the files of *The Times*, I could not find one case where there had been a diminution in the dividend last year as compared with the previous year.").

[74] *Hansard*, HC, vol. 436, ser. 5, col. 1121, 1947.

[75] *Hansard*, HC, vol. 444, ser. 5, col. 401, 1947; "Parliament," *The Times* (London), November 13, 1947, p. 6. This may have been prompted in part by some members' calls for higher rates soon after Dalton's proposal was announced. *Hansard*, HC, vol. 436, ser. 5, cols. 1126–7, 1947, statement of Mr. Beswick:

> I do not think this tax of 12½ per cent. goes far enough to limit these profits. I have been surprised by the lack of energy with which the Opposition have attacked this Profits Tax. The reason why they have displayed such lack of energy is because, in my view, they were expecting a heavier Profits Tax. I think there was some reason for reducing the 60 per cent. E.P.T., but I do not think there was any reason for reducing it down to 12½ per cent."

[76] "Profits, taxes and dividends," *The Times* (London), November 17, 1947, p. 7.

tax on distributed profits rose dramatically, to 30 percent in 1950 and 50 percent in 1951.[77]

In 1951, Labour lost control of government and the Conservatives took office with an eye toward reforming the profits tax. The tax on distributed profits was reduced from 50 percent to 22.5 percent and the tax on undistributed profits was lowered from 10 percent to 2.5 percent.[78] Even before the transfer of power took place, though, a Royal Commission on the Taxation of Profits and Income was convened to investigate the effectiveness of the current structure and to recommend changes if necessary. The Commission held hearings on the profits tax and most of the major business trade groups submitted reports and offered testimony.

During the hearings, it became clear that UK companies were less concerned with the differential nature of the profits tax than with the possibility that it was the proverbial camel's nose under the tent for conversion to a classical corporate income tax. As the Federation of British Industries had explained in its original testimony before the Royal Commission, "[a] profits tax is not deductible from a dividend that is paid."[79] Thus, unlike with the British income tax, the profits tax could be considered a tax on the company as a separate entity. In 1952, the Federation of British Industries emphasized this point in its second memorandum to the Royal Commission, stating that "[i]t is the *gravamen* of the criticism of Profits Tax, that it is a corporate tax which cannot be specifically passed on to shareholders."[80] When pressed to choose which tax was worse, that on distributed or that on retained profits, the Federation chose the undistributed profits tax in part because it was the most direct example of a separate entity tax.[81]

By the middle of the 1950s, opponents were aided in their cause by a growing sense that the profits tax had done little effective to stem the tide

---

[77] See Daunton, *Just Taxes*, p. 211 (noting that the 50 percent tax on distributed profits was proposed in conjunction with a statutory limit on dividends, which was never implemented).

[78] See Daunton, *Just Taxes*, p. 211.

[79] "Minutes of Evidence taken before the Royal Commission on the Taxation of Profits and Income," November 1, 1951, col. 84 (testimony of S. P. Chambers, C. D. Hellyar, and A. G. Davies on behalf of the Federation of British Industries).

[80] Federation of British Industries, "Second Memorandum to the Royal Commission on the Taxation of Profits and Income," 1952, p. 30.

[81] "Minutes of Evidence taken before the Royal Commission on the Taxation of Profits and Income," November 1, 1951, col. 84, para. 808 (testimony of S. P. Chambers, C. D. Hellyar, and A. G. Davies on behalf of the Federation of British Industries). The National Union of Manufacturers also argued against any tax on retained profits, arguing that the company-level tax had curtailed capital investment and cut into, rather than increased, retained earnings available to fund projects. See "Tax on undistributed profits, manufacturers' call for abolition," *The Times* (London), April 2, 1951, p. 3.

of dividends or increase the amount of productive investment.[82] In 1954, one British economist published a report questioning whether the profits tax was actually able to lower dividends.[83] The argument was that since British companies had a highly inelastic tendency to distribute dividends regardless of the amount of their profits, a punitive tax on dividends would not lessen the flow of dividends.[84] Businesses would simply pay the tax by further reducing savings.[85] This and other reports were apparently sufficient to convince a majority of the Royal Commission that the differential profits tax was no longer worth pursuing as an indirect limit on dividends. In its final report, it concluded that the tax

> has not prevented the increase in amounts distributed by way of dividend which has been noticeable since 1953, and we are disposed to think that, even with the present big difference between the distributed and undistributed rates, it can only have a minor influence on distribution policy when other influences combine to pull in the opposite direction.[86]

When coupled with the fact that there was no evidence that any retained earnings were profitably spent,[87] and that the differential only served to introduce complexity,[88] a majority of the Royal Commission recommended ending the differential feature.[89] Nicholas Kaldor authored a dissent on behalf of himself and two other members of the commission.[90] They disputed the majority's finding that dividends had not been affected by the differential rates, but conceded that a higher differential might be even more

---

[82] One business reaction which contributed to this development was the migration of British companies overseas in order to avoid the profits tax. See Arnold Rogow, "Taxation and 'Fair Shares' under the Labour Government," *Canadian Journal of Economics and Political Science* 21 (1955): 213. Labour even attempted to restrict this migration by inserting a provision in the 1951 Finance Act that made it illegal to migrate overseas if this resulted in evasion of tax liability.

[83] See A. Rubner, "The Irrelevancy of the British Differential Profits Tax," *Economic Journal* 74 (1964): 347, 353 (citing D. Walker, *Some Economic Aspects of the Taxation of Companies*, Manchester: Manchester School (Jan. 1954)).

[84] Rubner, "Irrelevancy of DPT."   [85] Ibid.

[86] Royal Commission on the Taxation of Profits and Income, Final Report, Cmd 9474 (1955), p. 159.

[87] Ibid.   [88] Ibid, p. 157.

[89] Ibid., pp. 159–60 ("The use of differential rates may have been of some value in the immediate post-war years but the arguments against such a tax structure increase with the years and in the end must prove decisive. We recommend that the differential rates should be brought to an end.").

[90] See Royal Commission on the Taxation of Profits and Income, Memorandum of Dissent to Final Report, Cmd 9474 (1955), pp. 354, 382–3 (signed by G. Woodcock, H. L. Bullock, and N. Kaldor).

effective.[91] The minority opposed repeal of the differential feature unless this was part of a larger reform including the taxation of capital gains.[92] In a move that foreshadowed developments to come later, Kaldor recommended that the UK eventually adopt a classical corporate income tax system.[93]

Initially, the minority's views appeared to carry the day.[94] The then-ruling Conservatives increased the tax on distributed earnings in each of the next two years.[95] When this failed to have the desired effect on dividend policy, however, the Conservatives implicitly declared the experiment with differential rates to be over when it omitted the differential rates from its 1958 Budget proposal.[96] The profits tax remained, but it applied equally to retained and distributed profits.[97]

2.5   1965-73

Not long after the repeal of the differential feature of the profits tax, the government once again became concerned with dividends and industrial investment.[98] In his Budget statement to Parliament in

---

[91] Ibid., p. 386, para. 99 ("The existence of the differential profits tax has undoubtedly been a major cause of the relative modesty of dividend distributions as compared with the rise of earnings.") and p. 388, para. 105 ("Nobody would dispute that a differential rate of say, 50 per cent. would not only prevent increased distributions but force companies to reduce the existing level of dividends.").

[92] Ibid., p. 388 ("We are strongly opposed therefore to the recommendation of the Majority that the differential profits tax should be abolished forthwith, quite independently of whether capital gains are taxed or not; though we would favour such a change as part of a wider reform which included the taxation of capital gains."). In the UK, capital gains were not taxed until 1965. See John Tiley, "United Kingdom," in Hugh Ault (ed.), *Comparative Income Taxation: A Structural Analysis* (Boston: Kluwer Law International, 1997), p. 113.

[93] See Royal Commission on the Taxation of Profits and Income, Memorandum of Dissent to Final Report, Cmd 9474 (1955), pp. 383-4.

[94] Some suggested that the minority also opposed the differential profits tax: see Thomas Balogh, "Differential Profits Tax," *The Economic Journal* 68 (1958): 528, but this is clearly untrue in at least the short term. See note 92, above.

[95] See Rubner, "Irrelevancy of DPT," at 354 (the minority's "prognosis was published in June 1955; in the autumn of the same year the Conservative Chancellor accepted this recommendation of the minority and widened the differential in the profits tax from 1:9 to 1:11.").

[96] Ibid.   [97] Finance Act 1958, 6 and 7 Eliz. II c. 56, s. 25.

[98] According to one account, "[w]hen the differentiated Profits Tax was abolished in 1958, and tax incentive for retentions was removed, there was an immediate upsurge in distributions, and that has continued to the present day." *Hansard*, HC, vol. 712, ser. 5, col. 52, 1965 (statement of Mr. Niall MacDermot). *Hansard*, HC, vol. 713, ser. 5, col. 1834, 1965 (statement of Chief Secretary to the Treasury, John Diamond: "previously we had a system which encouraged retention and that was replaced by a single-tier Profits Tax which removed that encouragement to retention. Therefore, there was further distribution, and the rate of growth of dividends went up by 50 per cent. as a result.").

November of 1964, James Callaghan, Labour's newly-appointed
Chancellor of the Exchequer, expressed concern at the current system.
According to Callaghan, the corporate income tax system "does not
provide sufficient incentive to companies to plough back profits for
growth rather than to distribute them as dividends."[99] While the government had enacted a generous set of depreciation deductions in 1954 with
the goal of increasing investment, Callaghan believed that they were
insufficient by themselves to make a difference.[100]

To further increase the incentive for corporations to retain earnings,
Callaghan proposed reforming the tax system. Rather than returning to
the 1950s differential profits tax feature, however, Callaghan advocated
repealing the profits tax and adopting the classical corporate income tax
recommended by Kaldor in 1955.[101] Since Kaldor's recommendation, a
series of writers had pushed the concept of a classical corporate tax in
subsequent years.[102] According to Callaghan, separating the corporate
and individual income taxes would help simplify the tax structure, end
certain abuses of the system, and permit the separation of corporate and
individual tax rates.[103] In the latter case, the ability to impose separate
rates at the corporate and individual levels was thought to permit
government to target tax incentives as an aid to national planning of
the economy.[104] Corporate income would thus be subject to tax both at
the corporate level when earned and at the shareholder level when
distributed as a dividend. Unlike in a classical corporate income tax

---

[99] *Hansard*, HC, vol. 701, ser. 5, col. 1041, 1964 (statement of Mr. Callaghan).

[100] Rt. Hon. James Callaghan, "The New United Kingdom Tax Structure in Relation to the
Needs of the Economy," *European Taxation* 5 (1965): 212, 214.

[101] *See* text accompanying note 93, above.

[102] *Hansard*, HC, vol. 712, ser. 5, col. 51, 1965 (statement of Mr. Niall MacDermot, citing
"Taxes for Today," a 1958 pamphlet published by the Conservative Political Centre,
"The Young Conservative," a 1963 pamphlet, and an article on Tory policy in the July
27, 1964 issue of the *Daily Telegraph*).

[103] *Hansard*, HC, vol. 701, ser. 5, cols. 1041–2, 1964 (statement of Mr. Callaghan). An
additional concern was that money was being invested overseas rather than in British
industry. See *Hansard*, HC, vol. 712, ser. 5, col. 57, 1965 (statement of Mr. MacDermot).
While this issue was heavily debated, some suspected that it was not an original
justification for the measure, but was only added as the balance of payments started
to become a concern. See *Hansard*, HC, vol. 713, ser. 5, col. 1828, 1965 (statement of
Mr. John Biffen: "I regard this argument [that the position of overseas investment has
necessitated the introduction of the Corporation Tax] with a great deal of suspicion,
not least because, when the Chancellor first announced the Corporation Tax, last
November, he made no reference whatsoever to the fact that it would be of some
assistance to our overseas situation.").

[104] See Daunton, *Just Taxes*, pp. 291–2.

system, where the shareholder-level tax is paid by the shareholders themselves, companies would be directed to withhold and remit the shareholder-level tax when dividends were paid.[105]

Callaghan conceded that this new system would subject company profits to double taxation, but he noted that Parliament had long since abandoned the single tax concept when it introduced the profits tax. According to Callaghan, "any idea of reforming the Tax system by introducing a Corporation tax in this country has foundered because of the widely held view that to levy a separate tax on company profits which is distinct from, and additional to, the Income Tax levied on individuals would constitute 'double taxation' of company profits. The Profits Tax already contradicts this argument."[106] Opponents countered that the differential profits tax only imposed a 15 percent burden while the proposed Corporation Tax would impose a double tax burden of between 35 and 40 percent.[107] As the Inland Revenue had itself concluded in 1959 when reviewing whether the profits tax opened the door for a full corporate tax, "[a]ll the history and tradition behind our tax code could be prayed in aid of this criticism."[108]

The classical corporate income tax was eventually adopted in 1965,[109] but it was a source of significant controversy almost from the beginning. One commentator warned, rather caustically, "it is the height of folly" to simultaneously attempt to effect the "euthanasia of the shareholder" while "pay[ing] lip service to the merits of private enterprise."[110] Adding to the seeming irony of the strategy was that Parliament imposed a tax on long-term capital gains for the first time, after subjecting short-term capital gains to tax under the Finance Act of 1962.[111]

---

[105] This was justified "[a]s a matter of administrative convenience." Shareholders who were exempt from tax or not subject to tax at the full standard rate were entitled to file a refund claim. See Callaghan, "New UK Tax Structure," at 214.

[106] See *Hansard*, HC, vol. 710, ser. 5, col. 254, 1965 (statement of Mr. Callaghan).

[107] See *Hansard*, HC, vol. 713, ser. 5, col. 1724, 1965 (statement of Mr. Barber).

[108] R. C. Whiting, "Ideology and Reform in Labour's Tax Strategy, 1964–1970," *The Historical Journal* 41 (1998): 1123 (quoting Board of Inland Revenue, *A Corporation Tax*, Public Record Office, Treasury Budget Papers T 171/508, December 30, 1959).

[109] Finance Act 1965, c. 25, ss. 46–89.

[110] A. R. Ilersic, "Taxes 1964–66: an Interim Appraisal," *British Tax Review* (1966): 373.

[111] This was ironic considering the tax on capital gains would likely reduce incentives for investment. One way to reconcile these two seemingly inconsistent prongs of Labour's tax strategy is by concluding that the Party wanted to encourage investment by business managers rather than by individuals. See Malcolm Crawford, "The 1965 Reforms in the British Tax System," *Moorgate and Wall Street*, August 1965, at 42, 44. Supporters also

Once the Conservatives regained office in 1970, they set about dis-
mantling the corporation tax.[112] In his March 30, 1971 Budget statement, Anthony Barber, the new Chancellor of the Exchequer, announced
the government's intention to replace the corporation tax and "the
substantial discrimination which it entails in favour of retained as
opposed to distributed profits."[113] Rather than doing so immediately,
though, Barber chose to publish his department's proposals in a "Green
Paper" that would be made available for further consideration.[114] In the
Green Paper, Barber advocated a two-rate system much like the German
approach in which distributed profits would be subject to tax at a lower
rate than undistributed profits, but he also indicated willingness to
consider a shareholder imputation system.[115] A Select Committee on
Corporation Tax was formed by the House of Commons to consider the
proposals contained in the Green Paper. In its report,[116] the Select
Committee recommended adoption of the shareholder imputation system in large part because of the concerns surrounding overseas income
earned by UK companies.[117]

On April 6, 1973, Parliament adopted the Select Committee's recommendations and thus ended the UK's short experiment with a classical

pointed out that it was possible to devise a capital gains tax that would not inhibit
investment, but would still achieve Labour's other goals. See ibid. at 50. A more
pragmatic way to reconcile the corporate tax and capital gains tax is that, since
companies would presumably increase their retained earnings, share values would
rise and corporations would extract their gains through sales of stock rather than
dividends. Those sales of stock, which had previously been tax-free, would now be
taxed. Thus, the capital gains tax served as a substitute for the tax revenue from
dividends. See Daunton, *Just Taxes*, at pp. 318–19.

[112] Daunton, *Just Taxes*, p. 326.

[113] *Hansard*, HC, vol. 814, ser. 5, col. 1383, 1971 (statement of Chancellor of the
Exchequer, Anthony Barber).

[114] *Hansard*, HC, vol. 814, ser. 5, col. 1383, 1971; *Reform of the Corporation Tax*, Cmnd
4630 (1971). Part of the justification for delay was to permit possible coordination with
the reform of corporation taxes among countries in the European Economic
Community. Ibid., col. 2.

[115] Ibid., col. 2.

[116] See Report from the Select Committee on Corporation Tax, Session 1970–71, HC 622,
October 20, 1971.

[117] Ibid., p. xiii, para. 24:

The arguments in favour of the imputation system spring basically from
this country's position as an international trader and investor. All whom
Your Committee questioned agreed that the imputation system was
preferable to the two-rate system as a basis for the renegotiation of double
taxation agreements (which will be necessary whatever system is finally
adopted).

corporate income tax.[118] In many respects, the new system was similar to the classical corporate tax that it replaced.[119] Corporations were subject to tax on their income and dividends were not deductible from corporate income for purposes of calculating tax. Shareholders were also subject to income tax on dividends received. The system also resembled that in place prior to 1965, however, in that Parliament relieved double taxation of corporate income by providing shareholders a credit to set against some of the tax paid at the corporate level. Much like the modern payroll withholding system, the dividend was grossed-up to reflect both the cash paid and the credit, with the credit calculated so as to equal the income tax liability on the dividend grossed-up at the basic rate. This meant that lower-rate taxpayers had no further liability or were eligible for a refund if their marginal rate was less than the base rate, such as with tax-exempt pension funds, while higher-rate taxpayers were subject to tax on the additional amount.[120]

The most significant innovation from both the pre- and post-1965 systems was the adoption of an Advance Corporation Tax ("ACT"). Under this provision, a corporation had to pay a tax on any dividends paid, irrespective of whether it actually had any tax liability.[121] The ACT could then be offset against the corporation's actual tax due.[122] If the actual tax due was low relative to a company's dividend payments, such as when it had a bad year or when much of its profits were generated and taxed overseas, then the company received surplus ACT credits that could be carried backward or forward over a period of years. In effect, the ACT acted as a prepayment for the corporation's actual tax liability. This responded to one of the concerns with the pre-1965 shareholder imputation system, which related to the potential for the tax credit to exceed the amount of the corporation's actual tax liability.

---

[118]   Finance Act 1972, c. 41.
[119]   See Andreas Tontsch, "Corporation Tax Systems and Fiscal Neutrality: the UK and German Systems and Recent Changes," *Intertax* 30 (2002): 175.
[120]   Ibid.
[121]   See Malcolm Gammie, "UK Imputation, Past, Present and Future," *Bulletin for International Fiscal Documentation* 52 (1998): 429.
[122]   Ibid.

3

The United States

While the United Kingdom maintained its integrated approach through most of the pre-World War II period, the United States soon diverged from this path. As it turned out, the *Pollock* case discussed in Chapter 1 was only a temporary bump in the road to a corporate income tax in the United States. In 1909, soon after it sent the Sixteenth Amendment to the states for ratification,[1] Congress passed a corporate excise tax as part of the Payne–Aldrich Tariff Act.[2] Although styled an "excise tax," it was effectively an income tax because the excise was measured by a corporation's net income. Since it was not accompanied by an individual income tax, however, the risk of double taxation was minimized. Upon ratification of the Sixteenth Amendment, a corporate income tax was once again adopted as part of the individual income tax imposed under the Revenue Act of 1913.[3] Just as in the 1894 Act, double taxation was avoided by excluding dividends from the individual income tax base. This method of integrating the corporate and individual income taxes served as a model until the dividend exclusion was removed in 1936.[4] Since that time, Congress has employed a variety of different methods to partially alleviate the burden of double taxation, but it has never seriously considered eliminating the corporate income tax altogether.

3.1   Revenue Act of 1913

Upon ratification of the Sixteenth Amendment,[5] Congress adopted a corporate income tax in conjunction with the individual income tax

---

[1] US Const. amend. XVI; See Sidney Ratner, *Taxation and Democracy in America* (New York: Octagon Books, 1980), p. 292.
[2] Act of August 5, 1909, ch. 6, § 38, 36 Stat. 112 (1909).
[3] See Ratner, *Taxation and Democracy in America*, pp. 335–6.
[4] See Jeffrey Kwall, "The Uncertain Case against the Double Taxation of Corporate Income," *North Carolina Law Review* 68 (1990): 619–20.
[5] US Const. amend. XVI.

imposed under the Revenue Act of 1913.[6] As mentioned above, Congress minimized the risk of double taxation by excluding dividends from what was called the "normal" tax on individual income.[7] Under the 1913 Act, all individual income was subject to a "normal", or base, tax levied at a flat rate of 1 percent. When income reached a certain level, a surtax was applied at progressive rates reaching as high as 6 percent. The corporate income tax rate was explicitly tied to the (individual) normal tax so that a rise in the normal tax rate would be matched by an identical rise in the corporate tax rate.[8] By exempting dividends from the normal tax, Congress ensured that corporate and non-corporate income was treated similarly. Corporate income distributed as a dividend was subject to both the 1 percent corporate income tax and the individual surtax, if applicable, but not to the normal tax, while non-corporate business income was subject to both the 1 percent normal tax and the surtax, if applicable, but not to the corporate income tax. As a result, the 1913 corporate income tax, like its predecessor under the 1894 Act, was a quasi-withholding provision for the individual income tax.[9]

Notwithstanding its use of the quasi-withholding tax structure, Congress was concerned with the trend toward the retention of corporate earnings. As Senator John Sharp Williams, one of the primary Democratic defenders of the income tax bill in the Senate,[10] explained, "it was thought for the purpose of obtaining revenue a corporation might now and then pass up a portion of its profits to surplus or otherwise refrain from distributing them."[11] The worry was that corporations

---

[6] Tariff Act of 1913, ch. 16, 38 Stat. 166–81 (1913).   [7] Ibid., § II(B), 38 Stat. 167–8.

[8] Ibid., § II(B), (G), 38 Stat. 166, 172 ("the normal tax hereinbefore imposed upon individuals likewise shall be levied, assessed, and paid annually upon the entire net income of . . . corporations.").

[9] As with the 1894 version, the 1913 Act did not completely eliminate the double taxation risk because individuals (but not corporations) were entitled to an exemption of $3,000 if single or $4,000 if married. Ibid., § II(C), 38 Stat. 168. Thus, if a stockholder's income fell below the applicable exemption amount, the corporate income tax subjected them to a tax when they would have had to pay none if the income had come from a non-corporate source. The bill's sponsors rationalized this failure to apply the exemption to corporate stockholders on the grounds that they enjoyed the benefits of investing through the corporate form. See *Cong. Rec.*, vol. 503, p. 509 (1913) (statement of Rep. Cordell Hull). In other discussions of the issue, however, it was clear that part of the obstacle was the administrative difficulties in rebating their share of the tax. See Ibid., p. 3848 (colloquy between Senators Williams and Cummins).

[10] See Steven A. Bank, "Origins of a Flat Tax," *Denver University Law Review* 73 (1995): 393.

[11] *Cong. Rec.*, vol. 50, p. 3774 (1913) (statement of Sen. Williams).

would become tax avoidance vehicles for high-income shareholders because retained earnings were subject to the 1 percent corporate tax, but not to the surtax until distributed as dividends.[12] This prompted the Senate Finance Committee and the Democratic caucus to adopt a provision for taxing individuals on the undivided profits of a corporation. An individual's "taxable income" was defined to include "the share of any taxable individual of the gains and profits of all companies, whether incorporated or partnership, who would be legally entitled to enforce the distribution or division of the same, if divided or distributed, whether divided or distributed or otherwise . . ."[13]

Because of its controversial nature,[14] and because of certain ambiguities, the provision was recommitted to the Senate Finance Committee and a less expansive tax on undistributed earnings was proposed.[15] Under this revised provision, an additional tax would be imposed only on companies "formed or fraudulently availed of for the purpose of preventing the imposition of such tax through the medium of permitting such gains and profits to accumulate instead of being divided or distributed."[16] While there was some dispute over how Treasury would determine whether a corporation had accumulated earnings beyond the reasonable needs of the business,

[12] Ibid., p. 3775 (statement of Sen. Borah: "The very difficulty which I presume this amendment was adopted to meet is the fact that they might incorporate, pay the 1 per cent upon their net earnings, and entirely escape the graduated tax or surtax. If there is not some way to meet that, that is precisely what may happen.").

[13] Ibid., p. 3774 (amendment introduced by Sen. Williams). The full text of the amendment is as follows:

> For the purpose of this additional tax, taxable income shall embrace the share of any taxable individual of the gains and profits of all companies, whether incorporated or partnership, who would be legally entitled to enforce the distribution or division of the same, if dividend or distributed, whether divided or distributed or otherwise, and any such company, when requested by the Commissioner of Internal Revenue or any district collector of internal revenue, shall forward to him a correct statement of such profits and the names of the individuals who would be entitled to the same if distributed.

[14] See "Attack new clause as double tax," *New York Times*, July 6, 1913, p. 5 ("Financial advisers of persons whose incomes are sufficiently large to make them liable for the surtax provided in the income tax bill have called their clients' attention in the last few days to a clause that has been inserted by the Senate Finance Committee and adopted by the Democratic caucus, which has occasioned a good deal of concern and has been criticized as indefensible double taxation.").

[15] *Cong. Rec.*, vol. 50, pp. 3774–5 (1913) (statement of Sen. Williams) (explaining the intent to recommit the amendment to Committee).

[16] Ibid., p. 4380.

and therefore presumably had done so to avoid the imposition of the surtax,[17] the provision no longer applied across the board. Senator Williams explained that the transformation of the bill was designed to be a more narrowly tailored solution to the problem of tax fraud:

> This clause gave us more trouble than perhaps anything in this bill . . . unless we provide for this evil in some way men might escape not the normal tax but escape the additional tax by merely forming themselves, or using a brother, wife, or somebody, or an office boy. Then, while perfectly willing to pay the normal tax as a corporation, they would escape the additional tax by not having their amount distributed by an arrangement so that they could draw upon the corporation, of course, for whatever they needed.[18]

This compromise version was adopted by Congress and is the forerunner of the modern accumulated earnings tax.[19] The problem of retained earnings generally, however, which the previous version of this provision addressed, continued to loom in the background.

3.2   Revenue Act of 1917

During World War I, it soon became obvious that the real threat to the surtax was not earnings fraudulently retained for the purpose of evading it,[20] but rather retained earnings generally. According to the sketchy data available to Congress, corporations were retaining an average of at least 50 percent of their earnings each year.[21] Based on aggregate corporate

---

[17]   Ibid., p. 5318 (statement of Sen. Borah).   [18]   Ibid., p. 5318 (statement of Sen. Williams).

[19]   Tariff Act of 1913, ch. 16, § II(A)(2), 38 Stat. 166–7 (1913). See IRC § 531 (West 2002).

[20]   According to several reports, the accumulated earnings tax was "a dead letter" upon passage. See *Cong. Rec.*, vol. 55, p. 6169 (1917) (statement of Sen. Andrieus Jones: "There is another provision of the law which was intended to prevent corporations from hoarding their earnings for the purpose of avoiding the payment of the surtax by the individual stockholders were the earnings distributed. But the law as it exists has proven a dead letter."); ibid., p. 6172 (statement of Sen. Simmons: "I think it is generally understood that by reason of the terms of that provision it was not really enforced and it became a dead letter upon the statute books."). Part of the problem was the difficulty in determining when a retention of earnings was in excess of the reasonable needs of the business. Even if Treasury could settle on an appropriate standard for establishing the reasonable requirements of a particular business, Senator Jones explained, this was "a task absolutely impossible of execution, not only as to the varied classes of business of the country but by reason of the enormous task of doing it. You would have to get experts in every line of business." Ibid., p. 6173 (statement of Sen. Jones).

[21]   See ibid., p. 6171 (statement of Sen. Jones) (quoting an average of the data from various sources).

income amounting to approximately $9 billion during the 1917 fiscal year,[22] Senator Andrieus Jones, a Democrat from New Mexico, argued that this meant that as much as $450 million in corporate income was not being subject to the individual surtax rates.[23] Moreover, with the surtax rates increasing from a top rate of 13 percent in 1916 to a top rate of 50 percent in 1917,[24] the magnitude of the lost revenue had increased significantly.

Senator Jones proposed applying an accumulated earnings tax to all undistributed profits, not just those retained for the purpose of evading the surtax. Under this proposal, which was originally approved by the Senate Finance Committee and reported to the Senate, a surtax of 15 percent would be imposed upon undistributed corporate earnings.[25] Additionally, corporations would be granted an exemption equal to 20 percent of earnings, while railroads would be entitled to an exemption equal to the amount the Interstate Commerce Commission determined should be retained for the purposes of extensions and improvements.[26]

As with the original 1913 Act provision, the accumulated earnings tax proposal was subject to "widespread criticism."[27] Corporate managers protested that the tax would impede their efforts to expand plant capacity to meet the needs of the war effort, especially at a time when investment capital was limited.[28] Perhaps most significantly, opponents argued that the trend toward more conservative dividend policies pre-dated the institution of corporate income tax and, therefore, the notion that all retaining of earnings was being done to avoid the surtax was false. This argument proved convincing. As Senator Furnifold Simmons, Chairman of the Senate Finance Committee, recounted:

> The suggestion had been made that the retention of earnings was for the purpose of escaping and avoiding the income surtaxes, but it was found

---

[22] Ibid., p. 6167 (statement of Sen. Jones).   [23] Ibid., p. 6171 (statement of Sen. Jones).

[24] Compare Revenue Act of 1916, ch. 463, § 1(b), 39 Stat. 757 (1916) (imposing a top surtax rate of 13 percent), with War Revenue Act of 1917, ch. 63, § 2, 40 Stat. 301 (1917) (imposing a top surtax rate of 50 percent).

[25] *Cong. Rec.*, vol. 55, pp. 5966, 6173 (1917).   [26] Ibid., pp. 5966, 6173.

[27] Ibid., p. 6004 (statement of Sen. Penrose).

[28] Ibid., p. 5966 (statement of Sen. Simmons: "It was pointed out to us that under present conditions, differing so materially from those of the past, it was not only absolutely necessary for them as heretofore to retain a portion of their surplus, but that if they did not do it to a very much larger extent than under ordinary conditions they would be utterly unable to meet the requirements of the present war and emergency situation."); see Roy Blakey and Gladys Blakey, *The Federal Income Tax* (London: Longmans, Green and Co., 1940), p. 141.

that before income taxes were imposed by our laws, before there was any possible advantage to be gained from such practice, it was the universal custom and practice.[29]

In response to this firestorm of protest, the undistributed profits tax proposal was rejected in favor of a 10 percent surtax that would exempt all income retained for the reasonable needs of the business.[30] In effect, Congress had simply retreated to the admittedly unworkable confines of the original accumulated earnings tax.

As an alternative to the undistributed profits tax proposal, in the War Revenue Act of 1917 Congress chose to raise the corporate income tax rate two percentage points above the individual normal rates.[31] It had severed the explicit link between the corporate and normal taxes in the Revenue Act of 1916,[32] but that had been a change of form rather than substance since both rates were set at 2 percent.[33] This was the first time the corporate and individual normal tax rates diverged.

While an increase in rates was at least partly necessitated by the country's entry into World War I and President Wilson's desire to pay for the war effort on an ongoing basis rather than through borrowing,[34] Senator Simmons explained that the divergence between the corporate and individual rates was designed to subject a corporation's retained earnings to a surtax similar in type, if not in degree, to the one applied to individuals:

> As it now stands in the corporation income-tax law, and as it has stood from the beginning, the normal tax of the individual and the normal tax, so to speak, of the corporation have been identically the same ... We

---

[29] *Cong. Rec.*, vol. 55, p. 5966 (1917) (statement of Sen. Simmons).

[30] Ibid., p. 6004 (statement of Sen. Penrose); War Revenue Act of 1917, ch. 63, § 1206, 40 Stat. 300 (1917). As in the original version, individuals would be directly subject to the surtax as if they were partners.

[31] See War Revenue Act of 1917, ch. 63, 40 Stat. 300 (1917). This was the second revenue measure enacted that year. The Revenue Act of 1917, enacted exactly seven months earlier on March 3, 1917, imposed the first excess profits tax on corporate and partnership income. See Ratner, *Taxation and Democracy in America*, p. 364.

[32] Revenue Act of 1916, ch. 463, 39 Stat. 756 (1916).

[33] Ibid., §§ 1, 10, 39 Stat. 756–7, 765–6. As part of an increase in the income tax rates to help meet expenses occasioned by the developing war in Europe, the income tax section was rewritten so as to improve the organization and clarify many of its provisions. See Roy Blakey and Gladys Blakey, *The Federal Income Tax*, p. 120. One byproduct of this rewrite was that the corporate income tax rate was disconnected from the individual income tax rate. Theoretically, this would allow the rates to move independently of each other, although there is no evidence that this was the motivation for the change.

[34] See Roy Blakey and Gladys Blakey, *The Federal Income Tax*, p. 130.

[increased the corporate income tax rate above the normal tax on individuals] chiefly for the purpose of equalizing any possible difference which might exist between the individual and the corporation with reference to surtaxes.[35]

According to the calculations of Treasury officials, this 2 percent increase in the corporate income tax rate was expected to raise an additional $180 million in revenue.[36] Senator Simmons noted that this "will very much more than equal the entire surtax if the whole amount had been distributed."[37] While Senator Jones and others disputed this conclusion, both as to the amount and as to the notion that a flat-rate increase would replicate a series of graduated surtax rates,[38] the Finance Committee's logic appeared sufficient to persuade a majority of Congress.

Thus, because of the problem of retained earnings and the imposition of the surtax, Congress had sanctioned the divergence of corporate and individual income taxes. Some contemporary observers suggested that

[35] *Cong. Rec.*, vol. 55, p. 6172 (1917) (statement of Sen. Simmons), p. 6330 (statement of Sen. Smoot) ("the committee undertook to equalize the taxes between the partnership and the corporation by imposing an additional normal tax upon corporations that is not imposed upon partnerships or individuals."), and p. 5966 (statement of Sen. Simmons) ("Taking all these matters into consideration, your committee decided that the equities of the situation would be best adjusted by imposing a surtax upon such portion of the retained surplus that is not necessary for the reasonable requirements of the business and by making the corporate tax 2 per cent in excess of the normal income tax."). See also *S. Rep.*, no. 103, p. 12, reprinted in 1939–1 C.B. 68 ("Under both the House bill and existing law the normal tax of the corporation and the normal tax of the individual is the same. In these conditions the earnings of the corporation escape surtax until distributed among its shareholders. This situation seemed to your committee to bring about an inequality between the corporation and the individual which should be remedied as far as practicable ... [Y]our committee believes that the situation would be best met by imposing the surtaxes above mentioned upon such portions of the retained surplus as is not retained for employment in the business and by imposing the additional tax of 2 per cent upon the corporate incomes ...").

[36] *Cong. Rec.*, vol. 55, p. 6172 (1917).

[37] Ibid., p. 6172, and p. 6336 (statement of Sen. Simmons: "The committee thought that if we put upon corporations an additional 2 per cent tax, thereby increasing their income tax $180,000,000, it would bring in the first place, into the Treasury four or five times as much money as would come to the Treasury from the surtax upon this 30 per cent or this 20 per cent or this 10 per cent, as the case might be, and that it would leave no injustice as between the corporations and the individuals, because the corporation in its entity dealing with the property of its stockholders would already have paid a much larger amount than the surtax would amount to if they had distribute[d] it.").

[38] Ibid., p. 6174 (statement of Sen. Jones), and p. 6331 (statement of Sen. McCumber) (noting that while the corporation pays 6 percent and the individual partners in a partnership only 4 percent under the normal tax, the partners pay an additional 30 percent under the surtax).

this development pushed the corporate income tax further away from its original focus on shareholder wealth.[39] As Frank Taussig noted, because of the divergence "[t]he [corporate income] tax comes even more to be regarded not as one that serves to reach shareholders' income, but one that is to be assimilated to other taxes, to be shifted to the general public, and to leave the shareholder's income undiminished."[40]

3.3   Revenue Act of 1918

Not surprisingly, the two percentage point increase in the corporate income tax rate under the 1917 Act served as a weak surrogate for the application of the surtax to retained earnings. Dissatisfied with the Treasury proposal for the taxation of corporate income, Claude Kitchin, chairman of the House Ways and Means Committee, proposed to subject corporate income to two different rates depending upon its use. Under Kitchin's proposal, distributed corporate income would be subject to tax at a 12 percent rate. By contrast, income retained by the corporation at the end of the year would be subject to an 18 percent rate. According to the House Committee report, the theory was that "the reduction of the rate to 12 per cent on an amount equal to the amount of dividends paid will have a wholesome effect in many cases in stimulating the payment of dividends, which will be subject to surtax in the hands of the stockholders."[41]

As in prior attempts to reach income retained for business, rather than tax evasion, reasons, the House Committee proposal evoked much protest. Even before the proposal was delivered to Congress for consideration, the *New York Times* predicted that it would be "opposed strenuously."[42] This quickly proved true. One representative claimed that the proposal "puts a premium upon bad business ... it is unjust, and there is no reason in the world why such a penalty should be placed

---

[39] See, e.g., Frank Taussig, "The War Tax Act of 1917," *The Quarterly Journal of Economics* 32 (1917): 20; Roy Blakey, "The War Revenue Act of 1917," *American Economic Review* 7 (1917): 808–9.

[40] Taussig, "The War Tax Act of 1917," 20. Although Taussig is correct that the corporate income tax could not be considered as burdening shareholders exclusively anymore, if it ever had, the notion that it could ever be wholly shifted to the consumer over the long term, with little or no impact on capital or labor, is generally rejected. See William Klein, "The Incidence of the Corporation Income Tax: a Lawyer's View of a Problem in Economics," *Wisconsin Law Review* (1965): 602.

[41] H. Rep., no. 767, p. 9 (1918), reprinted in 1939–1 C.B. 94.

[42] "Corporations face tax of 18 per cent.," *New York Times*, July 24, 1918, p. 17.

upon a good, conservative corporation."[43] Another representative echoed these concerns, calling it "dangerous" and the most objectionable . . . and unjust penalties on corporations imposed in this law."[44] In the House, such protests were to no avail, as the proposal's supporters successfully argued that the 6 percent difference in the taxation of distributed and retained income constituted a "bonus" or a "present" rather than a penalty.[45] Nevertheless, just as one House opponent predicted,[46] the proposal died in the Senate Finance Committee.[47]

Despite the demise of the undistributed profits tax proposal, Congress believed that the retained earnings problem would be alleviated to some extent by the application of the war-excess profits tax, as it came to be known,[48] to corporations only. Under the 1917 Act, businesses of all kinds, regardless of the form in which they operated, were subject to both the war profits and excess profits taxes.[49] In the 1918 Act, however, Congress elected to limit the application of the combined tax to only businesses operating in corporate form.[50] According to the Senate Finance Committee Report,

---

[43] *Cong. Rec.*, vol. 56, p. 10423 (1918) (statement of Rep. Chandler).

[44] Ibid., p. 10429 (statement of Rep. Fordney).

[45] Ibid., pp. 10423–4 (statement of Rep. Longworth: "The 18 per cent is the normal tax on all corporations as 12 per cent is the bonus for distribution . . . We have tripled the normal tax on individuals. We have raised it from 4 to 12 per cent. The present normal tax on corporations of 6 per cent is treated in the same way as the income on individuals, and therefore the normal tax on corporations, under this new law is 18 per cent and not 12 per cent . . . It is simply subjecting them, as we do individuals, to the normal tax and virtually offering them a present for distributing their profits.").

[46] Ibid., p. 10429 (statement of Rep. Fordney: "I am not going to offer any amendment, but I hope to see it go out in the Senate, and I have reasonable assurance that it will go out; and if it does I hope it will stay out.").

[47] See Roy Blakey and Gladys Blakey, *The Federal Income Tax*, p. 174. According to the Senate Finance Committee Report, "[f]ailure to permit without penalty all legitimate uses of earnings for financing corporations seemed inconsistent with the policy which has in the past been actually followed by well-managed corporations and which has been urged by the War Finance Corporation and the Capital Issues Committee. To retain the differential rate while exempting from the extra tax all income used by the corporation for legitimate purposes other than distribution would, however, make the law difficult of administration, because it would involve review by the Treasury Department of too many detailed questions of the administrative policy of individual corporations." *S. Rep.*, no. 617, p. 4, reprinted in 1939–1 C.B. 120.

[48] The war profits and excess profits taxes were effectively combined under the 1918 Act. In both cases, the intent was to reach profits in excess of some "normal" rate of return, whether due to the presence of wartime contracts and scarcity or simply occurring during a time of war. See Randolph Paul, *Taxation in the United States* (Boston: Little, Brown, 1954), p. 118.

[49] See ibid., p. 118.   [50] Ibid.

"[i]ndividuals and partnerships pay the heavy surtaxes upon all net income, whether left in the business or not, while corporations and their stockholders are relieved from surtaxes upon the portion of the earnings which is not distributed. This inequality is more than compensated for by the fact that the corporation is – while the individual and partnership are not – subject to the war excess-profits tax."[51] Thus, as a second-best alternative to the rate differential between distributed and retained income in the House bill, the war and excess profits taxes became a de facto surtax on corporate income.[52]

3.4   Revenue Act of 1921

The problem with the war-excess profits tax compromise to the retained earnings problem was that it was only as strong as the wavering political support for the war-excess profits tax. In his 1920 Annual Report, Treasury Secretary David F. Houston concluded that the excess profits tax was both impossibly complex and unjustifiably restricted to a small number of businesses.[53] Perhaps more importantly, he argued that the tax was a poor substitute for the surtaxes on individual income:

> The profits tax on corporations is evidently meant to be a rough equiv-alent for the surtaxes levied upon the reinvested or undistributed profits of other forms of business. But no true equivalence is reached. In 1918 the members of a well-known partnership paid nearly $1,125,000 more taxes than they would have paid had their business been organized as a corporation. And the contrary is frequently true.[54]

---

[51] S. Rep., no. 617, p. 8, reprinted in 1939–1 C.B. 124; Cong. Rec., vol. 61, p. 6834 (1921) (statement of Sen. Jones) ("the inequities of that old law became so apparent that the Congress repealed the excess-profits tax as to individuals and partners, the excess-profits tax upon corporate earnings being designed to take the place in a degree of the surtaxes upon individuals and partners."); ibid., p. 6861 (statement of Sen. Simmons) (explaining the understanding "was that this exemption on the part of the individual and the partnership from the excess-profits tax would equalize the difference in the taxes of these three groups of taxpayers.").

[52] See S. Rep., no. 617, p. 8, reprinted in 1939–1 C.B. 124 ("The situation as between the different forms of business organization having been thus brought into approximate balance, it was deemed proper to relieve the corporation from the 6 per cent differential income tax provided by the House bill.").

[53] David F. Houston, "Annual Report of the Secretary of the Treasury," 1920, p. 32.

[54] Houston, "Annual Report of the Secretary of the Treasury," p. 34. Houston appears to have been influenced by the support for the issue shown by his advisor, Thomas S. Adams. See Walter Lambert, The New Deal Revenue Acts: The Politics of Taxation (dissertation, 1970), p. 274; see also Thomas Adams, "Immediate Future of the Excess-profits Tax," The American Economic Review (Supplement) 10 (1920): 15.

Business groups echoed the Treasury Secretary's concerns about the excess profits tax.[55] At the Annual Meeting of the National Industrial Tax Conference, for instance, James Emery of the National Association of Manufacturers delivered a keynote address entitled, "The Excess Profits Tax – An Unsound Fiscal Policy."[56] Emery complained about the tax's "indefiniteness, uncertainty, and complexity," arguing that the tax would lead to wasteful expenditures in deductible areas, encourage the public to equate "excess" with "illegal" returns, and depress investor returns.[57] While a chorus of business representatives joined Emery in his criticism of the tax, they were by no means alone. Public finance economists such as Carl Plehn and T. S. Adams rejected the application of the excess profits tax and President Wilson even acknowledged in his outgoing message to Congress that revision of the excess profits tax was necessary.[58] Not surprisingly, after both President Harding and Treasury Secretary Andrew Mellon advocated repeal of the tax,[59] Congress eliminated it entirely.[60]

Because of the failings of the excess profits tax, policymakers and interested groups once again turned to the possibility of an undistributed profits tax. Treasury Secretary Houston recommended replacing the excess profits tax with a tax on undistributed profits where the highest tax levied upon retained earnings would be the same as the highest surtax rate. This would make the tax the same on saved or distributed income. As Houston explained, "[w]hile it is vitally important that saving and reinvestment effected through the medium of the corporation should not be dealt with more leniently than similar savings made by the partnership or individual, it is equally important that the methods of taxation

---

[55] Roy and Gladys Blakey reported that "so intense was the campaign of business against the excess-profits tax that it might better be described as a crusade." See Roy Blakey and Gladys Blakey, *The Federal Income Tax*, pp. 190–91.

[56] James Emery, "The Excess Profits Tax – an Unsound Fiscal Policy," in *Proceedings of the National Industrial Tax Conference* (National Industrial Conference Board, 1920), Special Report No. 9, p. 3.

[57] Ibid., pp. 9–12.

[58] See Carl C. Plehn, "Substitutes for the Excess Profits Tax and the Higher Income Surtaxes," in *Proceedings of the National Industrial Tax Conference* (National Industrial Conference Board, 1920), Special Report No. 9, p. 23; T. S. Adams, "Should the Excess Profits Tax be Repealed?," *Quarterly Journal of Economics* 35 (1921): 369; Roy Blakey and Gladys Blakey, *The Federal Income Tax*, p. 197.

[59] See Roy Blakey and Gladys Blakey, *The Federal Income Tax*, p. 210.   [60] Ibid., pp. 215–16.

employed should in all cases penalize saving and investment as little as possible."[61]

The National Association of Credit Men also issued a proposal to replace the excess profits tax and the corporate income tax with a graduated undistributed profits tax "that will have a tendency to encourage payment of dividends."[62] Under the proposal, dividends would be subject to the normal tax, and, if applicable, the individual surtax, in the hands of the stockholder.[63] According to R. G. Elliott, chairman of the Association's Federal Tax Committee, "if the corporation is permitted to retain a portion of its earnings for working capital or expansion, and these earnings are not to be taxed to the individual stockholders as income, then we must find some means of taxing this undistributed income in a fair manner."[64] Elliott concluded that the undistributed profits tax was necessary to push the money into the hands of the stockholders where it would be taxed at their individual normal and surtax rates.[65]

In Congress, the undistributed profits tax also resurfaced as a solution to the problem of legitimately retained corporate earnings.[66] Senator Jones offered the National Association of Credit Men's proposal as a substitute for the excess profits tax.[67] While he continued to maintain that the excess profits tax was not a sufficient substitute for the surtaxes applicable to individuals and partners, Senator Jones argued that the repeal of the excess profits tax only exacerbated the retained earnings

---

[61] Houston, "Annual Report of the Secretary of the Treasury," p. 34.

[62] R. G. Elliott, "Income Taxation," in *Proceedings of the National Industrial Tax Conference* (National Industrial Conference Board, 1920), Special Report No. 9, p. 23 (Elliott was chairman of the Federal Tax Committee of the National Association of Credit Men).

[63] Ibid., p. 23.   [64] Ibid., p. 66.   [65] Ibid., p. 66.

[66] Earnings retained for the purpose of evading the individual surtaxes were still subject to the accumulated earnings tax, but because of the decision in *Eisner* v. *Macomber*, Congress felt it could not continue to impose the tax on the stockholders directly as if they were partners. See *H. Rep.*, no. 350, 67th Cong., 1st Sess. 10 (1921), reprinted in 1939 C.B.–1 177. Instead, the surtax rate was raised from 10 to 25 percent, although the stockholders could still consent to be taxed at their individual surtax rates like partners and avoid the flat-rate penalty.

[67] See *Cong. Rec.*, vol. 61, p. 6833 (1921) (statement of Sen. Jones), and p. 6845 (Appendix to Jones' statement containing the National Association of Credit Men's proposal to his statement). One interesting additional amendment offered by Senator Jones was to permit partnerships and corporations the option of electing whether for tax purposes they would be treated as partnerships or corporations. Ibid., p. 6845.

problem.[68] Another, somewhat more modest, proposal for an undistributed profits tax was offered by Senator Simmons, the former Senate
Finance Committee Chair and current minority leader on the
Committee. He proposed to retain the corporate tax while imposing a
graduated surtax on retained corporate earnings.[69] According to
Simmons, under a flat-rate corporate income tax, income derived from
corporate operations would only contribute to the government coffers
about one-half of that derived from sole proprietorships and two-thirds
that coming from partnerships.[70] Simmons believed that not only would
his proposal allow the government to reach more corporate earnings, but
also it would equalize the tax treatment of distributions and retentions.[71]
He explained "I do not think it is a bad business policy [to retain earn-
ings], but because it is a good policy to pursue in business is no sufficient
reason why they should be exempt from taxes which all the balance of the
citizens of this country pay."[72]

Despite the force of these various undistributed profits tax proposals, Congress again rejected them in favor of increasing the differential between the corporate and individual normal tax rates.
Congress had reunited the corporate and individual normal tax
rates in the Revenue Act of 1918,[73] albeit at the higher rates of 12
percent in 1918 and 10 percent thereafter.[74] Under the Revenue Act

---

[68] Ibid., p. 6834 (statement of Sen. Jones). Retained earnings was declining as a percentage
of income because of the business downturn, but Senator Jones noted that corporations
still "do not distribute a large percentage." Ibid., p. 6840 (statement of Sen. Jones).
Additionally, Jones reported that high-income individuals "are still organizing corporations with their watered stock on which they do not expect to pay any dividends for
years to come. They expect the corporation to be one great repository of the gain on
which they will pay no tax except this 15 per cent. They are buying these other stocks in
corporations already organized which were made up largely of water, where the undistributed income is accumulating." Ibid.

[69] Ibid., p. 6862 (statement of Sen. Simmons).

[70] Ibid., p. 6862. In fact, the Actuary of the Treasury reported that between 1917 and 1921,
$810 million in revenue was lost because of the failure to tax undistributed earnings.

[71] Ibid.   [72] Ibid.   [73] See Revenue Act of 1918, ch. 18, § 230, 40 Stat. 1075 (1918).

[74] See ibid., 40 Stat. 1075–6. See Roy Blakey and Gladys Blakey, *The Federal Income Tax*,
pp. 185–6. This increase in rates tracked the upward trend in surtax rates during the war.
The top marginal surtax rate rose from 15 percent in 1916 to 67 percent in 1917 and then
77 percent in 1918 as part of an effort to keep pace with war expenditures that caused
government spending to rise from 1.8 percent of gross national product in 1913 to 21
percent in 1917 and 24.1 percent in 1918. See Carolyn Webber and Aaron Wildavsky, *A
History of Taxation and Expenditure in the Western World* (New York: Simon and
Schuster, 1986), pp. 422, 441, and tbl. 12.

of 1921,[75] the maximum individual normal rate dropped to 8 percent.[76] While the maximum corporate income tax rate dropped as well, it only went down to 10 percent.[77] Moreover, this rate only applied for the 1921 calendar year. Under the 1921 Act, the corporate rate was scheduled to rise to 12.5 percent in 1922 to partially make up the revenues lost from the repeal of the excess profits tax after 1921.[78]

Perhaps most influential in the decision to reject an undistributed profits tax was the effect of the business downturn on the retained earnings problem. Republican Senator Reed Smoot of Utah summed up the views of the majority:

> I do not think we need worry about undistributed earnings for this year or for a few years to come. Very few corporations in the United States will make a profit more than sufficient to pay their regular dividends for the year 1921, and where one company will do it, I predict now that a thousand companies will not do it. During war times ... there may have been some reason for taxing undistributed earnings; but just as surely as we stand here to-day there is not much danger of undistributed earnings for the year 1921, and, I think, for a number of years to come.[79]

Although Smoot's statement may have suggested that Congress could repeal the excess profits tax and reduce the corporate income tax rate to equal the normal tax on individuals, the legislators did not go that far. On the contrary, they more than doubled the differential between the normal tax on individuals and the corporate income tax, raising it from 2 to 4.5 percent. At this point, it became clear that, in responding to the retained earnings issue, Congress had transformed the corporate income tax from its original pass-through

---

[75] Revenue Act of 1921, ch. 136, § 210, 42 Stat. 227 (1921).
[76] Ibid.; see Roy Blakey and Gladys Blakey, *The Federal Income Tax*, p. 190.
[77] Revenue Act of 1921, ch. 136, § 230(a), 42 Stat. 252 (1921).
[78] Ibid., § 230(b), 42 Stat. 252–3. See Ratner, *Taxation and Democracy in America*, p. 409. This latter tax was part of a controversial attempt to extend the former war profits tax, which had been adopted to prevent companies from unduly profiting from the country's entry into World War I, into a permanent levy against profits in excess of some predetermined "normal" return. See Roy Blakey and Gladys Blakey, *The Federal Income Tax*, p. 164. While originally it had applied to all businesses regardless of form, in the 1918 Act it was restricted to corporations only. Ibid., p. 168.
[79] *Cong. Rec.*, vol. 61, p. 6861 (statement of Sen. Smoot).

vision to a separate, and at least partially additional, tax at the entity level.[80]

3.5 Revenue Act of 1924

In 1924, flush from two consecutive years of budget surpluses,[81] Treasury Secretary Andrew Mellon introduced a program for the reduction of the high individual surtaxes.[82] Under the Mellon Plan, the normal taxes on individuals would be reduced from a top rate of 8 percent under the 1921 Act to a top rate of 6 percent.[83] Additionally, the maximum individual surtax rate would be reduced from 50 percent to 25 percent, although it would apply to incomes of $100,000 and above rather than the then-current $200,000, and surtax rates would only apply to incomes in excess of $10,000, rather than $6,000 under the 1921 Act.[84] As Mellon explained, "[e]xperience has shown that the present high rates of surtax are bringing in each year progressively less revenue to the Government. This means that the price is too high to the large taxpayer and he is avoiding a taxable income by the many ways which are available to him."[85] Unlike past policy prescriptions, where the retained earnings problem was acknowledged and addressed through either an undistributed profits tax or a higher normal

---

[80] A tax attorney for the General Electric Company made this point in a speech before the National Industrial Conference Board:

> The normal tax paid by corporations is not imposed upon the corporation at all. The theory of it is that it is upon the stockholders, and the corporation is made the agent only for the purpose of collecting the tax from the stockholders, and that is why dividends, the tax on which is paid direct by the stockholders, are exempted from the normal tax in the hands of the individual stockholders. That being the case, the normal rate on corporations ought to be the same as the normal rate on individuals, and whoever consented to tax individuals at the rate of 8 per cent for the normal tax, and corporations 10 per cent, permitted a violation of one of the sound principles of taxation. The rate should be the same on both.

J. F. Zoller, "Is the Excess Profits Tax the Lesser Evil?," in *Proceedings of the National Industrial Tax Conference* (National Industrial Conference Board, 1920), Special Report No. 9, pp. 15, 20.

[81] Roy Blakey and Gladys Blakey, *The Federal Income Tax*, p. 223. President Coolidge announced in a 1924 speech that not only was the budget balanced, but the country had accumulated a surplus of over $300 million: "Address of the President of the United States before the National Republican Club at the Waldorf-Astoria, New York, February 12, 1924," in Andrew Mellon (ed.), *Taxation: The People's Business* (New York: Macmillan, 1924), p. 217 (Appendix E).

[82] See "Address of the President," p. 54.   [83] Ibid.   [84] Ibid.   [85] Ibid., p. 17.

or excess profits tax on corporations, retained earnings were not specifically mentioned or targeted under the Mellon Plan.[86] Despite evidence of a growing change in attitude toward retained earnings, Senator Andrieus Jones attempted to revive the undistributed profits tax concept.[87] Under his proposal, Jones established a normal corporate income tax of 9 percent, with a graduated surtax on retained earnings that imposed a 5 percent tax if a corporation retained 30 percent of its earnings.[88] Since the Senate Finance Committee had proposed raising the corporate income tax rate from 12.5 to 14 percent, Jones' proposal meant that a corporation could retain a reasonable amount of earnings – in his estimation 30 percent – without being worse off than under the flat corporate tax.[89] Buoyed by a coalition of Democrats and radical Republicans,[90] the proposal passed as an amendment to the revenue bill,[91] albeit "with considerably less than a full Senate present."[92]

---

[86] Although he did propose an increase in the corporate income tax rate, it was justified as a replacement for the repeal of the administratively burdensome capital stock tax. See *S. Rep.*, no. 398, 68th Cong. 1st Sess (1924), reprinted in 1939–1 C.B. 271 ("The committee recommends that the income tax on corporations be increased from 12 ½ per cent contained in the House bill to 14 per cent and that the capital stock tax be repealed. This will add only slightly, if at all, to the tax burden on corporations, will apportion that burden more equitably among the different corporations, will relieve corporations from the necessity of preparing two returns upon entirely different bases, and will greatly simplify the work of the Treasury Department in auditing returns."); *Cong. Rec.*, vol. 65, p. 8024 (1924) (statement of Sen. McLean) (explaining that the increase in the tax was designed to relieve corporations from "having to make the duplicate returns – the capital-stock tax and the income tax."). Despite this official explanation, some still suggested that the increase in the corporate income tax rate was designed to address surtax avoidance. See ibid., p. 8031 (statement of Sen. Adams) ("The Mellon amendment, if I may so speak of it, I think it is intolerable. I think the Senate of the United States and the Congress ought not to sit down supinely and say, 'We can not enact a just statute, but we must enact an unjust one, and in order to reach the big evader of taxes we must trample upon the rights of the small man.'")

The increase in the corporate income tax rate from 12.5 to 13.5 percent under the Revenue Act of 1926 was also justified as a replacement for the repeal of the capital stock tax, since that repeal was not ultimately passed in the Revenue Act of 1924. See *H. Rep.*, no. 1, 69th Cong. 1st Sess. (1926), reprinted in 1939–1 C.B. 338 ("the rate has been increased slightly as an offset for the repeal of the capital stock tax.").

[87] See *Cong. Rec.*, vol. 65, p. 8011 (1924) (statement of Sen. Jones).

[88] Ibid., pp. 8014–15.   [89] Ibid.

[90] See "New Corporate Tax urged by Democrats, adopted by Senate," *New York Times*, May 8, 1924, p. 1 ("Six of the insurgents voted with the minority. None of the regular Republicans voted for the Jones Amendment.").

[91] See *Cong. Rec.*, vol. 65, p. 8033 (1924) (yeas 43, nays 32).

[92] John Witte, *The Politics and Development of the Federal Income Tax* (Madison, Wis.: University of Wisconsin Press, 1985), p. 92. The vote was taken at 7:45 in the evening,

Support for the undistributed profits tax still appeared to be shaky, notwithstanding the approval of Senator Jones' proposal. In the debates on the Senate floor, some voted in favor of the amendment because of their interest in a graduated corporate tax or an excess profits tax rather than their concern for retained earnings.[93] Still others apparently voted in favor of the amendment for strategic reasons. A *New York Times* editorial speculated that "this tax was not intended to become law. It may be that the scheme is to load this and other objectionable provisions upon the Revenue bill so as to invite a veto by the President."[94] Alternatively, the *New York Times* suggested that "this corporation tax is thought by the combination temporarily in control of the Senate as simply one more item in the bill of goods which they hope to 'sell' to the Administration leaders when the time comes to strike a bargain for something else."[95] When the Senate voted the bill out to conference, with the support of ardent opponents such as Republican Senator Smoot, it appeared to be with the expectation that the undistributed profits tax would be cut out of it.[96] Not surprisingly, at the conference committee to the House bill the Senate receded on the issue of the corporate income tax rates and dropped the undistributed profits tax.[97] Because the individual normal rate

after "a long day of speeches." "New Corporate Tax urged by Democrats, adopted by Senate," *New York Times*, May 8, 1924, p. 1.

[93] For example, Senator Walsh saw Senator Jones' proposal as a good start toward alleviating the burden on small corporations by applying a graduated tax to corporations. See *Cong. Rec.*, vol. 65, p. 8029 (1924) (statement of Sen. Walsh: "The Senator from New Mexico suggests to meet the situation an amendment which does this one thing, if nothing else: it lowers the flat tax for the first time since the war upon the corporation making reasonably small profits . . . I would vote for it on that ground alone."). Similarly, Senator Brookhart noted that he supported Jones' proposal because it "would accomplish the same purpose" as his own excess-profits amendment. p. 8027 (statement of Sen. Brookhart). According to Brookhart, "[n]early every one of those institutions is a criminal institution, and its purpose is to increase its profits. I want to tax those profits. [Senator Jones'] amendment, if agreed to, will do it in a very effectual way. For this reason I am for it."

[94] Editorial, "Penalizing prudence," *New York Times*, May 9, 1924, p. 18. [95] Ibid.

[96] See "Minority all Republican," *New York Times*, May 11, 1924, pp. 1, 2 ("It was said this evening that some of the standpat Republican Senators will urge President Coolidge to veto the bill if the conferees fail to drop out the clauses which are most objectionable to them, including the Jones graduated tax on corporations and full publicity of income tax returns. As both differ radically from the House bill, they hope the House managers will succeed in diluting them.").

[97] See *H. Rep.*, no. 844, 68th Cong., 1st Sess. Amendment No. 72 (1924), reprinted in 1939–1 C.B. 305. See also Roy Blakey and Gladys Blakey, *The Federal Income Tax*, p. 245 ("Jones' proposal was unacceptable to the House managers. The Senate managers were doubtless not convinced of its desirability, hence receded.").

was dropped to 6 percent under the Revenue Act of 1924,[98] the spread between the corporate income tax and the normal tax on individuals, which represented the amount of each dividend that was subject to double taxation, grew more substantial.

3.6 Revenue Act of 1926 and the creation of the Joint Committee on Internal Revenue Taxation

In the Revenue Act of 1926, Congress acknowledged the existence of the retained earnings problem, but did not offer new legislation. Because of the continuing budget surpluses, Secretary Mellon again requested a reduction in the individual surtaxes and normal rates.[99] As the House Ways and Means Committee realized, however, this would widen the gap between the corporate and individual income tax rates, creating an increasingly greater burden on corporate income.[100] Accordingly, the Ways and Means Committee proposed that the newly-minted Joint Committee on Internal Revenue Taxation undertake a "thorough study of the situation ... [contemplating] that some method will be devised later whereby the inequalities between different business methods may be obviated."[101] The Ways and Means Committee noted that what had now become the double taxation of corporate income could not be alleviated through a reduction in the corporate income tax rate because of revenue concerns.[102]

At this point, Congress was at a crossroads in the taxation of corporate income. Because it desired to reach retained earnings through the corporate income tax rate, the corporate and individual normal income taxes had diverged considerably between 1917 and 1927.[103] A committee of the National Tax Association advocated returning to the conduit model of the corporate income tax.[104] Because of the complexity and questionable legality of directly taxing stockholders on the undivided

---

[98] Revenue Act of 1924, ch. 234, §§ 210, 230, 43 Stat. 282 (1924).
[99] Roy Blakey and Gladys Blakey, *The Federal Income Tax*, p. 255.
[100] H. Rep., no. 1, 69th Cong., 1st Sess. reprinted in 1939–1 C.B. 338 ("The majority of the committee do not approve any reduction in the corporation income tax at this time. To the contrary, the rate has been increased slightly as an offset for the repeal of the capital stock tax ... There are bound to be instances of inequality in the light of a comparison with the reduction in the individual rates.").
[101] Ibid.   [102] Ibid.
[103] In 1917, the differential was 2 percent, but by 1927 it had increased more than four-fold to 8.5 percent.
[104] Report of the Committee of the National Tax Association, "Simplification of the Income Tax," *Proceedings of the National Tax Association* 20 (1928): 133.

profits of the corporation, however, the committee proposed taxing corporations on their undistributed profits only and then subjecting stockholders to both the normal and surtax rates.[105]

A month after the National Tax Association recommended an undistributed profits tax as an alternative to the creeping double taxation of corporate income, the Joint Committee on Internal Revenue Taxation released its report. In this, the Joint Committee noted the need for a plan that "would automatically encourage reasonable distributions on the part of corporations and discourage unreasonable accumulations."[106] After considering a variety of alternatives, the Committee recommended a hybrid approach. Corporations would be allowed to deduct dividends in an amount not to exceed some fixed percentage of net income, such as 25 percent.[107] The advantage of doing so, according to the report, is that while similar to an undistributed profits tax, "this method is unlikely to cause unwise distributions from a business standpoint . . ."[108]

Despite the moderate tone set by the Joint Committee's report, neither body of Congress ever acted upon it. The spread between the corporate income tax and the normal tax on individuals remained steady at 7 percent until the end of the decade.[109] By then, however, the surtax, which had been as high as 65 percent in 1921, was down to 20 percent. The failure to subject undistributed profits to the individual surtax was less important when the difference between the corporate rate and the highest surtax rate was only 7 or 8 percent.

3.7   New Deal and the Undistributed Profits Tax

The corporate income tax and the associated retained earnings problem did not attract attention again until the country was in the throes of the Great Depression. During this period, commentators were absorbed in the search for possible causes of the Depression and for methods of stabilizing the

---

[105] Ibid., 133–4 (the tax would be set at 10 percent).
[106] *Report of the Joint Committee on Internal Revenue Taxation* (1928), p. 54.
[107] Ibid., pp. 55–6.   [108] Ibid., p. 56.
[109] It originally widened from 6.5 to 8.5 percent under the Revenue Act of 1926, before settling at 7 percent under the Revenue Act of 1928. Revenue Act of 1926, ch. 27, §§ 210, 230, 44 Stat. 39 (1926) (imposing a normal tax of 5 percent and a maximum corporate income tax of 13 percent in 1925 and 13.5 percent starting in 1926); Revenue Act of 1928, ch. 852, §§ 11, 13, 45 Stat. 797 (1928) (imposing a normal tax of 5 percent and a maximum corporate income tax of 12 percent); Joint Resolution Reducing Rates of Income Tax for 1929, ch. 2, 46 Stat. 47 (1929) (reducing, for 1929 only, the normal tax to 4 percent and the corporate income tax to 11 percent).

economy.[110] One culprit immediately identified was the unreasonable accumulation of corporate profits. According to a memorandum prepared by his advisors during then-Governor Roosevelt's campaign for the Presidency, the prosperity of the 1920s had led to "a greater accumulation of surpluses than were ever before realized in economic history."[111] Rather than distributing such excess profits to stockholders, "corporate administrators have assumed that they were private funds, capable of being withdrawn from personal uses and used to satisfy unrestrained ambitions for expansion."[112] This practice of "corporate hoarding," the memorandum charged, "upset the balance of production and consumption" and contributed both to the crash and the ensuing Depression.[113]

Though the memorandum's conclusions may have been suspect,[114] many shared its view that retained earnings were a serious

---

[110] See, e.g., Marriner Eccles, "Controlling Booms and Depressions," in Rudolph Weissman (ed.), *Economic Balance and a Balanced Budget* (New York, London: Harper & Bros., 1940), p. 69; Eleanor Lansing Dulles, *Depression and Reconstruction: A Study of Causes and Controls* (Philadelphia: University of Pennsylvania Press, 1936); Leonard Ayres, *The Economics of Recovery* (New York: The Macmillan Co., 1933); Paul Einzig, *The World Economic Crisis, 1929–1931* (London: The Macmillan Co., 1931); Richard Ely, "Real Estate in the Business Cycle," *The American Economic Review* 22 (1932): 138; William Cumberland, "Factors Operating toward Recovery from Depression," *Journal of Business of the University of Chicago* 5 (1932): 114.

[111] "Memorandum of May 19, 1932 of Raymond Moley and others for Franklin Delano Roosevelt outlining national program for recovery," in Box 282, Folder 3, Raymond Moley Papers, Hoover Institution Library and Archives, Stanford University. The May 19 memorandum was written in response to a request by Roosevelt to keep him updated during his pre-campaign vacation trip to Warm Springs. The memorandum provided the opportunity to prepare a series of specific recommendations for various aspects of the economic crisis and was the foundation of many of Roosevelt's campaign speeches and eventually his acceptance speech. See Raymond Moley, *After Seven Years* (New York: Harpers, 1939), pp. 21–2; Daniel Fusfeld, *The Economic Thought of Franklin D. Roosevelt and the Origins of the New Deal* (New York: Columbia University Press, 1954), p. 219. Many, if not most, of the memorandum's recommendations were eventually enacted into law.

[112] "Memorandum of May 19, 1932," 4.

[113] Ibid., 2–3. The theory was that profits, which might have been distributed to shareholders or paid to employees and made available for consumption, were instead left idle. To combat the overcapacity problem, companies closed plants and prices rose (because the company had to spread the overhead costs over fewer products) while workers went unemployed and shareholders failed to see a return on their investment. Furthermore, managers' investment of liquid surplus in the market enhanced volatility since they quickly withdrew money and parked it in short-term securities or in savings accounts.

[114] See Sergei Dobrovolsky, *Corporate Income Retention, 1915–1943* (New York: National Bureau of Economic Research, 1951), p. 26 (arguing that the rate of corporate savings did not increase substantially during the 1920s, even though the absolute numbers grew); Benjamin Anderson, "Eating the Seed Corn," *The Chase Economic Bulletin*, May 12, 1936,

problem.[115] During the debates over the Revenue Act of 1932,[116] Representative McFadden went beyond the undistributed profits tax to propose a tax on accumulated surplus itself.[117] According to McFadden, "[t]hese accumulated profits would have paid taxes to a far greater amount

p. 23 (claiming that the argument that corporate oversaving caused the Depression is an economic "fallacy"); John Martin, Jr., "Taxation of Undistributed Corporate Profits," *Michigan Law Review* 35 (1936): 55 ("While it is true that cash holdings of corporations increased 5.6 billions between 1926 and 1929, we cannot ignore the conclusions of the Brookings Institution that between 1900 and 1930 the unutilized margin of productive capacity in the United States *did not increase* in manufacturing, electric power utilities, agriculture, mining (except for the dislocation of the war), and probably also construction and merchandising.") (emphasis in original); Maurice Leven, Harold Moulton, and Clark Warburton, *America's Capacity to Consume* (Washington, DC: The Brookings Institution, 1934), pp. 100–108 (concluding that corporate additions to surplus, while increasing in absolute numbers, did not substantially increase as a percentage of national income). Some of the confusion over the extent of the problem may be due to the fact that corporate "savings" or surplus is itself an elusive concept to define. See J. Ellwood Amos, *The Economics of Corporate Saving* (Urbana: University of Illinois Press, 1937), p. 12.

[115] See, e.g., "Memorandum from George Haas to Roswell Magill dated September 1937 regarding Tax Revision Studies, 1937 – General Statements, Revenue Estimates, Summaries and Recommendations," 17, in Records of the Office of Tax Analysis/Division of Tax Research; General Records of the Department of Treasury, Record Group 56, Box 63, National Archives, College Park, Md ("it has been argued by very respectable economic authorities, that among the causes of the depression was the starving of consumption through the withdrawal of too large a proportion of our national income for corporate capital expenditure. It is also held by many that one of the vicious influences contributing to the beat stock market boom of the late Twenties was the piling up of liquid corporate resources through excessive retention of corporate earnings. Stock market speculation, which had already been stimulated by the rapid growth of corporate earnings, was further stimulated by the volume of funds representing undistributed earnings that was poured into brokers' loans by corporations."). See also Alfred Buehler, *The Undistributed Profits Tax* (New York, London: McGraw-Hill Book Company, Inc., 1937), p. 16 ("During the depression there was much criticism of corporate saving, which was popularly held to be an important cause of the depression."); "The tax debacle," *The Nation* 142 (1936): 266 ("The studies of the Brookings Institution have shown that the tendency toward oversaving underlies many of our economic difficulties"); "A sound tax," *The Nation* 142 (1936): 337 ("Recent studies have shown that one of the primary causes of the depression is to be found in the tendency toward oversaving on the part of wealthy individuals and corporations."); Donald Gilbert, "Should the Undistributed Profits Tax be repealed?," *The Tax Magazine* 14 (1936): 755 (noting that "consumption [is] obstructed and a recession in the durable goods industries invited" by hoarding earnings); Mark Leff, *The Limits of Symbolic Reform: The New Deal and Taxation, 1933–1939* (Cambridge University Press, 1984), p. 172 (noting that the concern about excessive corporate surpluses was "pervasive" throughout the 1930s).

[116] Revenue Act of 1932, ch. 209, §§ 11, 47 Stat. 174 (1932). Congress actually cut the gap in half when it raised the individual normal rate from 4 to 8 percent: see ibid. at § 13, 47 Stat. 177; but it soon reversed itself in the Revenue Act of 1934 when the normal tax was reduced to its original 4 percent. Revenue Act of 1934, ch. 277, §§ 11, 13, 48 Stat. 686 (1934).

[117] *Cong. Rec.*, vol. 75, p. 6341 (1932) (statement of Rep. McFadden) (the proposed tax would be at a rate of 4 percent).

if they had been distributed as dividends when they were earned. If they had been so distributed, we might not have come to the depths in which we find ourselves to-day."[118] While this proposal received little support, there was substantial concern about retained earnings and the leakage inherent in the accumulated earnings tax.[119]

These and other ideas clearly made an impression on Roosevelt.[120] In his July 1932 acceptance speech at the Democratic national convention, Roosevelt attributed the Depression to heavy "corporate surpluses" used to finance "unnecessary plants" and rampant, pre-Crash, stock market speculations.[121] Although Roosevelt did not immediately take action against retained earnings upon becoming President,[122] the undistributed profits tax notion resurfaced a few years later. Perhaps inspired by Treasury's support for an undistributed profits tax in its 1934 annual tax package,[123] Roosevelt declared in his June 1935 message to Congress that the USA might need to use taxation to "discourage unwieldy and unnecessary corporate surpluses."[124] This might never have translated into a concrete proposal,[125] however, absent a major budgetary crisis at the beginning of 1936. In order to fill two gaping holes in the budget, one

---

[118] Ibid.

[119] See, e.g., ibid., p. 6478 (statement of Rep. Frear), and p. 6483 (statement of Rep. Blanton).

[120] Other rationales forwarded in favor of an undistributed profits tax included the stabilization of the economy and the destruction of monopoly. See John Morton Blum, *From the Morgenthau Diaries: Years of Crisis, 1928–1938* (Boston: Houghton Mifflin Co., 1959), p. 307; Robert Jackson, "The proposed revision of corporation taxes" *Vital Speeches* 2 (1936): 432 (arguing that "antiquated tax laws" permitted corporate managers to use surpluses "to finance monopolistic practices").

[121] Franklin D. Roosevelt, "July 2, 1932 speech," in Samuel Rosenmann (ed.), *The Public Papers and Addresses of Franklin D. Roosevelt*, 13 vols., vol. I (New York: Random House, 1938), p. 651; Buehler, *The Undistributed Profits Tax*, p. 18.

[122] This was in part because Roosevelt was worried that an undistributed profits tax might arouse sufficient opposition to threaten his other New Deal programs. See W. Elliot Brownlee, "Historical perspectives on US tax policy toward the rich," in Joel Slemrod (ed.), *Does Atlas Shrug?: The Economic Consequences of Taxing the Rich* (New York: Russell Sage Foundation; Cambridge, Mass.: Harvard University, 2000), p. 51.

[123] Leff, *The Limits of Symbolic Reform*, p. 173; Marriner Eccles, *Beckoning Frontiers: Public and Personal Recollections* (New York: Knopf, 1951), p. 256.

[124] Buehler, *The Undistributed Profits Tax*, p. 19. Additionally, in response to President Roosevelt's call for measures to reduce economic concentration (see *Cong. Rec.*, vol. 70, pp. 9711–12 (1935)) Congress enacted a graduated tax on corporations in the Revenue Act of 1935. See Revenue Act of 1935, § 102(a), 49 Stat. 1014 (1935) (rates ranged from 12.5 percent on incomes below $2,000 to fifteen percent on incomes above $40,000).

[125] See Ellis Hawley, *The New Deal and the Problem of Monopoly* (Princeton University Press, 1966), p. 352 (suggesting that, at the end of 1935, it appeared that Roosevelt would postpone consideration of the undistributed profits tax proposal indefinitely).

caused by the Supreme Court's striking down of the processing taxes funding the Agricultural Adjustment Act and the other caused by Congress's overriding a presidential veto to accelerate payment of bonuses to World War I veterans,[126] Roosevelt turned to the undistributed profits tax. In a supplemental budget message to Congress on March 3, 1936, Roosevelt suggested Congress make up the $620 million shortfall by replacing the corporate income tax with an undistributed profits tax. According to Roosevelt, "[a] proper tax on corporate income ... which is not distributed as earned, would correct the serious twofold inequity in our taxes on business profits" by forcing corporations to distribute profits to their shareholders where they would be subject to the same high surtax rates as partnerships and sole proprietorships.[127] Most significantly, Roosevelt's proposal would completely exempt distributed income from double taxation because the repeal of the corporate income tax would be accompanied by a repeal of the exemption of dividends from the normal tax on individuals.[128] This would ensure that distributed income would be subject to one layer of tax, but no more than one layer.[129]

Managers soon mounted a fierce opposition to Roosevelt's proposal. While they had opposed previous attempts to impose an undistributed profits tax during the first decade of the income tax, those proposals generally arose from the concern of one senator – Senator Andrieus Jones – and did not have the support of the Administration or, in most cases, Treasury. Moreover, the emergence of the New Deal and Roosevelt's popularity, achieved to some extent at the expense of business, had raised the stakes. Thus, both directly and through lobbying organizations that they effectively controlled during the period, such as the National Association of Manufacturers and the US Chamber of Commerce,[130] corporate managers

---

[126] See *United States* v. *Butler*, 297 US 111 (1936) (holding that the Agricultural Adjustment Act "invades the reserved rights of the states. It is a statutory plan to regulate and control agricultural production, a matter beyond the powers delegated to the federal government. The tax, the appropriation of the funds raised and the direction for their disbursement, are but parts of the plan. They are but means to an unconstitutional end."); "Revenue Act of 1936: Hearings on H.R. 12395 Before the Sen. Comm. on Fin.," 74th Cong., 2nd Sess. 2 (1936) (statement of Henry Morgenthau, Jr., Secretary of the Treasury) (identifying the two budgetary concerns necessitating the undistributed profits tax proposal).

[127] Franklin D. Roosevelt, "A supplemental budget message to Congress (March 3, 1936)," in Rosenmann, *The Public Papers and Addresses of Franklin D. Roosevelt*, vol. V, p. 105.

[128] Ibid., p. 106.

[129] Undistributed income would be subject to double taxation because of the application of the undistributed profits tax and the individual normal tax.

[130] See Leff, *The Limits of Symbolic Reform*, p. 244 ("To some extent, this unity [of the business community in opposition to the tax] reflected the dominance of giant corporations in industrial

appeared in force during the hearings in the House Ways and Means Committee on a bill to enact Roosevelt's proposal.[131] While they claimed to be concerned with the effect of the proposal on small business,[132] many of their comments suggested that their underlying concern was the potential interference with the decisions of corporate managers and boards of directors. Enacting an undistributed profits tax, G. L. Walters of the Illinois Manufacturing Association complained, would "take from business management one of the most essential matters of management involved in business. Government would just as well take away from all those who have the responsibility of driving automobiles their control over the brakes, the clutch, the throttle, or the steering wheel."[133] Most seriously, Fred Clausen of the US Chamber of Commerce worried that the undistributed profits tax "would engender such uncertainties concerning the sound course to pursue as to subject the management to grave difficulties with shareholders and creditors."[134]

associations."). For instance, while the National Association of Manufacturers nominally represented a broad cross-section of industry, large corporations dominated its decision-making body throughout the New Deal and the World War II period. See Philip Burch, Jr., "The NAM as an Interest Group," *Politics and Society* 4 (1973): 103 ("Throughout the New Deal–World War II years an average of about sixty-five to seventy percent of the membership of the executive committee was composed of representatives of big industrial concerns, and in some years eighty percent or more of these important figures was drawn from such select business circles."); Alfred Cleveland, "NAM: Spokesman for Industry?," *Harvard Business Review* (May 1948): 365 ("the identity of the inner policy-making group indicates that active leadership within the NAM comes primarily from among the very largest manufacturing corporations"); Richard W. Gable, "NAM: Influential Lobby or Kiss of Death?," *The Journal of Politics* 15 (1953): 259, 260 (1953) ("In practice, therefore, the board has constitutionally unlimited power in making all policy decisions. This group has been heavily weighted in favor of an active minority which represents conservative, big businesses and which is an unrepresentative sample of NAM members in terms of size, wealth, and number of employees... Between 1933 and 1937 a total of almost $4 million was collected. A group of 262 companies – among the largest and most powerful in the nation – supplied almost 50 per cent of that total."); Richard W. Gable, *A Political Analysis of an Employers' Association: The National Association of Manufacturers* (unpublished Ph.D. dissertation, University of Chicago: 1950), pp. 242–3 (on file with The University of Chicago library) ("in terms of corporate size and number of employees, the leadership of the Association since 1933 has not been, on the whole, reflective of NAM members, much less of American industry").

[131] While small, undercapitalized businesses, which were most likely to be affected by the tax, were also active opponents of the bill, corporations with professional managers led the charge.

[132] See "Revenue Act of 1936 Hearings on H.R. 12395 Before the Sen. Comm. on Fin.," 74th Cong., 2nd Sess. 352 (1936) (statement of G. L. Walters, Illinois Manufacturing Association).

[133] Ibid., 339.

[134] Ibid., 739–40 (statement of Fred H. Clausen, Chairman of the Committee on Federal Finance, Chamber of Commerce of the United States).

The opposition was unsuccessful: the bill emerged from Committee unscathed and passed in the House with surprisingly little dissent.[135] Under the bill, the corporate income tax would be replaced by an undistributed profits tax graduated according to the percentage of net income retained.[136] For corporations with an annual net income of $10,000 or less, the rates ranged from 1 percent on the first 10 percent of undistributed net income to 29.7 percent on undistributed net income of 70.3 percent or more.[137] For corporations with annual income in excess of $10,000, the bill proposed rates ranging from 4 percent on the first 10 percent of undistributed net income to a maximum of 42.5 percent on undistributed net income of 57.5 percent or more.[138]

Republicans changed their strategy in the Senate, choosing both to oppose the undistributed profits tax and to seek to limit its force. To reduce the bill's exclusive reliance on the undistributed profits tax, opponents questioned its revenue-raising ability and harped on its lack of a track record of success. M. L. Seidman of the New York Board of Trade summarized these concerns:

> At a time like the present, when the need for revenue is so great, when we are spending so much more than what we are taking on, when business is recuperating from the worst depression in our history, and when industry is so sensitive to every disturbing influence, how can we possibly afford to gamble such a vast sum of known public revenue for what is so much an adventure into the wilderness?[139]

---

[135] See "$803,000,000 tax bill wins by vote of 267–93 in House; business attacks New Deal," New York Times, April 30, 1936, p. 1. Republican opposition was considered "perfunctory" and the chamber called "indifferent" to their pleas. See Turner Catledge, "House Democrats wind up tax bill; final vote today," New York Times, April 29, 1936, p. 1 (calling the proceedings "the most perfunctory witnessed in the House on an important measure in many years"); Editorial, "On the Senate's lap," New York Times, April 30, 1936, p. 18 ("After little debate worthy of the name, conducted for the most part before an indifferent chamber whose seats were less than one-quarter filled" the House passed the measure). This was due in part to the Republicans' decision to make "campaign material" out of the tax bill rather than attempt to lessen its impact through amendments. See "Republicans bar tax amendments," New York Times, April 28, 1936, p. 12.
[136] "Revenue Act of 1936: Hearings on H.R. 12395 Before the Sen. Comm. on Fin.", 74th Cong., 2nd Sess. 5 (1936).
[137] Ibid., 5–6.   [138] Ibid., 6.
[139] See ibid., 93 (statement of M. L. Seidman, Chairman, Tax Committee, New York Board of Trade), 679, 682 (statement of James A. Emery, general counsel, National Association of Manufacturers) ("it is not ... a reliable source of revenue, for it is subject to the variations of business policy rather than the net income of the business itself"), and 220–21 (statement of Fred H. Clausen, United States Chamber of Commerce) ("The added revenue to be derived is

These arguments served to reinforce the criticism that the tax was just a thinly veiled attempt to control corporate governance and drive a wedge between managers and their stockholders.[140]

The attack on Treasury's revenue projections proved fatal to the House bill's all-or-nothing strategy, but did not defeat the undistributed profits tax altogether. Thus, a group of nine Democrats on the Senate Finance Committee joined the Republican minority to announce an alternate revenue proposal.[141] Under the proposal, which was prepared with the substantial assistance of the US Chamber of Commerce and its representatives,[142] the undistributed profits tax would assume a greatly reduced role. In its place, the senators planned to raise the corporate income tax from the current top rate of 15 percent to rates ranging from 17.5 percent to 20 percent and to eliminate the exemption from the normal tax for dividends.[143] The undistributed profits tax would remain a part of the bill only as a "temporary" tax for three years.[144]

A second proposed alternative emerged that made the tradeoff between double taxation and the undistributed profits tax even starker. Originally set forth in a *New York Times* editorial, this proposal provided that the existing tax on corporate incomes would be retained, but at a flat rate of 15 percent rather than the graduated rates ranging from 12.5

---

highly uncertain and insufficient. It is less than the budgeted increase in ordinary expenditures for the next fiscal year.").

This theme was also emphasized in the popular press. See, e.g., "Taxing and destroying," *Business Week*, May 9, 1936, p. 48 ("Nobody knows how much revenue the bill would actually produce; it might be less than the billion dollars obtainable by the present taxes, which the bill would recklessly abolish ... If the things nobody knows about this bill were laid end to end, they would constitute an aggregate of ignorance as enormous and formidable as American statesmanship has ever been able to boast.").

[140] Editorial, "Punishing prudence," *New York Times*, March 13, 1936, p. 22 ("[i]t has become increasingly obvious that in the eyes of most of its sponsors the proposed tax on corporation surpluses is not primarily a revenue measure, but a new economic 'reform'"); "Revenue Act of 1936: Hearings on H.R. 12395 Before the Sen. Comm. on Fin.," 74th Cong., 2nd Sess. 520 (1936) (statement of Herman H. Lind, National Machine-Tool Builders Association) ("[t]he determination of dividend policy within an individual company will bring to the fore conflicts among various types of stockholders. A very different interest in the amount of earnings to be distributed will be found between stockholders of large incomes and those of small incomes – between those engaged in the management of a business and those who are purely investors."), and 722, 724 (statement of H. W. Story, Allis-Chalmers Manufacturing Co.) ("the normal pressure on management by stockholders for the payment of larger dividends" would grow, making it "more difficult for management to pursue a conservative policy of utilizing a large proportion of its earnings for the purpose of promoting the growth of the company.").

[141] See "Senate group plans complete tax bill revision," *Wall Street Journal*, May 9, 1936, p. 1.
[142] Ibid., p. 2.   [143] Ibid.   [144] Ibid.

percent to 15 percent.[145] In addition, the proposal would eliminate the exemption of dividends paid to individuals from the 4 percent normal tax and would impose a 4 percent undistributed profits tax.[146] The identity of rates between the dividend tax and the undistributed profits tax was no mere coincidence. As the *New York Times* acknowledged, "[s] uch a tax should raise substantial revenue at the same time as it would be likely to have very little effect on dividend policy, for it would penalize even the relatively low-incomed stockholders no more to retain these profits than to pay them out."[147] Senator William King, a Democrat from Utah, thought the concept worthy enough that he entered the editorial into the records during the Hearings.[148]

This latter proposal eventually won out in the Senate Finance Committee, although a late push by Committee Chair Pat Harrison helped restore a modicum of substance to the undistributed profits tax. As finally passed by the Senate, the undistributed profits tax was set at 7 percent and dividends were subjected to the 4 percent normal tax on individuals.[149] While business still grumbled about the introduction of even the principle of an undistributed profits tax,[150] they had substantially blunted the plan's distributive pressure. The bill was also a far cry from the 42.5 percent rate passed by the House.

In part because of the substantial gap between the House and Senate bills, it was not surprising that the Conference Committee arrived at a compromise satisfactory to no one. As finally adopted, the Revenue Act of 1936 imposed a surtax on the "undistributed net income" of corporations at rates ranging from 7 percent to 27 percent.[151] In addition to imposing this surtax on undistributed profits, the 1936 Act retained the normal corporate income

---

[145] Editorial, "A compromise tax bill," *New York Times*, May 4, 1936, p. 18.

[146] Ibid. The American Institute of Accountants simply suggested that the undistributed profits tax be applied at a "low rate." "Revenue Act of 1936: Hearings on H.R. 12395 Before the Sen. Comm. on Fin.', 74th Cong., 2nd Sess. 603 (1936).

[147] Ibid.

[148] Ibid., 352 (statement of Sen. King) ("I should like to insert in the record an editorial that the *New York Times* has in this morning's issue, a very excellent editorial, and by that I do not mean to give my approval to it in all respects, as to the terms of a bill.")

[149] See Turner Catledge, "18% corporate income tax and 7% on undivided profit agreed on by Senate group," *New York Times*, May 22, 1936, p. 1.

[150] See Turner Catledge, "New tax program is held adequate by the Treasury," *New York Times*, May 17, 1936, pp. 1, 27 (describing a US Chamber of Commerce statement objecting the proposal).

[151] Revenue Act of 1936, ch. 690, § 14(b), 49 Stat. 1655 (1936).

tax, with rates ranging from 8 percent to 15 percent,[152] and removed the exemption from the 4 percent normal individual tax for dividends received.[153] The result was the imposition of a full two layers of tax on corporate income, in addition to the surtax, whereas income from other sources was only subject to one layer of tax, in addition to the surtax. Because of the increase in the highest undistributed profits tax rate from 7 percent in the Senate bill to 27 percent in the final Act, however, this additional 4 percent normal tax on dividends did not appear to offer much to counterbalance the push to distribute earnings. The net penalty on retained earnings was still a quite hefty 24 percent at the highest marginal rates.

Although seemingly one-sided, this compromise was structured so as to minimize the coercive force of the undistributed profits tax. The top rate on the undistributed profits tax was identical to the lowest surtax rate for incomes in excess of $44,000.[154] This may have been designed to subject corporate income to the same tax – whether it was retained or distributed – assuming the shareholder's income fell within this surtax bracket. Application of the 4 percent normal tax on dividends, therefore, ensured that permitting the corporation to retain profits rather than subjecting them to an additional tax was still logical to that class of shareholders.[155] Only those shareholders not subject to any surtax – who were presumably the least powerful equity holders – were still likely to clamor for distributions as a result of the ultimately enacted undistributed profits tax.

Double taxation emerged because Congress recognized that undistributed profits avoided the high individual surtax rates and because managers pushed for a solution that would preserve their discretion to retain earnings. After the passage of the Revenue Act of 1936, business opposition to the undistributed profits tax continued. John Morton Blum recounted that, "[b]ecause that tax tended to return to stockholders the decision about how to spend or invest their money, it challenged the power of professional managers of large corporations. These managers, their lawyers, and accountants, in all an able, articulate, and influential group, were aggressive opponents of the tax."[156] Business

---

[152] Ibid., § 13(b), 49 Stat. 1655.   [153] Ibid., § 11, 49 Stat. 1653.

[154] See Revenue Act of 1935, ch. 829, § 101, 49 Stat. 1014 (1935) (both were set at 27 percent).

[155] Of course, if the corporation retained the profits and became subject to the tax, the shareholder would eventually be subject to a heavy tax upon distribution. If no distribution was ever made, however, the shareholder could recoup his profits in the form of capital gains upon sale of the stock.

[156] Blum, *From the Morgenthau Diaries*, p. 321.

leaders seized on the recession in the late summer of 1937 as an opportunity to blame the undistributed profits tax for a whole assortment of
economic ills.[157] Eventually, this proved successful, especially when
business began to point to the undistributed profits tax as the principal
cause of a crisis in business confidence.[158] In the Revenue Act of 1938,[159]
business leaders once again traded higher corporate rates and double
taxation for the nullification of the undistributed profits tax. Thus, the
corporate income tax rate was increased to 19 percent with a 2.5 percent
credit available to companies that distributed all of their earnings.[160] As
in the 1936 Act, dividends were subject to the normal tax on individuals.
To appease corporate managers who feared that the maintenance of even
a symbolic undistributed profits tax would allow it to come back from the
dead at a later date,[161] Congress agreed that the credit for distributed
earnings would expire in two years.[162] Managers made little attempt to
revive the dividend exemption after this point, choosing instead to focus

---

[157] "Profits Tax slows recovery, he says," *New York Times*, August 28, 1937, p. 20 (blamed for
decline of retail credit); "Levy on profits halts expansion," *New York Times*, August 27, 1937,
p. 24 (blamed for delay and termination of expansion plans); "15 criticisms made of the Profit
Tax," *New York Times*, September 26, 1937, p. 24 (US Chamber of Commerce study);
"Surplus tax repeal held labor benefit," *New York Times*, October 31, 1937, p. 8 (National
Association of Manufacturers Study); Editorial, "A tax theory demolished," *Wall Street
Journal*, October 22, 1937, p. 4; "Our taxes too high, periling business, Tremaine asserts,"
New York Times, October 1, 1937, p. 1 ("[New York State Controller] Tremaine blamed the
stock market slump directly upon the Federal Capital Gains and Losses Tax, and the
Undistributed Profits Tax"); "Ballantine finds New Deal harmful," *New York Times*,
October 20, 1937, p. 10 (highlighting the undistributed profits tax among New Deal programs
"as responsible for the current stock market slump").

[158] Lambert, *The New Deal Revenue Acts*, p. 414.

[159] Revenue Act of 1938, ch. 289, 52 Stat. 447 (1938).

[160] Ibid., § 13(c), 52 Stat. 455. *See* "Business tax aids retained in new compromise bill," *Wall
Street Journal*, April 23, 1938, p. 1; "Tax revision bill conferees adopt compromise
measure," *New York Times*, April 27, 1938, p. 3.

[161] "Revenue Act of 1938: Hearing on H.R. 9682 Before the Sen. Comm. on Finance,"
75th Cong., pt. 2 183 (1938) (statement of J. W. Hooper, Chairman of the Federal
Tax Committee, Brooklyn Chamber of Commerce) (warning that the retention of
the undistributed profits tax principle would make it "an ever-constant threat"), 257
(statement of M. L. Seidman, Chairman of Taxation Committee, New York Board of
Trade) ("it would remain to haunt business, not only for what it is, but also for
what it may eventually grow into if permitted to remain as a permanent part of our
tax structure"), and 469 (statement of Ellsworth Alvord, US Chamber of
Commerce) ("if you impose 3½ percent this year ... what is there to assure a
businessman that you will not boost that penalty to 42½ percent as was proposed
two years ago?").

[162] "Modified surplus tax for two years retained in Senate–House compromise," *New York
Times*, April 23, 1938, p. 1. By this time, even Treasury officials opposed continuing the

on a business tax aid program that would increase managers' flexibility and independence.[163]

3.8   Corporate tax reform in the post-World War II period

Interest in corporate tax reform began even before the conclusion of World War II. Businesses claimed that high corporate and individual rates on dividends combined with taxes on excess profits to stifle economic recovery. The *Wall Street Journal* opined that "with the return of peace it will be vital to our economy that capital flow into new enterprise to provide employment and to increase the national income. It is so difficult to see how this can happen as long as the present cramping system of double taxation exists."[164] Within two years after the conclusion of the war, as many as sixty proposals had been forwarded for the reform of the taxation of corporations, many offering quite radical alternatives.[165] George Barnes, a banker and a Governor of the Association of Stock Exchange Firms, noted that "[a]mong the most-discussed proposals with business men, at least, are those for elimination of corporation taxes as a means to encourage business expansion and end the double taxation of the shareholder's dividends."[166] For a variety of reasons, however, including initially budget deficits and later the

---

tax. According to Treasury Secretary Morgenthau, it had become one of the system's "tax irritants." "Revenue Revision – 1939: Hearings Before the House Committee on Ways & Means," 76th Cong., 1st Sess. 5 (1939) (statement of Henry Morgenthau, Jr., Secretary of the Treasury).

[163] See "Congress leaders plan to expedite tax aid legislation," *Wall Street Journal*, May 17, 1939, p. 1; "Leaders to push business tax aid at present session," *Wall Street Journal*, May 16, 1939, p. 1. Under this program, business would receive four major tax benefits: (1) Replace the undistributed profits tax and corporate income tax at rates ranging from 16.5 percent to 19 percent with a flat 18 percent corporate income tax; (2) Permit an annual revaluation of capital stock for purposes of the capital stock tax; (3) Eliminate the limit on capital loss deductions for corporations; and (4) Permit corporations to carry losses forward for two or three years. Alfred Flynn, "Four point plan for tax revision being considered," *Wall Street Journal*, May 13, 1939, p. 1. The latter provision was eventually extended to individuals and partnerships in the final House bill. See "Two new concessions to business included in House tax bill," *Wall Street Journal*, June 17, 1939, p. 1; "House passes tax revision bill; approval by Senate likely," *Wall Street Journal*, June 20, 1939, p. 2.

[164] Editorial, "Why venture?," *Wall Street Journal*, May 4, 1944, p. 4. See George Bryant, Jr., "Peace will bring little relief for individuals but some for business," *Wall Street Journal*, December 5, 1944, pp. 1, 6.

[165] "Tax report," *Wall Street Journal*, January 30, 1946, p. 1.

[166] George E. Barnes, "A Plan to Simplify Corporation Taxes and a Solution of Double Taxation of Corporate Earnings," *The Exchange* 5 (1944): 1.

focus on excess profits taxation during the Korean War,[167] this flurry of activity did not result in legislative movement.

Concern about declining equity investment helped to prompt a revival of interest in corporate tax reform. In 1951, Godfrey Nelson of the *New York Times* reported that "[o]nly about 6 per cent of our huge national income is now finding its way into" business enterprise, compared with up to 18 percent under normal conditions.[168] According to estimates prepared by the Securities and Exchange Commission, a mere 8 percent of aggregate liquid individual savings went toward the net purchase of equity securities such as common stock.[169] Moreover, not only did the percentage of new investments drop, but there was a drop in the total number of shareholders from approximately 10 million in 1930 to 6 million by 1952.[170] By 1953, the volume of trading on the New York Stock Exchange (NYSE) had reached a low point of fewer than 1 million shares and G. Keith Funston, the president of the Exchange, subsequently complained that "[n]ew enterprises seeking to create new wealth and productivity are unable to attract the equity capital we need."[171] Moreover, the net acquisition of corporate stocks dropped sharply during and immediately following the Korean War, from a high of $1.6 billion in 1951 to $1 billion in 1952, $700 million in 1953, and a post-World War II low of $300 million by 1954.[172]

The double taxation of corporate income was blamed for the drop in equity investment. At a Tax Institute symposium held in 1950, William Casey remarked that the effect of double taxation and the

[167] John H. Crider, "Doubts tax cuts till budget is met," *New York Times*, December 20, 1945, p. 16; C. P. Trussell, "Tax commitment with GOP in 1945 is laid to Truman," *New York Times*, June 10, 1947, p. 1; "Business group formed to urge alternative to Excess Profits Tax," *Wall Street Journal*, November 10, 1950, p. 8.

[168] Godfrey N. Nelson, "Tax course is held road to Socialism," *New York Times*, September 23, 1951, p. 137.

[169] J. Kirk Eads, "The Tax Man rings twice," *Nation's Business* 41 (1953): 81–2.

[170] Jonathan Barron Baskin and Paul J. Miranti, Jr., *A History of Corporate Finance* (Cambridge University Press, 1997), p. 232; John Micklethwait and Adrian Wooldridge, *The Company: A Short History of a Revolutionary Idea* (New York: Modern Library, 2003), p. 117.

[171] Jerry Markham, *A Financial History of the United States*, 3 vols., vol. II (Armonk, NY: M. E. Sharpe, 2002), p. 293; G. Keith Funston, "Double taxation of dividends, before the House Ways and Means Committee (July 15, 1953)," *Vital Speeches of the Day* 19 (1953): 723.

[172] Richard Sutch, "Derivation of Personal Saving: 1946–2002 [Flow of funds]," in Susan B. Carter, Scott Sigmund Gartner, Michael R. Haines, Alan L. Olmstead, Richard Sutch, and Gavin Wright (eds.), *Historical Statistics of the United States: Earliest Times to the Present, Millennial Edition*, 5 vols., vol. 3 (Cambridge University Press, 2006), part C: Economic Structure and Performance, at tbl. Ce91–121.

growing availability of more favorably taxed investments such as municipal bonds and real estate "have clearly reflected themselves in the fact that corporate stock has so consistently sold at a lower ratio to earnings, and is still doing so in the current bull market, than ever before."[173] The NYSE's Funston told the House Ways and Means Committee in July of 1953 that "[t]axation of capital gains and double taxation of dividends are Federally-erected twin dams holding back the free flow of life-giving venture capital into American industry."[174] While there were dissenters in this attempt to pin an equity crisis on double taxation,[175] there was at least some acknowledgment that the tax provisions, in combination with an economic downturn, may have had some effect.[176] In any event, the notion that the taxation of dividends was hurting equity investment had clearly become a mainstream view. Even the *Saturday Evening Post* observed that "double taxation can only retard the flow of risk capital into new ventures."[177]

President Dwight Eisenhower eventually accepted this logic and pushed for corporate tax reform to address it. In his 1954 State of the Union Address, Eisenhower called for a complete overhaul of the entire tax system to "remove the more glaring tax inequities."[178] In his Budget Message later that month, Eisenhower specifically identified double taxation as one such "glaring inequity," proposing to remove it "by allowing stockholders a credit against their own income taxes as a partial offset for the corporate tax previously paid."[179] Under the proposal, which was quickly approved by the Ways and Means Committee, the first $50 of dividends would be excluded from income, rising to the first $100 of dividends starting in 1955. In addition, a tax credit of 5 percent would be permitted on dividend income beyond the exclusion, rising to 10 percent in 1955

---

[173] William Casey, "Double Taxation of Dividends," in Tax Institute (ed.), *Taxation and Business Concentration: Symposium Conducted by the Tax Institute, June 15–16, 1950* (Princeton, NJ: Tax Institute, 1952), p. 211.

[174] Funston, "Double taxation of dividends, before the House Ways and Means Committee," 723.

[175] See Editorial, "Taxes and investment," *America* 91 (1954): 493.

[176] Eugene N. Feingold, *The Internal Revenue Act of 1954: Policy and Politics* (dissertation, Princeton University, 1960), p. 192.

[177] Raymond Rice, "The double tax on dividends deters venture investment – also it's unfair," *Saturday Evening Post*, February 13, 1954, p. 12.

[178] Alan Otten and David Ives, "The State of the Union message has something for almost everyone," *Wall Street Journal*, January 8, 1954, p. 1.

[179] "Complete text of tax proposals," *Los Angeles Times*, January 22, 1954, p. 13.

and 15 percent in 1956.[180] The decision to rely on a shareholder exemption and tax credit, rather than a corporate credit or deduction, was apparently so as not to discriminate between distributed and undistributed profits and thereby revive the hated undistributed profits tax.[181]

The dividend tax proposal was structured in large measure to respond to the equity crunch. A Ways and Means Committee spokesman said that the proposal was "designed to stimulate a flow of equity capital," while the *New York Times* reported that "[o]ne of the avowed aims of the plan is to encourage the purchase of stocks and thus give business the capital needed for modernization and expansion that will help keep the country at a high level of economic activity."[182] The Administration's supporters used this argument frequently. Treasury Secretary George M. Humphrey testified that double taxation "has restricted the market for shares of a stock in companies which want to expand and has forced them to borrow money instead of selling shares in their future. In the past ten years better than 75 per cent of private industry financing has been done by going in debt instead of selling shares."[183] Similarly, Representative Thomas E. Martin of Iowa declared that "[d]ouble taxation of dividends on corporation stock causes many people to invest their funds in tax-exempt bonds rather than invest them as risk capital." According to Martin, this has "caused corporations to turn to bonded indebtedness rather than common stock to keep their business going, even though heavily bonded indebtedness makes any business organization especially vulnerable to adversity when their continued operation is most important."[184] The *New York Times* predicted that this provision "would do about as much as any proposal of the President's tax program to give business a much wanted shot in the arm."[185]

The dividend tax relief proposal "proved to be one of the thorniest and most controversial considered in writing the revenue bill."[186] While the

---

[180] Alan Otten, "President asks Congress to put corporate income taxes partially on a pay-as-you-go basis, starting in 1955," *Wall Street Journal*, January 22, 1954, p. 5.

[181] Feingold, *The Internal Revenue Act of 1954*, p. 203.

[182] "House unit votes to lift large part of double levy on dividends," *Wall Street Journal*, January 15, 1954, p. 2; John Morris, "Cut in taxes on dividends approved by House group," *New York Times*, January 15, 1954, p. 1.

[183] Charles Egan, "Humphrey views the business dip as readjustment," *New York Times*, February 3, 1954, pp. 1, 13.

[184] Benjamin Masse, "Tax on dividends: a moral inquiry," *America*, May 15, 1954, pp. 185, 186.

[185] John Morris, "What's behind the tax reforms," *New York Times*, January 24, 1954, p. E5.

[186] Daniel Holland, *Dividends Under the Income Tax* (Princeton University Press, 1962), p. 147.

bill as a whole was developed with remarkable speed considering its comprehensive nature, the dividend tax provisions were the one speed bump. As one attorney involved with the legislation explained: "Such Congressional speed was possible because there was little Congressional controversy over the technical portions of the bill. Only on policy questions, especially the provisions for dividend tax relief, was there strong differences of opinion."[187] Democrats, in a calculated campaign to develop the issue for the fall elections,[188] "ridiculed the administration's program as a 'trickle down' policy that attempted to indirectly help the unemployed by granting tax relief to corporations and the rich."[189]

While Republicans succeeded in enacting some dividend tax relief, it was ultimately a "limited" victory.[190] The 4 percent dividend tax credit under the legislation was called a "watered down version" of Eisenhower's initial proposal for a 15 percent shareholder credit within three years.[191] Columbia economics professor Carl Shoup noted "the amounts of change are so small that in most cases they make no notable difference in the pattern of tax distribution, from the viewpoint of tax equity . . . [and] a credit of only 4 per cent and an exclusion of only $50 are not likely to influence the sum total of investment appreciably."[192] Not only was the relief limited, but it was short-lived. The dividend tax credit was ultimately repealed in 1964 as part of John F. Kennedy's plan to reduce corporate and individual tax rates and broaden the base.[193] The exemption remained for much longer, but eventually was repealed as well as part of the 1986 tax reform.[194]

This is not to suggest that the push for integration disappeared completely. Most notably, Congress enacted an elective pass-through scheme – Subchapter S – in 1958, although it was limited to small business corporations where the concern about double taxation was

---

[187] Norris Darrell, "Internal Revenue Code of 1954 – a Striking Example of the Legislative Process in Action," *Major Tax Problems* 1955 (1955): 15.

[188] Edward Collins, "A synthetic controversy," *New York Times*, March 29, 1954, p. 29.

[189] John W. Sloan, *Eisenhower and the Management of Prosperity* (Lawrence: University Press of Kansas, 1991): 135.

[190] Feingold, *The Internal Revenue Act of 1954*, p. 179.

[191] John Morris, "Eisenhower sets 1956 for tax cut," *New York Times*, January 21, 1955, p. 10.

[192] Carl Shoup, "The Dividend Exclusion and Credit in the Revenue Code of 1954," *National Tax Journal* 8 (1955): 141–2. See Witte, *The Politics and Development of the Federal Income Tax*, pp. 147–8; Masse, "Tax on dividends," 185.

[193] Julian Zelizer, *Taxing America: Wilbur D. Mills, Congress, and the State, 1945–1975* (Cambridge University Press, 1998), p. 205.

[194] Joint Committee on Taxation, *General Explanation of the Tax Reform Act of 1986* (Englewood Cliffs, NJ: Prentice-Hall, 1987), p. 276.

never particularly great.[195] Several integration proposals garnered significant support during the 1980s and 1990s,[196] but none were adopted. At the end of the century, the corporate income tax looked remarkably similar to the one criticized at the end of World War II.

[195] Zelizer, *Taxing America*, pp. 99–100; Note, "Optional Taxation of Closely-held Corporations under the Technical Amendments Act of 1958," *Harvard Law Review* 72 (1959): 723.

[196] See Department of the Treasury, *Tax Reform for Fairness, Simplicity, and Economic Growth – The Treasury Department Report to the President*, 3 vols., vol. 2 (Washington, DC: Office of the Secretary, Department of the Treasury, 1984), pp. 134–44; United States President, *The President's Tax Proposals to the Congress for Fairness, Growth, and Simplicity* (Washington, DC: President of the United States, 1985), pp. 120–29; Department of the Treasury, *Report of the Department of the Treasury on Integration of the Individual and Corporate Tax Systems: Taxing Business Income Once* (Washington, DC: Department of the Treasury, 1992); Alvin Warren, *Federal Income Tax Project: Integration of the Individual and Corporate Income Taxes: Reporter's Study of Corporate Tax Integration* (Philadelphia: American Law Institute, 1993).

PART II

Explaining the divergence

4

Profits

The growth of the corporation and corporate earnings and profits was important to the development of tax systems in both countries over this period. Although United States industrial corporations were much larger than their British counterparts prior to the start of World War II,[1] corporate profits in each country became increasingly significant over the nineteenth and early twentieth centuries. The issue for policymakers was how best to reach such profits through conventional methods of taxation. Ultimately, this turned on what corporations did with the profits they earned. In the nineteenth century, when corporations on both sides of the Atlantic had liberal dividend policies, a corporate-level tax was effectively a withholding tax on dividends. In the twentieth century, however, when corporations in the USA began to retain a higher percentage of their earnings, that characterization was no longer accurate and a new approach was inevitable.

4.1 Era of liberal dividend policies

Among most nineteenth-and early twentieth-century corporations on both sides of the Atlantic Ocean, dividends flowed freely. "It was the common practice to divide all profits in sight and to finance new construction by the issue of securities. Such policies were fully sanctioned by the public opinion of the day."[2] This "strong preference for debt financing in both the United States and Britain during the nineteenth century" existed "even in the absence of any substantial tax benefits."[3] Robert

---

[1] Christopher Schmitz, *The Growth of Big Business in the United States and Western Europe, 1850–1939* (Basingstoke: Macmillan, 1993), p. 26.

[2] William Ripley, *Railroads: Finance and Organization* (New York: Longmans, Green, 1915), p. 244; Ken Brown, "So, will stock dividends get back their respect?," *Wall Street Journal* Online, December 10, 2002 (quoting Roger Ibbotson, Professor of Finance at Yale) ("In the 19th century, it was common practice to pay out everything.")

[3] Jonathan Barron Baskin and Paul Miranti, Jr., *A History of Corporate Finance* (Cambridge University Press, 1997), p. 159.

Sobel suggests that the practice of liberal dividend policies continued into the early twentieth century, explaining that "[b]efore the war, most large corporations considered earnings after taxes and payments to bondholders and preferred stockholders a 'surplus,' and much of this was divided among the common stockholders."[4] According to Sobel, "[t]his meant that such firms would have to depend heavily upon the capital markets for funds needed for expansion, and large bond issues were considered normal."[5]

There were at least two factors contributing to this relatively liberal dividend policy. First, the inadequate financial reporting during this period made dividends one of the few sources of reliable information for potential and current investors. Second, the absence of an active market for most corporations' stock made dividends one of the few sources of shareholder liquidity. While the British were ahead of the Americans on both of these issues during the nineteenth century, shareholders in each country were motivated by these concerns to focus on corporate dividend policy.

4.1.1   Inadequate financial reporting

USA

One of the principal factors contributing to the free flow of dividends in the USA was the inadequacy of contemporary financial reporting. Financial disclosure was essentially non-existent for small and even large, non-public corporations, especially in the manufacturing sector. This non-disclosure prevailed in part because most such firms had never developed a tradition of financial reporting during their formative years when they were essentially owned and controlled entirely by family members.[6] Long after their stockholder base had expanded, however, managers still considered the corporation's internal financial data to be as private and personal as the financial circumstances of their own families.[7]

---

[4] Robert Sobel, *The Great Bull Market: Wall Street in the 1920s* (New York: Norton, 1968), p. 32.
[5] Ibid., p. 32.
[6] David Hawkins, "The Development of Modern Financial Reporting Practices among American Manufacturing Corporations," *The Business History Review* 37 (Autumn, 1963): 137. See William Ripley, *Main Street and Wall Street* (Boston: Little, Brown, and Co., 1927), p. 23 ("In such branches as cotton manufacture, for instance, soon after the industrial revolution it was necessary to assemble more capital than could customarily be provided by individuals or families. Yet even for these companies the capital stocks were usually owned by those who managed the enterprise. They were largely family concerns.")
[7] Hawkins, "The Development of Modern Financial Reporting Practices," 142.

The situation was not much better in the case of public corporations. The managements of many turn-of-the-century public corporations have been described as "notoriously secretive," providing little or no financial disclosure.[8] For instance, the Westinghouse Electric and Manufacturing Company, which built the world's first commercial AC electrical system in 1891 and founded a British subsidiary in 1899, neither distributed an annual report nor held an annual meeting for stockholders between 1897 and 1905.[9] This secrecy was true even among the heavily regulated railroad corporations, where a company such as the New York Central and Hudson Railroad did not prepare an annual report for stockholders during the 1870s or the 1880s.[10] The stock exchanges appeared to provide little help in establishing a norm of financial reporting among these companies. For example, in 1866, when the New York Stock Exchange asked the treasurer of the Delaware, Lackawanna, and Western Rail Road Company about its financial reporting, the treasurer replied "the Delaware Lackawanna R.R. Co., make no reports and publish no statements and have done nothing of the sort for the last five years."[11]

Even when a corporation did distribute regular financial statements to stockholders, these statements were often inadequate to inform investors of the true financial condition of the corporation.[12] One early financial commentator, Arthur Dewing, noted that information supplied by the corporation was "invariably colored by the point of view of the corporation, and frequently unreliable because of 'sins of omission'."[13] In 1906, the *Journal of Accountancy* began a column devoted to scrutinizing and, often criticizing, the reports of various large corporations, noting that the "officers [of the corporation] . . . have been permitted to render such an account and report of their stewardship as they may deem fit."[14]

---

[8] Ibid., 140 (labeling the International Silver Company, the Virginia–Carolina Company, and the American Tin Plate Company some of the worst offenders).

[9] Ibid., 137.   [10] Ibid., 136.   [11] Ibid., 135–6.

[12] Some commentators distinguished between the very early reports and those that were issued around the turn of the century, praising the former and criticizing the latter. See J. W. Garner, "Personal and Bibliographical," *The American Political Science Review* 3 (1909): 267 ("It is an interesting commentary on corporate methods to find that the early reports to the stockholders were sources of real information while recent ones are often conspicuous for their lack of such information.")

[13] Arthur Dewing, *Corporate Promotions and Reorganizations* (Cambridge, Mass.: Harvard University Press, 1914), p. 12.

[14] "The Reports of American Corporations" (Oct. 1906) *Journal of Accountancy*, in Richard Brief (ed.), *Corporate Financial Reporting and Analysis in the Early 1900s* (New York: Garland Publishing, Inc., 1986), p. 458.

Compounding the problem of vague or incomplete public financial statements was the absence of any uniform standards governing financial reporting.[15] The accounting profession was still in its infancy during this period and accounting practices ranged from the relatively unsophisticated to the positively barbaric.[16] In fact, audited financial statements were relatively unheard-of prior to 1900.[17] As a consequence, modern accounting experts have observed, "financial reporting during the nineteenth century was in disarray and failed to provide the needed measurements."[18] For companies not subject to such regulation, the situation was even worse. When the Federal Trade Commission sent a questionnaire and request for financial information to every manufacturer in the country, only 30 percent of the replies were reported in useful form.[19] Thus, even in the case where a company provided financial statements, it was difficult for a stockholder to interpret the information or to use it to make comparisons among different investments.

Part of the problem was that both the content and the frequency of disclosures often "depended upon the whim of managers" rather than the requirements of state corporation laws or corporate charters.[20] By 1900, only sixteen states required corporations to submit detailed financial reports on an annual basis and stockholder access to such reports was only upon demand in most of those states.[21] As part of the corporate excise tax in 1909,[22] Congress mandated that corporate tax returns would be open to the public, in part to provide a Federal lever for the production of such financial

---

[15] See Baskin and Miranti, Jr., A History of Corporate Finance, p. 183.

[16] See William Hewett, The Definition of Income and its Application in Federal Taxation (Philadelphia: Westbrook, 1925), p. 81 (commenting on "the relatively unsatisfactory nature of accounting practice in its present stage of development"); Robert Haig, "The Concept of Income – Economic and Legal Aspects," in Robert Haig (ed.), The Federal Income Tax (New York: Columbia University Press, 1921), p. 18 (lamenting the "wide gap which stretches between theory and practice in the field of accounting.")

[17] Hawkins, "The Development of Modern Financial Reporting Practices," 137.

[18] Baskin and Miranti, Jr., A History of Corporate Finance, p. 183. In 1887, the Interstate Commerce Commission imposed a requirement that railroads regularly submit uniform financial statements, but Congress did not authorize the establishment of uniform accounting methods for the preparation of such statements until 1906. Ibid., p. 145.

[19] See John Wildman, "The Place which Accounting should Occupy in any Scheme of National Preparedness," American Economic Review (Supp) 7 (1917): 226.

[20] Hawkins, "The Development of Modern Financial Reporting Practices," 136.

[21] Marjorie Kornhauser, "Corporate Regulation and the Origins of the Corporate Income Tax," Indiana Law Journal 66 (1990): 69.

[22] Act of August 5, 1909, ch. 6, § 38, 36 Stat. 112–17 (1909) (imposing a 1 percent excise tax on the privilege of doing business in the corporate form, with the tax measured by corporate income).

information.[23] This publicity requirement, however, was removed after business leaders waged an intense campaign to defeat it, arguing that "it infringed intolerably on corporate privacy."[24] Thus, even in the late 1920s, the Northern Pipeline was able to issue a one-line "income account" statement and a balance sheet described as "bare bones."[25]

One factor contributing to managerial reluctance to distribute full and complete financial statements was the fear that these would aid a company's competitors.[26] According to a witness testifying before the Industrial Commission on Trusts and Industrial Combinations in 1899, "[t]he public may not be your competitors; but you may have competitors, and in giving it to the public you would have to give it to your competitors."[27] While the Industrial Commission's final recommendations contained some safeguards against divulging trade secrets in publicly available financial reports,[28] they would have been unlikely to

---

[23] Ibid., § 38(6), 36 Stat. 116 (providing that all returns "shall constitute public records and be open to inspection as such.")

[24] Joe Thorndike, "Promoting Honesty by releasing Corporate Tax Returns," *Tax Notes* 96 (2002): 325; Marjorie Kornhauser, Letter to the Editor, "More historical perspective on publication of corporate returns," *Tax Notes* 96 (2002): 746. The Senate passed a bill to impose a publicity requirement for corporate income tax returns in the Revenue Act of 1924, but the provision was removed in conference. See Roy Blakey and Gladys Blakey, *The Federal Income Tax* (London, New York: Longmans, Green, and Co., 1940), p. 245. A publicity requirement was passed as part of the 1934 Act's "pink slip" requirement for all returns, but it was quickly repealed after only one year. Ibid., p. 364. Ironically, there are efforts in Congress to revive such a publicity requirement as a tool to aid in the fight against corporate financial misconduct. See Sheryl Stratton, "Closing the Credibility Gap by Disclosing Corporate Returns," *Tax Notes* 96 (2002): 322 (describing letter from Senator Charles Grassley to Treasury Secretary Paul O'Neill and Securities and Exchange Commission Chair Harvey Pitt, dated July 8, 2002, asking them to consider disclosure of corporate tax returns). The impetus for this latest campaign appears to be a *Wall Street Journal* editorial on the subject. Ibid., 322 (citing Alan Murray, "Companies should close credibility gap in books," *Wall Street Journal*, July 2, 2002).

[25] Rick Wartzman, "An original activist showed shareholders it's best to be skeptical," *Wall Street Journal*, June 15, 2002, p. B1.

[26] Hawkins, "The Development of Modern Financial Reporting Practices," 141 ("managers feared that by revealing financial information they would unwittingly assist their competitors.")

[27] Ibid. (quoting Charles W. King, secretary and general manager of the New Jersey Corporation Agency).

[28] See Thomas Phillips, "Recommendation as to publicity," *US Industrial Commission, Final Report*, vol. XIX (1902), in Brief, *Corporate Financial Reporting and Analysis*, p. 10 ("No examiner shall be assigned to examine any corporation who is himself interested in the business thereof, or of any competing concern, or who has relatives who are so interested . . . It shall be unlawful for an examiner to divulge private business except by his report to the auditor.")

assuage the fears of most businesses even if Congress had adopted the Commission's recommendation for increased publicity. This tension between the corporate desire for confidentiality and the public demand for disclosure was a continuing difficulty for accountants and legislators throughout the early twentieth century.[29] During the 1909 debate over the bill to impose an excise tax on corporations, there was strong opposition to the proposal to require that corporate tax returns be made public.[30] Small corporations, in particular, complained that the publicity requirement would put them at a disadvantage *vis-à-vis* their larger competitors who were well positioned to use such information to defeat them.[31]

UK

Even in the UK, where accounting rules and the accounting profession started much earlier than in the USA, financial disclosure was not particularly useful. Throughout most of the nineteenth century, there was no legal requirement that British companies maintain any kind of formal books or financial accounts, let alone distribute such information to shareholders.[32] Under the Joint Stock Companies Act of 1844 and a variety of related legislation, companies seeking to register joint stock companies were required to produce audited balance sheets and publicize them to shareholders.[33] In the Companies Act of 1856, however, the requirement to furnish audited financial statements was removed, apparently as part of a *laissez-faire* approach to internal corporate governance matters.[34]

Although many firms did actually provide some form of disclosure to non-insider shareholders despite the absence of a legal requirement to do

[29] See Wildman, "The Place which Accounting should Occupy," 227.
[30] See Kornhauser, "Corporate Regulation," 113–18.
[31] Ibid., 116–17; Kornhauser, "Letter to the Editor," 745; John Buenker, *The Income Tax and the Progressive Era* (New York: Garland Publishing, 1985), p. 117.
[32] P. L. Cottrell, *Industrial Finance 1830–1914: The Finance and Organization of English Manufacturing Industry* (London: Methuen, 1979), p. 256.
[33] R. H. Parker, "Regulating British Corporate Financial Reporting in the Late Nineteenth Century," *Accounting, Business and Financial History* 1 (1990): 51, 62–3.
[34] Stewart Jones and Max Aiken, "The Significance of the Profit and Loss Account in Nineteenth Century Britain: a Reassessment," *Abacus* 30 (1994): 196; Stewart Jones, "UK Companies Legislation: Accounting Publicity and 'Mercantile Caution': a Response to Maltby," *Accounting History* 4 (1999): 73, 77. For a contrary view on the *laissez-faire* motivation, see Josephine Maltby, "UK Joint Stock Companies Legislation 1844–1900: Accounting Publicity and Mercantile Caution," *Accounting History* 3 (1998): 11–12.

so, the quality of what was disclosed was often inadequate. According to Janette Rutterford, "the content of the income statement was very limited, the dividend payment being the key disclosure and the profit figure given as an afterthought, designed mainly to provide cover for the dividend."[35] Moreover, the absence of uniform standards for reporting financial data meant that it was often difficult to compare the financial positions of different companies. An 1849 report of a Select Committee of the House of Lords on the auditing of railroad accounts reported that

> Each Company is left, at its own will and pleasure, to adopt the form considered by them to be the most convenient, and to vary that form from time to time . . . The result is, that no adequate means are afforded by which to compare the financial affairs of any two Railways, or even to compare the Accounts of the same Railway from time to time; the form of the Balance Sheet submitted by one Railway to its Shareholders and Auditors has been found to vary in the very same year.[36]

It was not until the latter third of the nineteenth century that the government mandated any kind of uniform accounting treatment, but even this was done only in certain industries and generally did not extend to commercial and industrial concerns.[37]

In part because of the insufficient standardization in the accounting profession, British company financial statements were subject to "the risk of deliberate fraud."[38] As one contemporary publication revealed in 1887, "an honest accountant's certificate honestly applied is one of the rarest features in an industrial prospectus."[39] Josephine Maltby explained that "[a]ccounts could readily be 'cooked' by dishonest directors."[40] The use of hidden reserves to disguise a company's profitability made valuation through any means other than the dividend payment virtually impossible. As a result, opponents charged that the financial statements were more misleading than helpful. Henry Prescott, a banker, testified to the Mercantile Law Commission that

---

[35] Janette Rutterford, "From Dividend Yield to Discounted Cash Flow: a History of UK and US Equity Valuation Techniques," *Accounting, Business and Financial History* 14 (2004): 131.

[36] Parker, "Regulating British Corporate Financial Reporting," 64–5 (quoting Third Report of the Select Committee of the House of Lords on Audit of Railway Accounts (1849)).

[37] Ibid., 65–6.   [38] Maltby, "UK Joint Stock Companies," 24.

[39] James Jefferys, *Business Organisations in Great Britain 1856–1914* (New York: Arno Press, 1977), p. 402 (quoting *The Statist* I (1887): 284).

[40] Maltby, "UK Joint Stock Companies," 24.

Public statements of the accounts of trading concerns have been found by general experience to be very fallacious, and if the tendency of such statements shall be to generate confidence which would not otherwise exist on the part of the public, we think such publication may probably do more harm than good.[41]

In an 1855 edition of *The Economist*, the magazine advocated the repeal of the requirement that companies distribute audited financial statements, noting that "any attempt to give legal guarantee which falls at all short of its object is attended with mischievous consequences, as raising a presumption of security which does not exist, and which induces a dependence upon the provision of Acts of Parliament."[42] Later, Edward Campbell argued on the floor of the House of Commons that requiring publication of audited financial statements is "altogether useless, if not eminently mischievous."[43]

One possible explanation for the deficiency of disclosure in the UK, despite the availability of a more sophisticated group of accounting practitioners than in the USA, is that many British companies objected to disclosure on grounds of "commercial confidentiality."[44] In testimony to the Mercantile Law Commission in 1854, opponents claimed that the requirement to publish audited financial statements "improperly open[s] up the transactions of the concerns," noting that "mercantile affairs require secrecy in many cases; pending transactions involve long periods of time and cannot be published."[45]

In firms with widely dispersed shareholders, the claims of confidentiality may have been designed to shield directors from shareholder interference. When the Select Committee on the Companies Acts of 1862 and 1867 revisited the issue of publicity, one solicitor reminded it that this had been a key objection in the past:

If you make it obligatory in every case, you will limit the operation and scope of this Act [the Companies Act of 1862] very much indeed, because the Act is intended to embrace a large class of cases where parties carry on a trading business and do not want their affairs to be known, or even to be printed and published among their own shareholders, except to the extent they wish.[46]

---

[41] Ibid. (quoting testimony in the Report of the Royal Commission on the Mercantile Laws and Amendments to the Law of Partnership 98 (1854)).

[42] Ibid., 25 (quoting *The Economist*, January 6, 1855).

[43] Ibid. (quoting *Hansard*, HC, vol. 139, col. 345, 1856).   [44] Ibid., 23.

[45] Ibid., 23–4 (quoting testimony in the Report of the Royal Commission on the Mercantile Laws and Amendments to the Law of Partnership 77 (1854)).

[46] Ibid., 24 (quoting from testimony of J. Morris, solicitor, to the Select Committee on the Companies Acts 1862 and 1867, at 907).

According to one 1893 investors' journal, "[m]any Boards of Directors evidently consider that so long as dividends are paid, the shareholders have no claim to learn how they have been earned or what provisions have been made as to the future."[47] More recently, James Jefferys confirmed this account, writing that "[i]n companies where the ordinary shares were held by the public, the directors often frightened the shareholders into agreeing to stay in darkness with the argument that the publication of any light on the subject of profits might lead to competition and labour troubles."[48]

In firms controlled by blockholders rather than by directors, it is also possible that the concern for confidentiality may have been a product less of competitive concerns, than of privacy issues resulting from the dominance of large investors in many mid-nineteenth-century UK companies. As Stewart Jones notes, "large investors in possession of fairly undiversified portfolios would be more likely to find accounting disclosures an embarrassing intrusion into their private business affairs."[49] Regardless of the source of their concern, the consequence was that non-insider investors got either little or no information from the statements that were released.

Dividends as a form of disclosure

Given the weakness of contemporary financial disclosure in both the USA and the UK, a liberal dividend policy may have served an important signaling function for current and potential stockholders. Dividends suggested (in the absence of financial reporting) or confirmed or refuted (in the face of potentially incomplete or unreliable reports) a company's earnings and financial viability. Dividends, therefore, were one of the few objective resources available in setting a market valuation for the firm's stock.[50] As Rutterford observed, "British investors looked to the dividend as the only trustworthy number in the accounts."[51] Graham and Dodd described a similar phenomenon in the USA:

> Until recent years the dividend return was the overshadowing factor in common-stock investment. This point of view was based on simple logic ... Since the idea of investment is closely bound up with that of dependable income, it follows that investment in common stocks would

---

[47] Jefferys, *Business Organisations*, p. 432, n. 2.   [48] Ibid., p. 433.
[49] Jones, "UK Companies Legislation," 82.
[50] Baskin and Miranti, Jr., *A History of Corporate Finance*, pp. 18–19.
[51] Rutterford, "From Dividend Yield to Discounted Cash Flow," 131.

ordinarily be confined to those with a well-established dividend. It would follow also that the *price* paid for an investment common stock would be determined chiefly by the amount of the dividend.[52]

This explains why at least early market prices in both the USA and the UK were linked to a company's dividend policy.[53] According to Rutterford,

> [t]his emphasis on income reflected the fact that investors valued equities as quasi-bonds that differed from bonds only in the uncertainty of their maturity and of their dividend payments. This approach to valuation lasted on both sides of the Atlantic until the early twentieth century, when a number of factors caused a shift in emphasis, in the USA, from dividend yield to Price/Earnings Ratio (P/E).[54]

With nineteenth-century stock prices linked to dividend yields, companies were more reluctant to forgo a dividend or retain a large amount of earnings. Thus, when the United States Steel Corporation was threatened by outside competitors at the turn of the century, it contemplated, but rejected, choosing not to pay dividends because of the significant damage that decision would inflict on its stock price.[55] This decision was made notwithstanding the fact that US Steel was one of the few companies to issue relatively detailed income statements that provided investors with sufficient earnings data to calculate returns for each of the companies within the corporate group.[56] The corporation instead chose to raise new capital by issuing additional shares to the public.[57] In an era of erratic financial reporting, dividend rates effectively served as the basic means

---

[52] Benjamin Graham and David Dodd, *Security Analysis: Principles and Techniques* (New York, London: Whittlesey House; McGraw-Hill Book Co., Inc., 2d edn., 1940), p. 372 (emphasis in original). This was not always seen as an unmitigated good. See Hartley Withers, *Stocks and Shares* (London: Smith, Elder & Co., 1910), p. 158 ("[U]nfortunately the amount of dividend paid by a company is too often taken as the only test of its welfare.")

[53] There are many studies making such a link using modern data. See, e.g., Pyung Sig Yoon and Laura Starks, "Signaling, Investment Opportunities, and Dividend Announcements," *Review of Financial Studies* 8 (1995): 1015; Jonathan Barron Baskin, "Dividend Policy and the Volatility of Common Stocks," *The Journal of Portfolio Management* 15 (1989): 19–25; Jean Crockett and Irwin Friend, "Dividend Policy in Perspective: Can Theory Explain Behavior?," *The Review of Economics and Statistics* 70 (1988): 610.

[54] Janette Rutterford, "Gross or net? The role of taxation in the history of equity valuation," *Accounting History* 15 (2010): 51.

[55] See Edward Meade, "The Genesis of the United States Steel Corporation," *The Quarterly Journal of Economics* 15 (1901): 543.

[56] Rutterford, "Gross or net?," 51.

[57] Meade, "The Genesis of the United States Steel Corporation," 544.

of valuation until, at least in the USA, the price/earnings ratio supplanted it early in the twentieth century.[58]

4.1.2   Liquidity

A liberal dividend policy was important not only as a source of information, but also as a source of shareholder liquidity as well. In the early days of the Anglo-American corporation, cash distributions were effectively the only way for an investor to extract a return from the company. From 1601 to 1613, the British East India Company, for example, distributed the entire proceeds of a voyage to shareholders, without any distinction between the income and the original capital, "because they were doubtless viewed as elements in the total liquidation of a completed voyage."[59] To avoid flooding the market and thereby depressing the price of their goods, quarterly auctions were held throughout the year, with proceeds paid after each auction in an early version of the quarterly dividend payment.[60] Paying liquidating dividends "obviated the need for objective accounting data, since the success of a venture could be ascertained by actual cash flows," but it also "reduced the need to rely on embryonic financial markets for liquidity, and shares could be purchased without undue concern about whether they could be readily sold at a fair price."[61] This practice stood in stark contrast to the Dutch East India Company. With the benefit of a functioning stock exchange and a more robust debt market, the Dutch East India Company locked capital in for a period of ten years rather than distributing it along with the profits after each trip.[62]

Although nineteenth-century companies did not liquidate after each transaction, dividends frequently continued to comprise the only foreseeable source of return on a shareholder's investment.[63] During most of the century, the largest corporations were private, family-controlled

---

[58]   See Richard Schabacker, *Stock Market Theory and Practice* (New York: B. C. Forbes Publishing Co., 1930), p. 405.
[59]   Baskin and Miranti, Jr., *A History of Corporate Finance*, p. 71.   [60]   Ibid., pp. 71–2.
[61]   Jonathan Barron Baskin, "The Development of Corporate Financial Markets in Britain and the United States, 1600–1914: Overcoming Asymmetric Information," *The Business History Review* 62 (1988): 202.
[62]   See Ron Harris, "Law Finance and the First Corporations," in James Heckman, Robert Nelson, and Lee Cabatingan (eds.), *Global Perspectives on the Rule of Law* (Abingdon: Cavendish Pub., Ltd., 2009); Baskin, "The Development of Corporate Financial Markets," 202.
[63]   Baskin and Miranti, Jr., *A History of Corporate Finance*, p. 19.

enterprises and most publicly traded securities up until 1870 were government-issued.[64] The New York Stock Exchange did not experience its most substantial growth until after the turn of the century.[65] Prior to the Civil War, the number of shares trading hands each day reached as high as 70,000.[66] It was not until 1886 that as many as one million shares changed hands in a single day.[67] Moreover, throughout this period the New York Stock Exchange was primarily a market for railroad securities and the few publicly traded manufacturing company stocks were not widely held.[68] While there were stock exchanges besides the New York Stock Exchange and there were other ways to sell securities beside listing them on an official market,[69] the entire picture was one of thinly trading public markets and a virtually non-existent market for stock in closely held corporations. Not surprisingly, therefore, to induce individuals to invest in a new corporation promoters often promised them that all profits would be distributed as dividends on an annual basis.[70]

The London Stock Exchange was more established than its New York counterpart,[71] with membership more than doubling between 1852 and 1881,[72] but its experience during most of the nineteenth century was comparable. In the mid-1850s, a mere 2.6 percent of the capital stock of

[64] Ibid. at 193; Robert Sobel, *Inside Wall Street: Continuity and Change in the Financial District* (New York: Norton, 1977), p. 32; Baskin, "The Development of Corporate Financial Markets," 207.

[65] See Morton Horwitz, *The Transformation of American Law, 1870–1960: the Crisis of Legal Orthodoxy* (Oxford University Press, 1992), p. 95; see also Martin Sklar, *The Corporate Reconstruction of American Capitalism, 1890–1916: the Market, the Law, and Politics* (Cambridge University Press, 1988), p. 4, n. 1 (describing the transition from closely held to publicly traded corporations); Sobel, *Inside Wall Street*, pp. 26–7; Stuart Banner, "The Origin of the New York Stock Exchange, 1791–1860," *Journal of Legal Studies* 27 (1998): 115; J. Edward Meeker, *The Work of the Stock Exchange* (New York: The Ronald Press Co., 1922), p. 29.

[66] See Meeker, *The Work of the Stock Exchange*, p. 32.

[67] See Edward Kirkland, *Industry Comes of Age: Business, Labor, and Public Policy, 1860–1897* (New York: Holt, Rinehart, and Winston, 1961), p. 226.

[68] See Meeker, *The Work of the Stock Exchange*, p. 36; Baskin and Miranti, Jr., *A History of Corporate Finance*, p. 193; Thomas Navin and Marian Sears, "The Rise of a Market for Industrial Securities, 1887–1902," *The Business History Review* 34 (1955): 109–10. There were only twenty industrial corporations listed on the Exchange as late as 1896, although the number more than doubled by 1900. See Kirkland, *Industry Comes of Age*, p. 226.

[69] See Kirkland, *Industry Comes of Age*, p. 216.

[70] See Meade, "The Genesis of the United States Steel Corporation," 525.

[71] Ranald C. Michie, *The London and New York Stock Exchanges, 1850–1914* (London, Boston: Allen & Unwin, 1987), p. 3 (noting that in 1876 the London Stock Exchange was referred to as "the most highly organized market in the world").

[72] Cottrell, *Industrial Finance 1830–1914*, p. 152.

British companies was quoted on the Exchange.[73] That number had grown by 1883, but only to 6.2 percent, leading R. A. Breyer to note that "[f]rom 1856 to 1885 the London Stock Exchange provided little capital for industrialized companies."[74] Even among quoted securities, there was relatively little trading outside the large issuers. P. L. Cottrell explained that "securities arising from small issues were generally unmarketable on the London Stock Exchange during the 1870s."[75] While the increase in brokers facilitated higher trading in subsequent years, this was mostly concentrated in shares in which there was already significant trading. This "eroded further the liquidity of some industrial shares."[76] In many respects local stock exchanges were much more significant in providing liquidity than the London Stock Exchange, but they primarily specialized in individual industries and many of them did not experience their most significant growth until the end of the nineteenth century.[77]

Given the relatively limited ability to cash out an investment on nineteenth-century exchanges, dividends were an important source of liquidity. Dividends often fluctuated with a company's earnings rather than remaining stable and regular, but this was not inconsistent with shareholders' expectations. For many nineteenth-century equity investors,[78] their primary investing experience was as a partner in a partnership or investor in a voluntary association.[79] With these investments, they were accustomed to a division of the entire profits, and indeed of the capital itself, with little or no retention of earnings at the partnership or

---

[73] R. A. Breyer, "The Late Nineteenth Century Revolution in Financial Reporting: Accounting for the Rise of Investor or Managerial Capitalism?," *Accounting, Organizations and Society* 18 (1993): 665.

[74] Ibid., 665. See Michie, *The London and New York Stock Exchanges*, p. 26 ("Even by the late 1850s only the National Debt could be bought and sold without difficulty and delay, and the improvement by the 1870s had been slight.")

[75] Cottrell, *Industrial Finance 1830–1914*, p. 182.   [76] Ibid., p. 183.

[77] Janette Rutterford, "The Shareholder Voice: British and American Accents, 1890 to 1965," (forthcoming) *Enterprise and Society* 6–7.

[78] That is, those who elected to invest their money in something other than the traditional choice of real property or a debt instrument such as a municipal or corporate bond. Cf. Navin and Sears, "The Rise of a Market for Industrial Securities," 106 ("Before 1890 a man with excess capital to invest was likely to put his money into real estate"); See J. Edward Hedges, *Commercial Banking and the Stock Market Before 1863* (Baltimore: Johns Hopkins Press, 1938), pp. 30–7.

[79] Baskin and Miranti, Jr., *A History of Corporate Finance*, p. 177; Shaw Livermore, *Early American Land Companies: Their Influence on Corporate Development* (New York: The Commonwealth Fund; London: Oxford University, 1939), pp. 7–8.

associational level.[80] Moreover, most stock was held in family-owned businesses where investors would be well apprised of the performance of the business and would be comfortable with a dividend that fluctuated along with profits.[81] Consistent with this description, many early corporations issued stock for only nominal amounts with future expenses financed by calls on the existing stockholders for additional capital contributions.[82] The implication was that the corporation would neither ask for nor retain more than was needed to finance the operation of the business.

4.2   The divergence in dividend policy

4.2.1   US corporations shift to more conservative dividend policies

In the United States, corporate finance theory regarding dividends began to change at the end of the nineteenth century, long before the enactment of the income tax in 1913. Whereas during much of the nineteenth century the conventional wisdom had been to distribute all or almost all of a corporation's earnings as dividends and raise expansion capital through the debt or equity markets, by World War I the conventional wisdom was that a corporation should "plow back" a substantial percentage of its earnings to fund expansion, protect against downturns, maintain regular dividend policies, and provide for unexpected expenses. In his 1917 treatise on business finance, William Lough noted that "[i]t is generally agreed that regular dividends combined with large – or at least adequate – savings out of annual income should be features of the financial management of most corporations."[83] A few years later, one observer reported that "[t]oday it is taken for granted that no corporation shall pay out more than a fraction of its earnings."[84]

---

[80] See ibid., p. 232 ("There is no clear demarcation in these companies between the idea that dividends were to be paid out of capital and the idea that current earnings should provide such payments ... Dividends were thus quite naturally thought of as a share in the distribution of previously acquired assets, earned or purchased.")

[81] William Lough, *Business Finance: A Practical Study of Financial Management in Private Business Concerns* (New York: The Ronald Press Co., 1917), p. 440 (early stockholders "were supposed to be familiar with the status and fluctuations of the business and were expected to share in its ups and downs. If the enterprise enjoyed an exceptionally good year, it was accepted as a matter of course that the dividend rate would be correspondingly increased. If in the following year there was a sharp decline in profits, the dividend rate should be correspondingly cut.")

[82] Ibid., p. 440; E. Merrick Dodd, *American Business Corporations Until 1860, with Special Reference to Massachusetts* (Cambridge, Mass.: Harvard University Press, 1954), p. 74.

[83] Lough, *Business Finance*, p. 477.

[84] Oswald Knauth, "The Place of Corporate Surplus in the National Income," *Journal of the American Statistical Association* 18 (1922): 164.

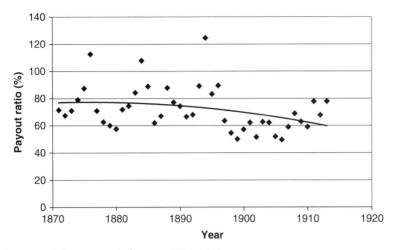

Figure 4.1 US payout ratio by year, 1871–1913
See Cowles Commission for Research in Economics, *Common-Stock Indexes 2* (2d edn.,
1939) ("Cowles Commission"); Jack W. Wilson and Charles P. Jones, *An Analysis of the
S&P 500 Index and Cowles's Extensions: Price Indexes and Stock Returns, 1870–1999*, 75 J.
Bus. 505, 527–31, Appendix: Table A1 (standardizing and updating the data originally
compiled by the Cowles Commission for the period 1871 through 1939). "Payout ratio" is
defined as the dividends divided by the earnings for the indicated year.

The available data suggest that this change in corporate finance theory
was reflected in a change in actual dividend policies for American
companies. As Figure 4.1 illustrates, while dividends hovered around
80 to 90 percent of earnings prior to the turn of the century, they
dropped to approximately 50 to 60 percent of earnings during the first
decade or so of the twentieth century.[85]
British companies, by contrast, paid dividends liberally long after US
firms had switched to policies geared toward higher retention of earnings. John Micklethwait and Adrian Wooldridge reported that the attitude of many was that British companies "were there to be harvested.
Before the First World War, for example, the ratio of dividends to
earnings in Britain was as high as 80 to 90 percent, far higher than in

---

[85] While the omission of closely held corporations and the inadequacy of nineteenth-century
financial reporting caution against reading too much into the data – see Steven Bank, "Is
Double Taxation a Scapegoat for Declining Dividends? Evidence from History," *Tax Law
Review* 56 (2003): 468–71 – the graph nevertheless highlights that corporate dividend payments dropped during the years preceding the adoption of the modern income tax in 1913.

the United States."[86] This gap in dividend payout rate continued through the interwar years. Graham and Dodd observed that, in 1934,

> [t]he typical English, French, or German company pays out practically all the earnings of each year, except those carried to reserves. Hence they do not build up large profit-and-loss surpluses, such as are common in the United States. Capital for expansion purposes is provided abroad not out of undistributed earnings but through the sale of additional stock.[87]

This was true even among railroads. Archibald Currie, a professor of political economy, noted in his study of British investment in North American railroads during the nineteenth and early twentieth centuries that "[a]s a rule, British railways paid out substantially all their earnings as dividends . . . whenever new capital was needed to finance additions and betterments, British railways relied on the sale of new securities."[88] Charles H. Grinling, writing in 1903 about British railroads, observed that "the net profits are divided up amongst the shareholders as far as they will go, an amount being 'carried forward' to next half-year, usually because it was not possible to squeeze out another ¼ percent."[89]

Although British railways eventually began to retain earnings at a more significant pace, they were still behind their American counterparts. Between 1870 and 1894, when only 14 percent of the common stock in British railroads paid no dividends, the practice among North American railroads "was to plow back earnings whenever possible. In this way the carriers tried to build up the value of the physical assets to the point where they equaled or exceeded the nominal value of the securities outstanding."[90] William Z. Ripley reported that "[b]etterments or improvements by the best of our railroads have commonly been in part paid for out of surplus income. Therein lies the great benefit of American over English practice. Dividends have been withheld, sometimes for years, in order to build up a road."[91]

The gap between American and British practices widened during World War I. By 1917, William Lough wrote that "[t]he tendency in European countries is much more strongly in favor of paying out the greater portion

---

[86] John Micklethwait and Adrian Wooldridge, *The Company: A Short History of a Revolutionary Idea* (New York: Modern Library, 2003), p. 84.
[87] Graham and Dodd, *Security Analysis*, p. 331.
[88] A. W. Currie, "British Attitudes towards Investment in North American Railroads," *The Business History Review* 34 (1960): 204.
[89] Charles Grinling, "British Railways as Business Enterprises," in William Ashley (ed.), *British Industries: A Series of General Reviews for Business Men and Students* (London: Longmans, Green & Co., 1903), p. 166.
[90] Currie, "British Attitudes towards Investment," 204, 211.
[91] William Ripley, "Stock Watering," *Political Science Quarterly* 26 (1911): 105.

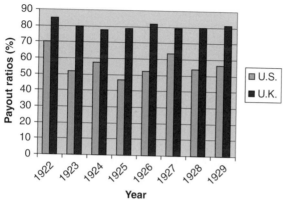

Figure 4.2 Dividend payout ratios in the USA and UK, 1922-9
USA: Jack W. Wilson and Charles P. Jones, *An Analysis of the S&P 500 Index and Cowles's Extensions: Price Indexes and Stock Returns, 1870-1999*, 75 J. Bus. 505, 527-31 (2002) (based on data compiled by the Cowles Commission for Research in Economics, *Common-Stock Indexes* (2d edn. 1939)); UK: W. A. Thomas, *The Finance of British Industry 1918-1976*, p. 89, tbl 4.2 (1978) (based on data compiled in *The Economist*, December 17, 1938, at 600).

of earnings in the form of dividends than it is in the United States."[92] As Figure 4.2 demonstrates, during the 1920s UK companies paid out dividends at approximately the same rate – 80 percent – as US firms did during the nineteenth century, while US firms were only paying out approximately 50 to 60 percent of earnings as dividends. Stated differently, British companies on average retained approximately 20 percent of their earnings while US companies retained approximately twice as much – between 40 and 50 percent of earnings.[93]

[92] Lough, *Business Finance*, p. 439.

[93] Cf. Sergei Dobrovolsky, *Corporate Income Retention, 1915-1943* (New York: National Bureau of Economic Research, 1951), Appendix C, Table C2, p. 110 (National Bureau of Economic Research study finding retained earnings for US companies in the study averaged approximately 45–50 percent during the 1920s); William Thomas, *The Finance of British Industry 1918-1976* (London: Methuen, 1978), Table 4.2, p. 89 (in an analysis of *The Economist's* compilation of published UK company accounts during the period, found retained earnings averaged approximately 20 percent); Colin Clark, *National Income and Outlay* (New York: A. M. Kelley, 1937), pp. 186–7 (noting that during the years 1924–35, the retained earnings of British companies were never as high as 25 percent of profits and in many years they were substantially less); A. Wilfred May, "American and European Valuation of Equity Capital: a Comparison," *The American Economic Review* 29 (1939): 735, Tbl. 1 (compilation of US data from 135 corporations during the period 1922-6 and 403 corporations from 1927-9, and British data from 420-59 companies, finding that the US firms retained between 45 and 65 percent and the UK firms retained between 70 and 80 percent).

By and large, US stockholders supported the move toward more conservative dividend policies. When stockholders either participated in management or were close to those who did, as was common during the nineteenth century, they generally understood the ups and downs of the business and accepted the proposition that their dividend would be similarly volatile.[94] This changed, though, as shareholders became more distant from the managers and the operation of the business. As William Lough pointed out in his 1917 treatise, "shareholders who are not active in the business or familiar with it ... regard their ownership of a company's stock purely as an investment of capital that will bring them an income."[95]

For this "investor stockholder,"[96] the focus was on regular dividends, even if that meant the corporation had to retain a larger percentage of its earnings in the lush years so as to be able to continue to pay dividends in the lean years. Lough warned that "dividends must not be allowed to rise, even in the most prosperous periods, above a conservative estimate of the minimum earnings of the company."[97] While corporations did sometimes deviate from this conservative dividend policy to distribute additional amounts in a particularly profitable year, they maintained a policy of regularity by referring to such amounts as an "extra" or "special" dividend paid on top of the regular dividend so as to signal the impermanence of the additional amount.[98]

Corporations used their move to regular dividends to signal their financial stability to the market.[99] The United States Rubber Company, for example, had been characterized by wildly erratic earnings and dividends since its founding in 1892.[100] In 1911, after an eleven-year drought in dividend payments, the company declared that it would

---

[94] See text accompanying notes 59–70, above.   [95] Lough, *Business Finance*, pp. 440–41.

[96] This type of investor stockholder has existed throughout the history of large corporations, but there was a gradual increase in their numbers as more corporations went public and the separation of ownership and control thereby became more pronounced.

[97] Lough, *Business Finance*, p. 444.

[98] See, e.g., "Dividends," *New York Times*, April 9, 1907, p. 13 ("At a meeting of the Board of Directors of the New York Produce Exchange Bank, held this day, a semi-annual dividend of Three (3%) Per Cent was declared and an extra dividend of One (1%) Per Cent payable April 15th"); Arthur Dewing, *The Financial Policy of Corporations* (New York: Ronald Press Co., 3rd edn., 1934) at 636–7 (noting that it is referred to as an "extra" dividend in order to signal to the shareholders that it is not permanent).

[99] In 1907, for example, the American Telephone and Telegraph Company announced an $8 per year regular dividend. See Dewing, *Financial Policy* (5th edn., 1953), vol. I, p. 763, n. ee.

[100] Ibid., vol. I, p. 761, n. dd.

commence paying a 4 percent regular annual dividend on its common stock.[101] In an announcement regarding the move, the company's president explained that "notwithstanding the fact that for some years past the surplus net earnings have been considerably in excess of the sum required for dividends upon the preferred stocks, the Directors have felt it for the best interests of the company to defer payments on the company."[102] He attributed the decision to restore the dividend to a substantial increase in profitability from their automobile tire line.[103] As a result of this move, United States Rubber's stock rose twelve points in less than two weeks, underscoring the importance of regularity for common stockholders.[104] By contrast, if a company cut or eliminated its dividend a negative signal was sent to the market. One observer noted that "the reputation of the management of many of the industrial combinations was seriously injured by their failure to redeem their promises of dividends on the common stock."[105]

As stock ownership spread in the USA, one observer noted that "new significance has been placed upon the importance of maintaining regular dividends year in and year out."[106] Whereas fewer than 4.5 million individuals owned stock in 1900, more than triple that number – almost 14.5 million – owned shares by 1922.[107] The growth in stock ownership not only increased the size of the stockholding population, it changed the face of the typical stockholder. For example, by World War I stock ownership had spread to middle-income individuals.[108] This new type of stockholder viewed dividends as one of his or her primary sources of income. One economist, writing in 1924, noted that over the last twenty-five years, "[t]he tendency toward a more democratic distribution of beneficiary interests in the corporations of the country has been attended by an increase in the number of people who are getting a portion of their income from their accumulated savings."[109] Although

---

[101] "Dividend on Rubber Common," *New York Times*, October 6, 1911, p. 15.   [102] Ibid.
[103] Ibid.   [104] Ibid.
[105] Meade, "The Genesis of the United States Steel Corporation," 525.
[106] See Donald Wilbur, "A Study of the Policy of Dividend Stabilization," *Harvard Business Review* 10 (1932): 373.
[107] H. T. Warshow, "The Distribution of Corporate Ownership in the United States," *The Quarterly Journal of Economics* 39 (1924): 15.
[108] Ibid., 17. It also spread to new demographic groups such as women: Lough, *Business Finance*, p. 441 (noting, for example, that "[a]pproximately half the stockholders of the New Haven Railroad are women.")
[109] Warshow, "The Distribution of Corporate Ownership in the United States," 15. Joseph Kennedy, writing a few years later, concurred in this assessment, observing that "millions

shareholders may have been worse off in the long term as a result of the more conservative dividend policies,[110] regularity was important both for stockholders who depended upon the dividends for monthly expenses and for those who saw dividends as a signal of a stable financial company.

4.2.2   British adherence to traditional perspectives on dividend policy

The emerging divergence between British and American attitudes toward dividend policy first appeared in shareholder disputes. These provided an increasingly important forum for such issues because of the rise in British holdings of US companies. Lured in part by the promise of "handsome dividends," the British had long been a significant source of investment for American companies, starting as far back as the early decades of the eighteenth century in the canal industry and becoming even more prominent with the advent of railroads in the 1830s.[111] After a brief interruption during the Panic of 1893,[112] British foreign investment in the USA grew from $1.1 billion in 1876 to $2.5 billion in 1898 and over $4 billion in 1914.[113] For railroads in particular, British holdings are estimated to have more than doubled from approximately $160 million in 1881 to as much as $350 or $400 million by 1898.[114]

of people have become investors in securities and count upon continuity of their dividend returns in budgeting their living expenses. Anything that would interrupt the continuous flow of dividends will rob the thrifty American investor of part of his livelihood." Joseph Kennedy, "Big business, what now?," *The Saturday Evening Post*, January 16, 1937, p. 80.

[110] See O. J. Curry, "Utilization of Corporate Profits in Prosperity and Depression," *Michigan Business Studies* 9 (1941): 1, 17; Graham and Dodd, *Security Analysis*, pp. 375–6.

[111] Currie, "British Attitudes towards Investment," 202; C. K. Hobson, "British Oversea Investments, their Growth and Importance," *Annals of the American Academy of Political and Social Science* 68 (1916): 26.

[112] Herbert Feiss, *Europe: The World's Banker 1870–1914* (Amherst, Mass.: Harvard University Press, 1930), p. 21.

[113] See Baskin and Miranti, Jr., *A History of Corporate Finance*, p. 130; Dorothy Adler, *British Investment in American Railways, 1834–1898* (Charlottesville: University of Virginia Press, 1970), p. 168; Hobson, "British oversea investments," 30; George Paish, "The Export of Capital and the Cost of Living," *The Statist* (Supplement), February 14, 1914, pp. i–viii. The higher figures are the subject of some dispute among economic historians. Compare D. C. M. Platt, *Britain's Investment Overseas on the Eve of the First World War: The Use and Abuse of Numbers* (New York: St Martin's Press, 1986), p. 5, with Charles Feinstein, "Britain's Overseas Investments in 1913," *Economic History Review* 43 (1990): 294.

[114] Adler, *British Investment in American Railways*, pp. 167–9.

While more of this investment was in the form of debt than of equity,[115] there was substantial stock investment as well.

Since American railroads were ahead of the curve in the trend toward retained earnings,[116] perhaps in part because they were also ahead of the curve in the separation of ownership and control, they were at the forefront of stockholder disputes over dividends. In 1881, for example, the Pennsylvania Railroad Company's relatively conservative dividend policy came under fire. Representatives of a group of British stockholders attended a stockholders' meeting "to express their views that all earnings should be distributed to the stockholders and all capital improvements financed by security issues."[117] According to the company records, "[t]hese efforts continued over a number of years, and as the amount of [British] holding continued to grow, President Roberts and the directors were required to put forth considerable effort to keep the domestic stockholders united in support of the more conservative policy."[118]

British reaction to the US controversy over imposition of an Undistributed Profits Tax in 1936 only further confirmed the large gulf in the two countries' attitudes toward dividends and the corporate tax. *The Times* (London) reported the substantial negative effect the undistributed profits tax appeared to be having on business confidence,[119] but

[115] Currie, "British Attitudes towards Investment," 208; Baskin, "The Development of Corporate Financial Markets," 218.

[116] See Ripley, *Railroads: Finance and Organization*, p. 244 ("But a few roads, undoubtedly well in advance of their time, during the '80s began to devote a good part of their earnings to new construction and betterment.").

[117] George Burgess and Miles Kennedy, *Centennial History of the Pennsylvania Railroad Company, 1846–1946* (Philadelphia: Pennsylvania Railroad Co., 1949), p. 441. For a general discussion of the advent of British stockholders' committees in the American railroad industry, see Adler, *British Investment in American Railways*, pp. 173–4.

[118] Burgess and Kennedy, *Centennial History*, pp. 441, 443. Foreign ownership of the Pennsylvania Railroad increased from 7.37 percent in 1871 to 47.46 percent in 1888. See Adler, *British Investment in American Railways*, p. 176, n. 30.

[119] See, e.g., "The Wall Street slump," *The Times* (London), May 4, 1936, p. 23 ("The largest single factor perhaps in the change of sentiment reflected in the fall of stock prices has been the proposal, and now the passing by a great majority in the House of Representatives, of the Administration's new Taxation Bill. That Bill ... is regarded generally by Business as an enormous obstacle in the road to recovery"); "Heavy spending in America; effect of new tax law," *The Times* (London), November 16, 1936, p. 21 ("The endorsement of the 'New Deal' by the electorate at the polls has by no means effected a miraculous reformation in the spirit of corporations. They are quite as desirous as they ever were to conserve their assets and build up comfortable surpluses for a rainy day ..."); "President and the US 'slump'," *The Times* (London), November 15, 1937, p. 22 ("Revision of that tax [the undistributed profits tax] – and of the Capital Gains Tax, too, if that were not too much to hope for – seems to most business men the most hopeful way of curtailing this present depression ...").

British business representatives were not entirely sympathetic. The president of the Society of Incorporated Accountants, Walter Holman, observed that "[t]he taxation of undistributed profits seemed particularly hard to Americans who had not previously been subjected to the process of taxing profits at the source, so that the accumulation of undivided profits became increasingly difficult."[120] Holman suggested that the problem was partly the result of an "inclination to speculation which was part of the makeup of the American temperament."[121] He explained, "the extension of the taxation of capital profits was a hard blow to a people brought up to invest more for capital increase than for immediate income."[122] Since the British were used to a relatively free flow of dividends as the primary source of return on their investment, the implication was that the Undistributed Profits Tax would not have produced the same malaise among businesses in the UK.

This divergence of dividend policies among US and British firms continued throughout the years up to World War II. In 1940, Benjamin Graham and David Dodd observed the following in their treatise on securities:

> It is important to note that this feature [tendency toward high retained earnings] is peculiar to American corporate finance and has no close counterpart in the other important countries. The typical English, French or German company pays out practically all the earnings of each year, except those carried to reserves. Hence they do not build up large profit-and-loss surpluses, such as are common in the United States. Capital for expansion purposes is provided abroad not out of undistributed earnings but through the sale of additional stock.[123]

While the British reserves might have been inflated to serve the same purpose as American surplus accounts,[124] Graham and Dodd note that "these reserve accounts rarely attain a comparable magnitude."[125]

4.3   Dividends and corporate income taxation

The divergence in both dividend policy and attitudes toward the retention of corporate earnings in the two countries had a noticeable impact

---

[120] "'Penal' taxation in the United States," *The Times* (London), December 17, 1937, p. 11.
[121] Ibid.   [122] Ibid.   [123] Graham and Dodd, *Security Analysis*, p. 379.
[124] In fact, the British worried about companies' "secret reserve accounts," which could be used to hide profits that were not distributed to shareholders. See Horace Samuel, *Shareholders' Money* (London: Sir Isaac Pitman & Sons, 1933), p. 269 ("One of the most classic variations of the technique of inflating or deflating profits at the will of the Board is that system of secret reserves which is one of the cornerstones of modern Company finance.")
[125] Graham and Dodd, *Security Analysis*, p. 379.

on the design of corporate income taxes. In the USA, the growth of retained earnings created an atmosphere that was conducive to the adoption of a tax system friendly to those earnings, while at the same time leading to calls for reform of taxes on retained earnings when concern about excessive corporate accumulation peaked. By contrast, in the UK the maintenance of high dividends called for a tax system friendly to those dividends, while at the same time leading to calls for reform of dividend taxation when corporate investment in growth and expansion was deemed critical. This helps explain the differences in the basic systems, while accounting for their convergence at various points throughout the twentieth century.

4.3.1   USA

The retained earnings-friendly aspect of the US corporate tax originates at least in part in the combination of dividend constraint, which held that shareholders had no claim to the earnings and profits of the corporation until a dividend was declared by the board, and the growth in the importance of retaining earnings as a business custom.[126] In the context of the graduated marginal rate structure adopted in 1913, with rates rising sharply during World War I, Congress was faced with a dilemma. During the nineteenth century, when most profits were distributed as dividends, Congress could afford to wait to levy a tax until a corporation's profits were distributed. Matters changed, however, with the rise of retaining earnings as a customary practice. If the government refrained from taxing shareholders on earnings and profits until they were distributed as dividends, the corporation could become a massive shelter for undistributed profits from the surtax rates.

One possible solution to this dilemma would have been to unify the corporate and partnership taxes under the pass-through rules applicable to partnerships. This was indeed considered in 1917. Under both then-current law and a bill passed in the House, partnership income was deemed to have been distributed and received by the individual partners regardless of whether any money had actually been paid out.[127] This meant that partners were automatically subject to the individual surtaxes

---

[126] Cyrus LaRue Munson, "Dividends," *The Yale Law Journal* 1 (1891): 193; H. W. R., "Dividends," *Central Law Journal* 9 (1879): 163.
[127] *Cong. Rec.*, vol. 55, pp. 5963, 5966 (1917) (statement of Sen. Simmons).

on money earned through the partnership.[128] As Senate Finance Committee Chairman Furnifold Simmons explained, the Committee recognized early on in its deliberations that this discriminated against partnerships and in favor of corporations because the income earned through the latter was not subject to the surtax until actually distributed to shareholders.[129] To remedy this discrimination, Simmons reported that "[t]he first suggestion was to apply to the corporation the rule that now applies to the partnership and to treat the surplus as distributed for the purpose of the income tax whether in fact distributed or not."[130]

According to Simmons, applying a partnership-style tax to corporate income was rejected for two reasons. First, the Finance Committee members were worried that it might be "open to constitutional objections," which presumably referred to the notion that the earnings of the corporation could not constitutionally be deemed income of the shareholders because the latter group's rights to the earnings were subject to the discretion of the directors.[131] Second, they saw that "it might work very great hardship, especially upon a minority shareholder, who would be required to pay a tax upon an income which he had not received and which he could not force the corporation, notwithstanding his property right, to declare."[132] This effectively argued in favor of an entity-level solution, resulting in a small rise in the corporate tax rate, and then the enactment of the war-excess profits tax of 1917, to make up for the effective exemption of earnings from the surtax rates while held by the corporation. Repeated proposals to subject undistributed profits to shareholder-level taxation were rejected even as increases in the surtax rates made the potential revenue losses more significant. As discussed in Chapter 3, Andrew Mellon made no attempt to change this approach after World War I when he took over as Treasury Secretary.

Mellon's failure to address the undistributed profits issue, or, stated, more positively, his embrace of the corporate income tax as a separate

---

[128] Ibid.   [129] Ibid.   [130] Ibid.
[131] Ibid. The Court later announced such a rule in *Eisner* v. *Macomber*, 252 US 189 (1920). In the immediate aftermath of *Macomber*, some suggested that a partnership-style tax could still be imposed on corporate earnings, but this was viewed as unlikely. See Thomas Powell, "Income from Corporate Dividends," *Harvard Law Review* 35 (1922): 364, n. 2 (arguing in favor of the constitutionality of such a tax, but conceding that others disagreed).
[132] *Cong. Rec.*, vol. 55, pp. 5963, 5966 (1917). Senator John Sharp Williams made a similar point when discussing the problem in 1913: "It is a very difficult problem, because there is no right to anybody to have a dividend unless the directors declare a dividend." *Cong. Rec.*, vol. 50, p. 5319 (1913).

tax system, may have been due less to the reasons stated by Simmons and more to the growing consensus during the 1920s that retained earnings were a valuable engine for the economy. While business leaders had made this claim for years in response to undistributed profits tax pro- posals, the argument was starting to take hold among policymakers as well. Dr. T. S. Adams, a Yale economist and advisor to the Treasury Department, had publicly advocated a shareholder-level tax on the undivided profits of a corporation in 1918.[133] By 1923, however, he had reversed course. According to Adams,

> [t]he proposal [to tax undistributed profits] has been rejected because Congress and the people will not face the prospect of applying fifty per cent surtaxes to the great volume of savings effected every year by the corporations of this country . . . We want corporations to save, to rein- vest, to plow back their profits into the business. We admit that it would be undesirable to apply the high surtaxes to the savings made by corpo- rations. Saving, reinvesting is beneficent; it is a renewal of the lifeblood of business; and that part of the business income of the country [that is retained] cannot stand surtaxes rising to fifty per cent.[134]

This change in approach may have been prompted by the country's experience during the economic downturn at the beginning of the decade. Senator Smoot pointed out that "those companies which in good years had accumulated a reasonable surplus got through the depression without bankruptcy, but that the companies which had used the greater part of their earnings in the past in distributions to their stockholders failed."[135] Even then-Secretary of State Charles Evan Hughes stressed the importance of corporate surplus in a speech before the National Institute of Social Sciences. Hughes reportedly exclaimed "[w]e must have a surplus and it must be used to develop enterprise. How fatuous to dry up this essential source of prosperity by plans of

---

[133] John Martin, Jr., "Taxation of Undistributed Corporate Profits," *Michigan Law Review* 35 (1936): 47, n. 16.

[134] Thomas Adams, "Evolution vs. Revolution in Federal Tax Reform," *Proceedings of the National Tax Association* 16 (1924): 308–9. One Senator quoted a statement by Dr. Adams supporting a graduated surtax on undistributed profits, although it appears that the statement offered "one of the solutions that may be suggested" to address the undistributed profits issue, rather than his own personal choice. See *Cong. Rec.*, vol. 65, p. 8018 (1924) (statement of Sen. King).

[135] Ibid., p. 8021 (statement of Sen. Smoot). See Arthur Ballentine, "The graduated corporation tax," *New York Times*, May 14, 1924, p. 18 ("At a time when the general economic welfare demands the fostering and development of business, Senator Jones would place upon it new, unreasonable and unadjusted burdens.")

taxation which discourage enterprise and yet are stridently proclaimed as being in the interest of the people."[136] The sense was that while retained earnings were a problem for the tax system, the cure might be worse than the disease.[137]

4.3.2   UK

If the American system reflected the importance of retained earnings to domestic corporations, the British system reflected the importance of dividends to shareholders. In the United Kingdom, the application of an imputation system assured that dividends would not be disadvantaged *vis-à-vis* retained earnings. Under the system adopted in the Income Tax Act of 1918, income earned at the corporate level would be subject to taxation at the rate applicable to income earned individually, plus any super-tax. This compared favorably to income earned outside the corporation, which was subject to the income tax and any super-tax, if applicable. The credit for tax paid on their behalf at the company level ensured that shareholders would not pay a second layer of the income tax simply because the money was received as a dividend rather than a partnership distribution or earned individually.

The British reaction to the application of the Corporation Profits Tax from 1920 to 1924 reflected the popular embrace of a dividend-friendly company tax system. Indeed, much of the uproar over the plan to layer an entity-level tax on the existing system was its potentially inequitable treatment of shareholders. Josiah Stamp, assistant secretary at Inland Revenue and a member of the 1919 Royal Commission on Income Tax, described the predicament in shareholder terms:

> Two companies might be identical in capital, pre-war profits and excess profits, and yet in the one instance the shareholders might be all poor, or might be persons whose total incomes were reduced, and in the other the shareholders might be millionaires, or persons whose total income had greatly increased, and if the effect of the payment of duty were traced

---

[136] "Hughes here pleads for swift justice," *New York Times*, May 16, 1924, p. 3.

[137] Max Rolink, the former Deputy Collector of Internal Revenue, wrote that he "agrees with those legislators who complain that accumulated corporate profits have paid no surtax and have thus been favored at the expense of distributed profits which have, of course, paid the surtax and that the burden on the two classes of profits should somehow be equalized. This, however, is no excuse for the passage of any unsound tax law proposing a remedy worse than the evil it attempts to cure." Max Rolink, "Letter to the Editor: Taxing corporate surplus," *New York Times*, May 18, 1924, sec. VIII, p. 19.

forward as an individual tax, in a reduction of potential dividend, we should find the principle of ability violated in the most extreme ways.[138]

John Butcher of the House of Commons expressed a similar sentiment, calling the burden on ordinary shareholders "an intolerable hardship" and writing in a letter to the editor of *The Times* that "the serious hardship which the corporation profits tax will inflict on Ordinary shareholders in railway, gas, canal, and all other companies paying low rates of dividend has hardly received sufficient public attention."[139] Butcher proposed to limit the imposition of the tax to situations in which dividends on the ordinary shares exceeded 10 percent.[140] A fellow member of the House of Commons, John Marriott, concurred with Butcher's assessment, calling the proposed tax's incidence "ludicrously unfair" on the "luckless shareholders."[141] A *Times* editorial concluded that it would hit ordinary shareholders particularly hard because of deductions for payments of interest and preferred dividends.[142] As Colonel Wedgwood stated, "I cannot understand why all the landed interests should be exempted, and this extra Income Tax should be

---

[138] Josiah C. Stamp, "The Special Taxation of Business Profits in relation to the Present Position of National Finance," *The Economic Journal* 29 (1919): 413.

[139] *Hansard*, HC, vol. 128, ser. 5, col. 355, 1920. J.G. Butcher, "Letter to the Editor: Corporation profits tax," *The Times* (London), June 22, 1920, p. 12. One commentator took issue, not with Butcher's focus on the harms to shareholders, but with his focus on the holder of ordinary shares when, in the case of companies that paid no ordinary dividend, "the tax will fall on the holders of the lower Preference stocks." F. H. Blackburne Daniell, "Letter to the Editor: Corporation profits tax," *The Times* (London), June 25, 1920, p. 12.

[140] *Hansard*, HC, vol. 128, ser. 5, col. 356, 1920. Chancellor of the Exchequer Austen Chamberlain responded that ordinary shareholders were already protected: "in no case is it to exceed one-tenth of the sum available as dividend or reserve for the benefit of ordinary shareholders after deduction of fixed charges in the nature of a fixed debenture interest or a fixed preference interest on debenture and preference shares already issued." Ibid., cols. 438–9.

[141] J. A. R. Marriott, "Letter to the Editor: Position of shareholders," *The Times* (London), July 7, 1920, p. 10.

[142] "Editorial: the Corporation Tax," *The Times* (London), July 14, 1920, p. 13; "City notes – important new issues – the Corporation Tax," *The Times* (London), March 1, 1921, p. 18. There was some evidence that it actually had this effect. The chairman of the Costa Rica Railway Company announced at the firm's 1921 annual meeting that the "unpopular and injurious" Corporation Profits Tax "is mainly – I might say wholly – responsible for the reduction in your dividend from 2 per cent to 1½ per cent." "Company meetings – the Costa Rica Railway Company, Limited – Corporation Profits Tax – hardships on ordinary stockholders," *The Times* (London), July 20, 1921, p. 19.

reserved for stocks and shares. It is a tax which falls upon ordinary shares and not upon debenture or preference shares."[143]

4.3.3 Reversals

During crises over the scarcity of profits and corporate or shareholder investment, the two systems have sometimes flipped entirely in their treatment of dividends and retained earnings. Several examples demonstrate this phenomenon, which only underscores the extent to which the development of the respective corporate income tax systems reflects, at least in part, the bottom-up issues of profits.

British Profits Tax – 1947

In 1947, the adoption of the British Profits Tax so soon after America's experience with the Undistributed Profits Tax in the late 1930s was a striking example. Contemporary observers immediately pointed out the divergence in approaches, noting that whereas the USA had previously shielded retained earnings from the surtax rates, they punished them with their profits tax levy, and whereas the UK had previously shielded dividends from an extra layer of tax, they now subjected them to a higher rate than the tax on retained earnings via a differential profits tax. One American scholar wrote that "[t]he [British] profits tax of 1947 is specifically designed to encourage retention of earnings, a policy which is in direct contrast to current American and Canadian tax policy aimed at discouraging excessive corporate accumulation."[144] John Maynard Keynes wrote in 1946 that he objected to the possibility of differential profits taxation in the UK, pointing out that the surtax creates a bias to under-, rather than over-declare dividends, as evidenced by the case of the USA: "In the United States this bias has now reached quite extravagant lengths. The New Dealers have tried to devise all sorts of ways of encouraging *larger* declaration of dividends."[145]

The more permissive taxation of retained earnings and concomitant punishment of dividends in the UK during this period were often attributed to a perceived need for increased savings. George May, an American accountant, noted there was a "different attitude" in England

---

[143] *Hansard*, HC, vol. 128, ser. 5, col. 113, 1920.

[144] Morris Beck, "British Anti-inflationary Tax on Distributed Corporate Profits," *National Tax Journal* 1948 (1948): 275.

[145] Martin J. Daunton, *Just Taxes: The Politics of Taxation in Britain, 1914–1979* (Cambridge University Press, 2002), p. 204 (*quoting* Keynes, *The Dividend Policy of Companies*, March 31, 1946, located in Public Records Office, T171/388).

than the one that had led to undistributed profits taxation in the USA before the war: "Grave doubt was felt about the adequacy of individual and corporate savings to maintain and expand the industrial economy, and there was a demand for relief from taxation on profits retained. Sympathy with this demand was frequently expressed both by ministers and by officials of the Inland Revenue."[146]

US dividend tax reform – 1954

At the same time that the UK had become concerned about excessive dividends, the USA had itself reversed course from its prewar stance and become worried about the excessive taxation of dividends. In 1948–9 an economic downturn appeared to be affecting the amount of available equity capital.[147] While there were naysayers who contended that savings were adequate,[148] those concerned about equity investment cited the larger equity needs of the postwar economy. According to Irwin Friend of the US Department of Commerce, the "huge capital requirements for expansion of plant and equipment facilities to take care of postwar markets and technological advances … inevitably led to a growing pressure of demand upon the available sources of funds for business investment – focusing attention for the first time in many years on possible deficiencies in the supply of capital, particularly equity capital."[149] Emil Schram, the president of the New York Stock Exchange warned "the market for equity securities is so anemic that it can absorb only a limited volume of new shares."[150]

Double taxation was frequently blamed for this shortfall in stock investing. The Chairman of General Electric Co. complained that "the present double taxation of dividends is not only inequitable, but it is a serious deterrent to investment in equity securities."[151] The *Wall Street Journal*

---

[146] George May, "Corporate Structures and Federal Income Taxation," *Harvard Business Review* 22 (1943): 16.

[147] See, e.g., Stanley Miller, "The Equity Capital Problem," *Harvard Business Review* 26 (1948): 672.

[148] Randolph Paul, "Cold War Taxation Policy," *Tax Law Review* 4 (1948–9): 42. See Paul Howell, "The Effects of Federal Income Taxation on the Form of External Financing by Business," *Journal of Finance* 4 (1949): 221 (concluding that while tax did affect the incentives to invest, the equity crunch had not yet reached a crisis of national proportions).

[149] Irwin Friend, "Business Financing in the Postwar Period," *Survey of Current Business* (March 1948): 10.

[150] *Wall Street Journal*, March 19, 1948, quoted in Paul, "Cold War Taxation Policy," 41.

[151] "GE chairman urges Congress to stimulate investment in common stocks by easing business tax laws," *Wall Street Journal*, December 15, 1949, p. 2.

concurred, writing "the double taxation of corporate profits paid out in dividends not only reduces the amount of capital available for investment in productive enterprises but goes a long way toward destroying the incentive to venture that has contributed so materially in this country's expansion."[152]

This reopened the door for corporate tax reform proposals. If double taxation was thought to hinder corporate financing, business and its supporters wanted it removed. Thus, Republican congressman John Byrnes of Wisconsin introduced a bill proposing shareholders be granted a tax credit equal to as much as 20 percent of dividends received up to a maximum of $2,000. Byrnes "noted 'serious implications' in the current shift from equity financing to debt financing . . . [explaining that] means must be found to attract individuals in the lower income brackets into corporate financing."[153] Similar proposals came from the other side of the aisle, as Democratic Representative Walter Lynch of New York offered a measure that included a 10 percent shareholder credit for dividends.[154] Private groups such as the Brookings Institution re-released integration plans from the World War II and postwar era.[155]

Although these proposals suggested a concern at the lack of money coming into corporations, there was a related concern at the lack of money going out of corporations in the form of dividends. Representative Wright Patman of Texas called for a study of the retention of corporate earnings to avoid double taxation, suggesting that corporations "should be required to pay out in dividends at least two-thirds of their earnings."[156] As the *Los Angeles Times* observed, "[t]he ghost of the undistributed profits tax walks again in Washington," with J. S. Seidman noting that "serious consideration is being given to some form of undistributed profits tax on corporations."[157]

The Korean War temporarily derailed integration plans, but concerns about declining equity investment remained. In 1951, Godfrey Nelson of the *New York Times* reported that "[o]nly about 6 per cent of our huge

---

[152] "Should be tax 'musts'," *Wall Street Journal*, December 12, 1949, p. 4.
[153] "Dividend credits in taxes proposed," *New York Times*, March 8, 1949, p. 37.
[154] "House Democrat asks cuts in Excise, Capital Gains, Dividend Taxes," *Wall Street Journal*, October 14, 1949, p. 3.
[155] "Brookings urges business tax cut," *New York Times*, May 29, 1950, p. 8. See Lewis Kimmel, *Postwar Tax Policy and Business Expansion* (Washington, DC: The Brookings Institution, 1943).
[156] "Patman demands study of firms' undistributed profits in last 3 years," *Wall Street Journal*, March 26, 1949, p. 1.
[157] "Undistributed Profits Tax under serious study," *Los Angeles Times*, November 4, 1949, p. 25.

national income is now finding its way into" business enterprise, compared with up to 18 percent under normal conditions.[158] According to estimates prepared by the Securities and Exchange Commission in the same year, a mere 8 percent of aggregate liquid individual savings went toward the net purchase of equity securities such as common stock.[159] Moreover, not only did the percentage of new investments drop, but there was a drop in the total number of shareholders from approximately 10 million in 1930 to 6 million by 1952.[160] By 1953, the volume of trading on the New York Stock Exchange (NYSE) had reached a low point of fewer than 1 million shares and G. Keith Funston, the president of the Exchange, subsequently complained that "[n]ew enterprises seeking to create new wealth and productivity are unable to attract the equity capital we need."[161]

Many observers attributed at least part of the blame for the lack of equity capital to the continued, high, postwar income tax rates, particularly on dividend income. At a symposium of the Tax Institute held in 1950, William Casey remarked that the effect of double taxation and the growing availability of more favorably taxed investments such as municipal bonds and real estate "have clearly reflected themselves in the fact that corporate stock has so consistently sold at a lower ratio to earnings, and is still doing so in the current bull market, than ever before."[162] The NYSE's Funston told the House Ways and Means Committee in July of 1953 that "[t]axation of capital gains and double taxation of dividends are Federally-erected twin dams holding back the free flow of life-giving venture capital into American industry."[163] While there were dissenters in this attempt to pin an equity crisis on double taxation,[164] there was at least some acknowledgment that the tax provisions, in combination with an economic downturn, may have had some effect.[165] In any event, the

---

[158] Godfrey Nelson, "Tax course is held road to socialism," *New York Times*, September 23, 1951, p. 137.

[159] J. Kirk Eads, "The Tax Man rings twice," *Nation's Business* 41 (1953): 81–2.

[160] Baskin and Miranti, Jr., *A History of Corporate Finance*, p. 232; Micklethwait and Wooldridge, *The Company*, p. 117.

[161] Jerry Markham, *A Financial History of the United States*, 3 vols., vol. 2 (Armonk, NY: Sharpe, 2002), p. 293; G. Keith Funston, "Double taxation of dividends, before the House Ways and Means Committee (July 15, 1953)," *Vital Speeches of the Day* 19 (1953): 723.

[162] William Casey, "Double Taxation of Dividends," in Tax Institute (ed.), *Taxation and Business Concentration* (Princeton, NJ: Tax Institute Symposium, June 15–16, 1950), p. 211.

[163] Funston, "Double taxation of dividends," 723.

[164] See Editorial, "Taxes and investment," *America* 91 (August 21, 1954): 493.

[165] Eugene N. Feingold, *The Internal Revenue Act of 1954: Policy and Politics* (Dissertation, Princeton University, 1960), p. 192.

notion that the taxation of dividends was hurting equity investment had clearly reached a mainstream consensus. Even the *Saturday Evening Post* observed that "double taxation can only retard the flow of risk capital into new ventures."[166]

Ultimately, Republicans succeeded in their effort to enact a bill that contained some dividend tax relief, though it was considered a "limited" victory.[167] The 4 percent dividend tax credit under the legislation was called a "watered-down version" of Eisenhower's initial proposal for a 15 percent shareholder credit within three years.[168] Columbia economics professor Carl Shoup noted that "the amounts of change are so small that in most cases they make no notable difference in the pattern of tax distribution, from the viewpoint of tax equity . . . [and] a credit of only 4 per cent and an exclusion of only $50 are not likely to influence the sum total of investment appreciably."[169]

One of the major reasons that the dividend tax relief was relatively limited was that the equity crisis had started to dissipate. By the time the bill reached the Senate in late June 1954, the chairman of the Council of Economic Advisors, Arthur Burns, announced in a cabinet meeting that "recovery was underway."[170] Total corporate cash flow, which had been relatively stagnant in 1953 and 1954, and retained profits, which dipped in 1954, both rose significantly in 1955.[171] The stock market also experienced a recovery, with the Dow Jones Industrial Average rising above its 1929 high in November of 1954 for the first time since the stock market crash and the number of shareholders jumping to 8.6 million by 1956.[172] At this point, managerial preference for internal financing

---

[166] Raymond Rice, "The double tax on dividends deters venture investment – also it's unfair," *Saturday Evening Post*, February 13, 1954, p. 12.

[167] Feingold, *The Internal Revenue Act of 1954*, p. 179.

[168] John Morris, "Eisenhower sets 1956 for tax cut," *New York Times*, January 21, 1955, p. 10.

[169] Carl S. Shoup, "The Dividend Exclusion and Credit in the Revenue Code of 1954," *National Tax Journal* 8 (1955): 141–2. The equity point was exacerbated by the fact that the credit was not refundable, which made it useless for shareholders with no federal income tax liability. See Scott Taylor, "Corporate Integration in the Federal Income Tax: Lessons from the Past and a Proposal for the Future," *Virginia Tax Review* 10 (1990): 286.

[170] Robert J. Donovan, *Eisenhower: The Inside Story* (New York: Harper & Brothers, 1956), p. 221; John W. Sloan, *Eisenhower and the Management of Prosperity* (Lawrence: University Press of Kansas, 1991): 143.

[171] Harold G. Vatter, *The US Economy in the 1950s: An Economic History* (New York: W. W. Norton & Co., 1963), p. 96 (table 3–7).

[172] Markham, *A Financial History of the United States*, vol. 2, p. 293.

resumed and there was simply no longer a desperate need to attract the equity financing that double taxation may have been inhibiting.

UK classical corporate income tax – 1965

The British adoption of a US-style classical corporate income tax in 1965 just a decade after the USA made a move toward UK-style integration was perhaps the most stunning reversal of traditional patterns. The change had its roots in Lord Kaldor's recommendation in his dissent to the 1955 Royal Commission report on the differential profits tax. Not surprisingly, though, the idea gained political traction amid controversy over the use of profits by UK companies.

When the proposal for a corporate tax was first introduced, debate centered at least in part on the claim that this would spur productive reinvestment of profits, although there was also dispute as to whether retentions would increase at all.[173] Gresham Cooke argued that the concept was "old-fashioned."[174] He noted that "other countries are seeing that old established, undynamic companies can go on adding to their retentions year after year without any great benefit to themselves or their country. They can have a long series of profitless expansions."[175] Jo Grimond confirmed that this phenomenon was occurring in the UK as well. According to Grimond, "[s]ome big companies appear to be diversifying their activities because they have nothing else to do with the large funds which they acquire. Some companies should curtail their activities and distribute their reserves rather than retain money on which they do not earn as high a rate as is needed in the national interest."[176] A newly-published study by the economist Ian Little, which tentatively concluded that as a result of the differential profits tax in the 1950s retained earnings were inefficiently employed,[177] was cited prominently in support of the Conservative opposition's arguments.[178] Terrence Higgins summed up the disagreement over the Corporation Tax as lying between "whether we believe profits should be ploughed back into companies

---

[173] Some opponents argued that the "stickiness" of dividend rates meant that companies would pay the additional corporate tax out of money that would otherwise be available for "ploughing back" into the firm. See, e.g., *Hansard*, HC, vol. 713, ser. 5, col. 1879, 1965 (statement of Mr. Antony Barber).

[174] Ibid., col. 1000 (statement of Mr. Gresham Cooke).   [175] Ibid.

[176] *Hansard*, HC, vol. 712, ser. 5, col. 94, 1965 (statement of Mr. Joseph Grimond).

[177] See I. M. D. Little, "Higgledy-piggledy Growth," *Bulletin of the Oxford University Institute of Economics & Statistics* 24 (1962): 412.

[178] *Hansard*, HC, vol. 713, ser. 5, col. 1885, 1965 (statement of Mr. Patrick Jenkin).

and taxes should encourage this, or whether we should encourage the distribution of profits and the operation of the capital market in such a way that capital is attracted into new uses by market forces."[179] According to Higgins,

> [w]e on this side believe strongly that it is better that the balance should be in favour of distribution rather than that there should be a very serious move in favour of ploughing back. If one ploughs back, it means that capital is retained by those companies which are already in existence. This in turn, means that there is less opportunity for new firms to obtain capital needed to expand and these firms are, indeed, the growth points of the economy. This is a fundamental difference between the two parties.[180]

Opponents concluded that companies were more efficient when they were subject to the scrutiny of the capital markets in order to obtain more funds.[181]

Proponents of the move to a classical corporate income tax argued that retentions were the most likely source of new investment in the British economy.[182] According to the Financial Secretary to the Treasury, Niall MacDermot, evidence presented to the 1955 Royal Commission had established that "the amount of new money raised through the market is marginal in relation to the total investment. It is retentions that are responsible for the far greater part of capital investment in the private sector."[183] The Chief Secretary to the Treasury, John Diamond, further substantiated such evidence, noting that only 9 percent of new investment came from cash raised through public issues of stock, while 65 percent came from retained earnings and the rest from borrowing.[184] Diamond explained that "[w]e are, therefore, framing a tax structure under which a business man will, out of his realised profits, have 50 per cent. more cash available for investment and plough-back

---

[179] *Hansard*, HC, vol. 710, ser. 5, col. 1051, 1965 (statement of Mr. Terrence Higgins).

[180] Ibid.   [181] Ibid. (citing Little's study).

[182] *Hansard*, HC, vol. 712, ser. 5, col. 53, 1965 (statement of Mr. Niall MacDermot) ("it is from retentions that the great weight of money comes for industrial and commercial expansion"); ibid., col. 130 (statement of Mr. A. E. P. Duffy) ("Many hon. Members recognise now that the bulk of firms get the bulk of their additional capital for necessary growth out of retained profits.").

[183] Ibid., cols. 52–3 (citing evidence offered by the Issuing Houses Committee). See Rt. Hon. James Callaghan, "The New United Kingdom Tax Structure in Relation to the Needs of the Economy," *European Taxation* 5 (1965): 215 ("in the United Kingdom it does seem that the main source of finance for industrial investment is nowadays 'plough back'.").

[184] *Hansard*, HC, vol. 713, ser. 5, cols. 1835–6, 1965 (statement of Mr. John Diamond).

than he has under the present system."[185] While he conceded that "[o]ne cannot make individuals who are inefficient efficient" simply by providing additional funds, Diamond suggested that the bill would "encourage them towards efficiency and give them the tools to achieve it."[186]

The classical corporate income tax's lifespan in the UK was short at least in part because of its apparent failure to deliver meaningful economic changes. In a 1970 study of 837 UK firms, two British economists reported that retained earnings was typically a residual item after dividend payouts were met and therefore "[i]t would appear that companies can be encouraged to retain profits only by a fiscal policy which gives them increased earnings."[187] Martin Daunton concluded that "[t]he Callaghan–Kaldor reforms were disappointing, for they produced little revenue and did not stimulate economic growth to any discernible extent."[188]

In effect, the demise of the classical corporate tax in the UK reflected the hardened dividend culture that pervaded among British firms and their shareholders. Just as the American commitment to integration wavered when the underlying economic crisis disappeared, the UK's attempt to restrain dividends proved unsustainable. As will be discussed in the next chapter, these apparent cultural differences reflected real differences in the British and American corporations.

---

[185] Ibid., col. 1833.   [186] Ibid.
[187] R. J. Brinston and C. R. Tomkins, "The Impact of the Introduction of Corporation Tax upon the Dividend Policies of United Kingdom Companies," *The Economic Journal* 80 (1970): 627.
[188] Daunton, *Just Taxes*, p. 299.

5

Power

The way corporations in the United States and the United Kingdom dealt with retained earnings and set dividend policy reflects an underlying difference in the location of power in corporations in the respective countries. This difference in the location of corporate power, in turn, contributed to the divergence of corporate income tax schemes. The notion is that the corporation itself was simply perceived differently in the two countries during the first half of the twentieth century when the income tax systems were still developing. Power in the large British public corporation was primarily located at the shareholder level, thus leading to a shareholder-focused corporate tax, while power in the large American public corporation was primarily located at the entity level, thus leading to an entity-focused corporate tax. These differences were then hard-wired into the respective national consciences and continued to influence corporate tax reform in ensuing years.

One possible version of this argument is that the UK and the USA each decided to treat corporations differently as a matter of law and this legal difference dictated the difference in tax schemes. This is the version that early twentieth-century commentators, influenced by entity theory conceptions of corporate development, forwarded in describing the two tax schemes. Under this argument, in the UK, the corporation was a mere aggregation of the individual shareholders and therefore was not itself subject to taxation. In his 1927 comparative study of the US and UK income tax systems Harrison Spaulding wrote that in the UK "[a] corporation is regarded merely as a device by means of which a number of individuals can conveniently do business, and it is not looked upon as a separate object of taxation. It is not in itself a potentially taxable person, but is an aggregation of persons who may or may not be taxable."[1] Although Spaulding conceded that "[i]t is necessary for some purposes

---

[1] Harrison Spaulding, *The Income Tax in Great Britain and the United States* (London: P. S. King & Son, Ltd., 1927), p. 87.

that corporations be regarded as separate legal entities," he explained that "the British do not extend this conception to the field of income tax."[2] This characterization continued to resonate in later descriptions.[3] Jonathan Barron Baskin noted that the British income tax "was originally based on the idea that corporations should be treated similarly to partnerships."[4] Martin Daunton offered a more modern and nuanced version of this entity theory explanation, stating that "[c]orporate taxation did not have a purchase in British fiscal policy, for it contradicted the assumption that firms were agents rather than taxable entities. Corporation taxation did not, as in the United States, connect with hostility to big business or with opposition to a federal income tax."[5]

By contrast, in the USA, in the early twentieth century the notion is that the corporation was considered a separate, or "real," entity. As such, it was a proper object of taxation quite apart from whether there was already a tax at the shareholder level. Spaulding asserted that

> [i]n the United States the doctrine of corporate entity has been carried much farther than in Great Britain. A corporation is looked upon by the courts of the United States as a legal entity entirely distinct from those who own and control it. This doctrine is so well settled, and it has been established so long, that it has no doubt had its effect on the popular mind. The Americans see a corporation as a thing different from other taxpaying persons, and, as we shall see, as a thing peculiarly suitable for specially heavy taxation.[6]

Modern observers in the USA continue to give credence to this characterization of early twentieth-century opinion. The American Law Institute, for example, wrote that

---

[2] Ibid.

[3] In later years, opponents sometimes harkened back to the entity theory argument to resist certain tax measures, even if the very adoption of the offensive provision casts doubt on the continued strength of the entity theory perspective. For example, in testifying against the profits tax in 1951, the Association of British Chambers of Commerce stated that "[a] company should be regarded as an association of individuals acting in common," rather than as a separate taxable entity. Memorandum submitted by the Association of British Chambers of Commerce, *Minutes of Evidence taken before the Royal Commission on the Taxation of Profits and Income* (1952), pp. 103, 108, para. 49.

[4] Jonathan Barron Baskin, "The Development of Corporate Financial Markets in Britain and the United States, 1600–1914: Overcoming Asymmetric Information," *The Business History Review* 62 (1988): 214.

[5] Martin J. Daunton, *Just Taxes: The Politics of Taxation in Britain, 1914–1979* (Cambridge University Press, 2002), p. 93.

[6] Spaulding, *The Income Tax in Great Britain and the United States*, p. 92.

> The origin of . . . the separate entity taxation of corporations as opposed
> to the conduit taxation of partnerships can be linked to some extent to a
> debate that raged during the last part of the 19th century and the early
> part of the 20th century concerning the nature of corporate and partner-
> ship personality . . . Gradually, the entity theory prevailed for corpora-
> tions but not for partnerships.[7]

Similarly, one modern text explains that "[t]he US separate corporate income tax is probably based on the (mistaken) notion that corporations are legal persons or aggregations of capital that can, do, and should pay taxes and bear tax burdens."[8]

This entity theory-based explanation for the divergence is not so much wrong as over-determined. There were numerous instances in the early part of the twentieth century in which the corporation was characterized as a real entity for tax purposes in the UK and as an aggregation of the individual shareholders for tax purposes in the USA. It would thus be incorrect to conclude that the different schemes were dictated by the formal legal distinctions announced in common law decisions or in legislation. Moreover, the explanation as a whole presumes that a "deci-sion" was made at some point based upon an intellectual or cultural divide over the proper legal characterization of what was essentially the same fundamental legal device. In reality, it is more likely that the differing treatment for tax purposes originated as a result of the gradual and unintentional development of actual differences in the operation of the underlying entities which affected popular and legal perceptions.

It is therefore appropriate to offer a more nuanced account of the evolution of the corporation in the two countries to understand how it diverged and how that affected the development of corporation taxation. The business vehicles that shared the common name of "corporation" in the United States and the United Kingdom were actually quite different in many important respects. As discussed in Chapter 4, one difference was in dividend policy, but this was symptomatic of a larger divergence in the corporate structure itself. The principal manifestation of this difference was in the location of power within the corporation.

Corporate scholars have often characterized countries as falling within two broad camps on the corporate governance spectrum:

---

[7] George Yin and David Shakow, *Federal Income Tax Project: Taxation of Private Business Enterprises: Reporter's Study* (Philadelphia: American Law Institute, 1999), pp. 35–6.
[8] Richard Westin, John McNulty, and Richard Beck, *Federal Income Taxation of Business Enterprises: Cases, Statutes, Rulings* (New York: Lexis Publications, 2d edn., 1999), p. 649.

"outsider/arm's-length" and "insider/control-oriented."[9] In the former, the larger corporations are publicly traded, widely owned, and no particular shareholder or group of shareholders is able to exercise the type of control typical of a corporate insider such as an executive.[10] The shareholders in such corporations are outsiders and they interact with the management at arm's length. In the latter, a country's larger corporations either are not publicly traded or, if they are, a sizeable stake is owned by blockholders such as individuals, families, or institutional investors and those blockholders choose to use that stake to exercise control over corporate operations.[11] The controlling shareholders operate like insiders in such corporations, blurring the lines between ownership and management. In outsider/arm's-length countries, power over the public corporation lies with the managers, while in insider/control-oriented countries power over the public corporation resides at the shareholder level.

Although both the USA and the UK could be characterized as having outsider/arm's-length systems today, the USA made the transition from the insider/control-oriented system earlier than the UK: in the first part of the twentieth century. This meant that at that point power resided at the entity level with the managers in the USA corporation while in the UK corporation it was still held by the shareholder. More specifically, managers and shareholders had different roles and enjoyed differing degrees of power under the laws and customs of the two countries.

This difference in the *locus* of power in British and American corporations not only affected decisions about the appropriate dividend policy discussed in Chapter 4, but it may have affected views on the appropriate role of corporate taxation in regulating corporate power and in reaching corporate wealth. To the extent that in the UK ownership separated from control much later than in the USA, UK policymakers may have conceived of a family-controlled corporation when they contemplated the taxation of the corporation. This would necessarily have suggested a more aggregate conception of the corporation, pointing toward an integrated approach to the taxation of corporate income. Conversely, if

---

[9] Brian R. Cheffins, *Corporate Ownership and Control: British Business Transformed* (Oxford University Press, 2008), pp. 4–5. See Erik Berglof, "A Note on the Typology of Financial Systems," in Klaus J. Hopt and Eddy Wymeersch (eds), *Comparative Corporate Governance: Essays and Materials* (Berlin, New York: Walter de Gruyter, 1997), p. 152.

[10] Cheffins, *Corporate Ownership and Control*, p. 5.   [11] Ibid.

in the USA the separation of ownership and control occurred much earlier, the rise of the manager-controlled enterprise may have made it easier to conceive of a classical system of corporate taxation in which the corporation (on its earnings) and the shareholders (on the dividends they received) were taxed separately. These perceptions were not fixed in law as part of an ideological or cultural decision, as suggested by the entity theory explanation. As a result, variations in tax treatment could occur at various points and as a result of individual provisions adopted in response to specific contingencies or because of shifts in the nature of corporate ownership and governance. Nevertheless, the justifications for such variations were often framed in a historical rhetoric. Accordingly, the adoption of an American-style classical corporate income tax in the UK was justified as an aid to stemming the tide of excessive dividends paid to wealthy shareholders, while the adoption of an undistributed profits tax in the USA was justified as a means of constraining abusive managers.

5.1   A critique of the formal entity theory explanation

The most basic objection to the simple form of the entity theory explanation is that there are numerous legislative counter-examples during this period. The real entity approach was evident at times in the UK, most notably with the Corporation Profits Tax from 1920 to 1924, while the aggregate approach was utilized in the USA in the Corporate Excise Tax of 1909 and in the original Undistributed Profits Tax adopted prior to World War I. In both cases, it is possible to write off the deviation to exigent circumstances preceding and following the war. Nevertheless, this argument suggests that each country's view of the corporation was more flimsy and malleable than is ordinarily assumed. More likely, the entity theory explanation itself is too facile to capture the essence of each country's perspective on corporation taxation.

5.1.1   The use of an entity approach in the UK

At first glance, in the early twentieth century the UK does appear to have had an aggregate perspective when it came to corporate taxation. It subjected corporations to taxation as a mere convenience, permitting shareholders a full credit for taxes paid on their behalf at the entity level. Moreover, its courts appeared to follow this approach when interpreting the application of the corporate income tax. In a 1904 case, for instance, Lord Vaughn Williams stated that the fact that the corporate tax was levied against the corporation and measured by the corporation's profits "in no way negatives the proposition that the company is paying the income tax on behalf of the shareholders amongst whom the profits, after payment of income tax, are distributed."[12]

Notwithstanding the fact that the law appeared to favor an aggregate perspective with respect to the tax treatment of corporations, there were certainly contrary indications. For example, British courts were considered much less likely to pierce the corporate veil than American courts at the turn of the century, although one comprehensive study of veil-piercing claims found that there were very few cases brought in the UK between 1880 and 1910 in which the litigants sought to disregard the corporate form.[13] Moreover, in a prominent 1906 case, *Automatic Self-Cleansing Filter Syndicate Co. Ltd.* v. *Cuninghame*, the Court of Appeal ruled that the company's directors were not agents of the shareholders and upheld the board's right to ignore a shareholder resolution.[14]

In taxation specifically, the courts appeared to be much less favorable toward an aggregate conception shortly after World War I. In an early 1920s case, Lord Viscount Cave declared that

> [p]lainly a company paying income tax on its profits does not pay it as agent for its shareholders. It pays it as a taxpayer, and if no dividend is declared the shareholders have no direct concern in the payment. If a dividend is declared, the company is entitled to deduct from such dividend a proportionate part of the amount of the tax previously paid by such company; and in that case the payment by the company operates in relief of the shareholder. But no agency, properly so called, is involved.[15]

Outside the courts, there were, in fact, many examples where the British taxed the corporation as an entity without adjustment for the circumstances of individual shareholders or constituents. Municipal corporations were one exception to the aggregate principle. As economist Douglas Knoop observed when commenting on the 1920 Royal Commission on the Income Tax, "municipal corporations and other local authorities are liable to income tax, under various headings, without any question of the amount of the tax being adjusted to the incomes of the individual ratepayers."[16] Similarly, philanthropic corporations in

---

[12] *Attorney-General* v. *Ashton Gas Co.* [1904] 2 Ch. 621; affirmed [1906] AC 10.
[13] Peter Oh, "Piercing v. Lifting," (work in progress on file with the author).
[14] [1906] 2 Ch 34.   [15] *Commissioners of Inland Revenue* v. *Blott* [1921] 2 AC 171.
[16] Douglas Knoop, "The Royal Commission on the Income Tax," *The Economic Journal* 30 (1920): 271.

England, such as certain colleges and schools, were initially subject to the Corporation Profits Tax despite being prohibited from earning any profit for shareholders or otherwise.[17] While these types of entity could be considered special cases, this entity theory-based guiding principle was extended to the private commercial sector as well. One such example is the debates over the proper tax treatment of the co-operative society. Co-operative societies are membership commercial trading organizations such as stores that pay dividends to each member in proportion to the member's purchases from the store.[18] Historically, they had been exempt from income taxation, but there was an "old-felt grievance" that this exemption was unfair, especially given the increased utilization of this form in manufacturing and trading.[19] A majority of the members of the 1920 Royal Commission on the Income Tax had recommended subjecting societies to the regular income tax on their undistributed profits.[20] According to the Royal Commission's report, "a registered Co-operative Society cannot be regarded merely as a group of individuals; it is as much a separate entity as any other body of persons."[21] The Report concluded that "a society should be treated exactly as a limited liability company trading in similar circumstances and under similar conditions," although the majority noted that, as a practical matter, "we believe that there will be very little difference between the liability of Co-operative Societies under our proposals and under the existing legal position that has given rise to so great an amount of feeling."[22] A group of dissenters, including Cambridge economist Arthur Pigou, argued that no part of the surplus of a co-operative society should be considered income. Their fundamental objection was that "[t]he Income Tax is not a

---

[17] *Hansard*, HC, vol. 153, ser. 5, col. 1100, 1922 (statement of John Rawlinson).

[18] Martin J. Daunton, *Trusting Leviathan: The Politics of Taxation in Britain, 1799–1914* (Cambridge University Press, 2001), p. 217.

[19] "Lighter burden of taxes – Appeal by FBI to Government – Cooperators' quota," *The Times* (London), January 31, 1923, p. 7.

[20] Report of the Royal Commission on the Income Tax, Cmd 615 (1920), p. 120, para. 550 ("we have come to the conclusion that any part of the net proceeds which is not actually returned to members as 'dividend' or 'discount' is a profit which should be charged to Income Tax."). See Alzada Comstock, "British Income Tax Reform," *The American Economic Review* 10 (1920): 503.

[21] Report of the Royal Commission on the Income Tax, Cmd 615 (1920), p. 120, para. 551.

[22] Ibid., p. 121, para. 555, p. 122, para. 566. See Knoop, "The Royal Commission on the Income Tax," 269–70.

corporation tax. It is a tax upon the incomes or profits of individuals, and though for convenience it is assessed in the first instance upon corporations in which they hold interests, the amount of it is always adjusted to the income not of the corporation, but of the individual shareholders."[23]

Ultimately, the recommendation to subject co-operative societies to the income tax was not enacted because it was considered too controversial.[24] Nevertheless, co-operative societies were subject to direct taxation under the Corporation Profits Tax. The theory was that the status of co-operative societies as separate entities made them eligible for entity-level taxation: The dissenters to the Royal Commission Report had pointed out that, "[i]f there were in the United Kingdom, as there is in the United States of America, a corporation tax, levied specially on corporations as such, it would, no doubt, be proper that a Co-operative Society should, as a separate legal entity, be made liable to that tax."[25] Chancellor of the Exchequer Austen Chamberlain subsequently highlighted this statement in the Parliamentary debates over the Corporation Profits Tax, noting that it provided "high and domestic authority for the proposal" to subject co-operative societies to an entity-level tax.[26]

The clearest example of the willingness to embrace an entity-level tax in early twentieth-century England was the Corporation Profits Tax itself. In responding to the concern that poorer shareholders not otherwise subject to the income tax would bear the burden of the profits tax, Chancellor Chamberlain stated that "[t]he Corporation Tax is not devised as a tax upon the individual, but as an impersonal tax upon the profits of a company chargeable thereto prior to distribution. No question of recovery by an individual shareholder can arise."[27] A concern about foreign shareholders elicited a similar response from future prime minister Stanley Baldwin: "I would remind my hon. Friend that the Corporation Profits Tax is not a tax upon dividends, but upon the profits of concerns with limited liability prior to the distribution thereof."[28] After the tax was implemented, companies complained that the profits

---

[23] Reservation to Part V, Section XII, in Report of the Royal Commission on the Income Tax, Cmd 615 (1920), p. 164.

[24] Rufus S. Tucker, "The British Finance Act, 1920," *The Quarterly Journal of Economics* 35 (1920): 168.

[25] Reservation to Part V, Section XII, in Report of the Royal Commission on the Income Tax, Cmd 615 (1920), p. 164.

[26] *Hansard*, HC, vol. 128, ser. 5, col. 439, 1920 (Rt. Hon. Austen Chamberlain).

[27] Ibid., cols. 1029–30.   [28] Ibid., col. 2081.

tax imposed double taxation, particularly for corporations holding stock in other corporations, despite assurances when it was adopted that this would not be the case.[29]

The Corporation Profits Tax also had structural elements of an entity-level tax. As originally passed, the tax exempted railroads and public utilities. Apparently, one of the criticisms of the tax as it was going through the House of Commons had been that it would disadvantage certain corporations subject to statutory rate controls because those corporations could not raise their prices to cover the additional tax.[30] As Colonel Josiah Wedgwood explained during debates over extending the exemption,

> when the Corporations Profits Tax was introduced, the Chancellor of the Exchequer of that day [Austen Chamberlain] . . . discovered as the tax was going through this House that certain companies – statutory companies – would not be able to pass the tax on, and that if the Corporations Profits Tax was levied upon those companies the unfortunate shareholders would have to bear it, and not the consuming public. When he discovered that, he said: "I did not mean that. We will exempt those companies from this tax, so that the shareholders shall not be penalized, and will levy it only on those businesses which can transfer it to the consumer."[31]

This undercuts the notion that the tax was intended to be a proxy for a tax on shareholders, since Chamberlain expressly approved the practice of passing the tax on to consumers.

Notwithstanding the arguments in favor of viewing the Corporation Profits Tax as an example of the entity view, there is potential to characterize the tax as reflecting an aggregate perspective. As discussed in Chapter 2, one of the justifications for the tax was to substitute for the failure to apply the super-tax at the shareholder level to retained

---

[29] "Company meetings – The Costa Rica Railway Company, Limited – Corporation profits tax – Hardships on ordinary stockholders," *The Times* (London), July 20, 1921, p. 19 ("It was emphatically stated, when this measure was before Parliament, that under no circumstances would any portion of the tax be exacted twice over; yet, as a matter of fact, this is repeatedly done, particularly where companies hold each other's shares. Again, a company, in arriving at the assessment for corporation profits tax, is not allowed to deduct what it may have already paid in respect of the ordinary 6s. income-tax.")

[30] *Hansard*, HC, vol. 128, ser. 5, cols. 2233–4, 1920.

[31] *Hansard*, HC, vol. 153, ser. 5, col. 1436, 1922. See also *Hansard*, HC, vol. 128, ser. 5, col. 354, 1920; Letter to the Editor, "Case of public utility companies," *The Times* (London), January 9, 1922, p. 6.

earnings. This could suggest an aggregate approach, on the theory that entity-level taxation was considered to be an indirect super-tax on shareholders. Perhaps the strongest evidence against that interpretation, though, is that the Corporation Profits Tax was retained even after the Chancellor proposed to impose the super-tax directly upon undistributed profits for private companies. The inconsistency led George Touche, Chairman of the Industrial and General Trust Company, to declare at the company's 1922 annual meeting that this "destroys the last shred of excuse for the corporation profits tax."[32] Sir William Perring offered a similar view in the House of Commons, noting that with the proposal "to levy Super-tax upon private companies in respect of undivided profits, there is no justification any longer to continue the Corporation Profits Tax."[33] While this extension of the super-tax was only imposed against certain instances of retained earnings, the popular criticism was that the tax was targeted at something other than the shareholders.

To the extent that the profits tax had originally been justified on grounds that it would better reach shareholders, it was characterized as an entity-level attack on the evasion of shareholder-level taxes, rather than as an indirect tax on the shareholder himself. The 1920 Royal Commission had raised concerns that "there is a very considerable leakage of duty from the less scrupulous minority."[34] According to the Commission's report, £1.25 million had been recovered in each of 1917 and 1918 as a result of taxpayer audits and they estimated that as much as an additional £5 to £10 million might still be collected with additional resources.[35] The Association of Tax Surveying Officers opined that £100 million may have escaped assessment in the previous several years.[36] While the Royal Commission did not disclose the methods of evasion so as not "to place a guide to improper practices in the hands of susceptible persons,"[37] there was a growing concern that companies were employing a number of tax avoidance devices, including the use of excessive retained earnings by overstating a company's reserve fund and the distribution of stock dividends in the form of "bonus shares" that allowed

---

[32] "The Industrial and General Trust, Limited: Sir George Touche on the Corporation Profits Tax," *The Times* (London), May 26, 1922, p. 24.
[33] *Hansard*, HC, vol. 153, ser. 5, col. 1283, 1922.
[34] Report of the Royal Commission on the Income Tax, Cmd 615 (1920), p. 135, para. 626.
[35] Ibid.; Comstock, "British Income Tax Reform," 504.
[36] Report of the Royal Commission on the Income Tax, Cmd 615 (1920), p. 135, para. 627.
[37] Ibid., p. 135, para. 628.

the company to retain the earnings.[38] In both cases, the point of the maneuver was to allow the company to retain the earnings so they would not be subjected to the progressive, individual super-tax rates. As former Prime Minister and Chancellor of the Exchequer Herbert Asquith maintained, the profits retained through such devices "really are, or ought to be, in the fullest sense of the term, subject not only to the Income Tax but to Super-tax, as in the case of a private firm they are subject now."[39] Although the Corporation Profits Tax was designed to counteract the evasion of the shareholder-level taxes, it needed to be imposed at the entity level. In this sense, the rationale was similar to the one that led to the development of the separate corporate-level tax in the United States.

Moreover, views were mixed as to whether the public thought of the Corporation Profits Tax as anything other than a tax on the entity itself. In Parliamentary debates over the extension to railroads and public utility companies of an exemption from the tax, John Marriott explained that "its existence is hardly realized by a considerable section of the general public," noting that "it is a more or less camouflaged addition to the Income Tax."[40] During the same debates, Wedgwood stated that "the Corporation Profits Tax ... is a tax transferred entirely to the consumer."[41] Others, however, felt that the tax was borne primarily by shareholders. Sir Arthur Fell, for example, explained that "[t]he feeling against the Corporation Profits Tax has steadily increased and spread throughout the country. The newspapers now understand much better than they did, and even the shareholders who suffer from it are beginning to associate with it the effect which it had upon them."[42]

Finally, court decisions underscored the uncertainty surrounding the appropriate method of characterizing corporations for purposes of the Profits Tax. For example, a 1923 decision of the High Court of Justice, King's Bench Division, held that a social club was subject to the Corporation Profits Tax notwithstanding the fact that no profits went to any "shareholders."[43] The holding was overturned on appeal, however, on the grounds that this was not a "trade or business" under the statute despite the fact that it used a limited liability corporate shell to operate.[44] In a similar case, the Court of Appeal held that a mutual fire

---

[38] *Hansard*, HC, vol. 128, ser. 5, col. 262, 1920 (statement of Asquith).   [39] Ibid., col. 263.
[40] Ibid., col. 1077.   [41] Ibid., col. 1436.   [42] Ibid., col. 2098.
[43] *Commissioners of Inland Revenue* v. *The Eccentric Club, Limited*, The Times (London), May 4, 1923, p. 5.
[44] *Commissioners of Inland Revenue* v. *The Eccentric Club, Limited*, The Times (London), December 18, 1923, p. 4.

insurance company was liable for the Corporation Profits Tax even though it had no subscribed capital, shares, or shareholders.[45] The Court cited Section 53(h) of the Act, which provided that "profits shall include in the case of mutual trading concerns the surplus arising from transactions with members."[46] The use of a corporation was sufficient to cause it to be deemed a separate taxpayer, despite the absence of any rationale for separate taxation under an aggregate theory.

5.1.2   The use of an aggregate approach in the USA

Around the same time that the UK system employed elements of an entity approach, the US system contained elements of an aggregate approach. The corporate tax adopted in 1909, which is commonly believed to be the first entity-level income tax levied on the corporation in America,[47] is an early example of this. Indeed, a large part of the justification for the tax was to reach the individual in the face of the Supreme Court's 1895 decision that an income tax was unconstitutional because it was an unapportioned direct tax.[48] Although there were regulatory arguments in favor of levying a tax on the corporation, support for the tax emerged as a compromise to a proposal to push through an income tax in defiance of the Court's earlier decision.[49] This strategy was facilitated in part by the prevailing aggregate conception of the corporation.

When the corporate excise tax was adopted, many believed that taxing corporations would burden the shareholders because the corporation was nothing more than a collection of individual shareholders. The *Commercial and Financial Chronicle* wrote "[a] tax on net earnings of corporations is an income tax on one class of persons who happen to own stock therein. The fact that, although corporations themselves are not 'natural persons,' they are composed of natural persons is over-looked; touch a corporation and the persons composing it are

---

[45] *Commissioners of Inland Revenue* v. *The Cornish Mutual Assurance Company, Limited*, The Times (London), November 8, 1924, p. 4.
[46] Ibid.
[47] Reuven S. Avi-Yonah, "Why was the US Corporate Tax Enacted in 1909?," in John Tiley (ed.), *Studies in the History of Tax Law*, 4 vols., vol. II (Oxford: Hart Publishing, 2007), p. 382.
[48] *Pollock* v. *Farmers' Loan & Trust Co.*, 157 US 429, 572 (1895).
[49] Steven A. Bank, "Entity Theory as Myth in the US Corporate Excise Tax of 1909," in Tiley (ed.), *Studies in the History of Tax Law*, vol. II, pp. 404–5.

touched."[50] In a letter to the editor of the *New York Times*, A. C. Pleydall, Secretary of the New York Tax Reform Association, explicitly compared it to the UK approach, noting that "[s]uch a tax would reduce dividends and really be a tax upon the individual stockholder . . . It was stated in a Washington dispatch that the tax on corporate dividends is similar to the English system of taxing incomes 'at the source'."[51]

This belief was central in the debate over the 1909 corporate tax. In a report on the state taxation of corporations,[52] which was released by the Bureau of Corporations as part of the Congressional debates over the corporate excise tax,[53] the problem of reaching individual wealth invested in corporations was one of the principal concerns. The report noted that "a growing fraction of each man's wealth is being invested in the shares and bonds of corporations."[54] Part of the difficulty was whether to tax the corporation's property in light of separate taxes upon individual property, including stocks and bonds, and the separate physical presence of corporate property and the individual holders of such property. In its analysis of this issue, the aggregate perspective was clearly evident. According to the Report, "[o]bviously a tax on the corporation is really a tax upon its stockholders, for otherwise then as a matter of legal reasoning a corporation and its stockholders are one. Hence the question whether both the corporation and the stockholders shall be taxed is an interesting problem as to double taxation."[55]

It is certainly possible that for some legislators the desire to reach the "accumulated wealth" of the country could be characterized as part of the desire to regulate corporations, and therefore, part of a real entity perspective.[56] This view was sometimes expressed in the press. In an editorial, the *New York Times* declared that

---

[50] "The financial situation," *The Commercial and Financial Chronicle* 88 (1909): 1525.

[51] A. C. Pleydall, "Letter to the Editor: The corporate tax," *New York Times*, June 19, 1909, p. 6.

[52] Report of the Commissioner of Corporations on the system of taxing manufacturing, mercantile, transportation, and transmission corporations, in the states of Connecticut, Maine, Massachusetts, New Hampshire, Rhode Island, and Vermont, May 17, 1909.

[53] See *Cong. Rec.*, vol. 44, p. 3628 (1909) (order that 2,000 copies of the report be printed). This Report also attracted the attention of the press in its coverage of the debates over the Corporation Tax bill. See "What the states do in the way of taxing corporations," *The Commercial and Financial Chronicle* 89 (1909): 133 (noting the relevance of the Report even though "[i]t has not been issued with any reference to the proposed Federal Corporation Tax.")

[54] Report of the Commissioner of Corporations, 15.   [55] Ibid., 11.

[56] See Avi-Yonah, "Why was the US Corporate Tax Enacted," p. 382.

[i]t is the outgrowth of the gust of passion that has beswept the land during the years when the public has been appealed to hate and to hamper the corporations, when it has been taught that the word corporation was well-nigh synonymous with chicane, that the people were oppressed and robbed by the managers of the corporations. This law is drawn with intent to gratify the passionate resentment thus awakened, and it is drawn, and, we suppose, will be enforced without the slightest discrimination between shameless offenders and perfectly innocent and law-abiding corporations.[57]

Notwithstanding this perspective, many in Congress believed that popular opinion was aligned with the aggregate theory of the corporation and that people would view the tax as a levy on shareholders. Senator Albert Cummins warned

I want Senators to understand what they are about to do, because the people of the country will understand that it is the shareholders, little and big, who will pay the sum ... They will know just one thing, and that is whereas their rich neighbors who are not engaged in corporate enterprise pay no tax, they, because they have endeavored to forward the progress and speed the development of their country, and have taken shares of stock in corporations of an almost infinite number of kinds, have been selected, as it would seem, by the folly of their Government, to bear a burden which they ought not to bear, except in company with others who are similarly situated.[58]

Senator Joseph Bristow read one constituent letter on the floor of Congress that summarized the fear that it would penalize shareholders:

Is it fair and consistent with the American idea of fairness and a "square deal" to tax our net earnings – taxes which will come out of the dividends to our stockholders, very many of whom are men in very moderate circumstances and working every day for a living and the support of their families – simply because we are doing business under a charter, while a neighbor doing business as an individual or under a copartnership is entirely free from said tax? And further, does the proposition reach the very wealthiest citizens, such as Rockefeller and Carnegie, whose holdings are not in stocks of corporations, but in bonds?[59]

Indeed, one of the criticisms levied against the corporate tax proposal was "that bondholders might escape payment of the tax while the small

---

[57] Editorial, "By direction of the President," *New York Times*, June 26, 1909, p. 6.
[58] *Cong. Rec.*, vol. 44, p. 4039 (1909) (statement of Sen. Cummins).
[59] Ibid., p. 4036; "Taft plan for tax splits Committee," *New York Times*, June 19, 1909, p. 5.

holders of stock would contribute all the revenue."[60] This was because of the fear that the use of the phrases "net earnings" or "net profits" would permit the deduction of bond interest and the resulting tax burden would fall exclusively on the dividends.[61] Senator Moses Clapp explained: "Not only does it fail to make such discrimination, but absolutely exempts the man who has gone still further in the process of accumulation and has laid his accumulated savings in the form of bonds."[62]

This potential impact on stockholders was considered particularly outrageous in comparison to the income or inheritance taxes because of the large amount of wealth, and income from that wealth, which was held outside the corporation by even the shareholders most identified with corporate growth. For example, Cummins observed "I do not wonder that a man like Harriman should favor this measure rather than the general income tax; because the part of his great fortune, which has been segregated from the corporations in which he is interested, lies beyond the operation of this law."[63] Senator Jonathan Dolliver concurred, stating that "I believe it will create in our market place a grave sense of injury to find that the rich men doing business without incorporation are exempted, while a score or a hundred men and women in very modest circumstances who have invested a small amount in the stock of organized corporations are required to submit to this public assessment."[64] From this perspective, although the tax was nominally levied against the corporation, it was simply viewed as another component of a tax on individuals.

A similar aggregate perspective governed when the first post-Sixteenth Amendment corporate income tax was adopted four years later. Although this tax was separate and in addition to the regular income tax, it was focused on the shareholder. Most importantly, dividends were

---

[60] See "Taft's corporation tax framed to reach the rich," *New York World*, June 18, 1909, p. 5B. See also *Cong. Rec.*, vol. 44, p. 4055 (1909) (letters expressing the same concern for small stockholders). For a contrary view, see "A tax on net earnings," *Wall Street Journal*, June 18, 1909, p. 1 ("The theory that they would seriously affect dividends will hardly bear examination in the light of the moderate amount involved in the proposed tax.").

[61] "Taft's corporation tax framed to reach the rich," p. 5B; Editorial, "Earnings, profit, income," *New York Times*, June 23, 1909, p. 6.

[62] *Cong. Rec.*, vol. 44, p. 4008 (1909) (statement of Sen. Clapp), and p. 4036 (statement of Sen. Bristow, R–Kans.) (favoring an income tax because "[i]t would then include the bondholders and those who have large fortunes that are not reached by this tax. It would more equitably distribute the burden as to population than this corporation tax.")

[63] Ibid., p. 4038 (statement of Sen. Cummins). See "The President takes a hand," *LaFollette's Weekly Magazine*, June 26, 1909, pp. 13, 14.

[64] *Cong. Rec.*, vol. 44, p. 4229 (1909) (statement of Sen. Dolliver, R–Iowa).

exempt from the normal tax on individuals, thus avoiding double taxation. Many wanted to go beyond that, though, by supporting an explicitly pass-through approach. The Senate Finance Committee and the Democratic caucus voted in favor of an amendment that would subject individuals to the surtax rates on the gains and profits of partnerships and corporations "whether divided or distributed or otherwise."[65] This rerun of the pass-through business taxation employed during the Civil War and Reconstruction was attacked not so much because it violated the corporation's status as a separate entity, but rather because it would subject stockholders to "indefensible double taxation."[66] Corporate income would be subject to the individual surtax once when earned and retained and a second time when distributed.[67]

This general undistributed profits tax was subsequently dropped, but Congress did adopt a more narrowly focused version that still employed the pass-through structure.[68] Under this provision, if a corporation retained earnings for the purpose of avoiding the shareholder tax on dividends,[69] the shareholders would be subject to a surtax on their pro

---

[65] *Cong. Rec.*, vol. 50, p. 3774 (1913) (statement of Sen. Williams, D–Miss.). The full text of the amendment is as follows:

> For the purpose of this additional tax, taxable income shall embrace the share of any taxable individual of the gains and profits of all companies, whether incorporated or partnership, who would be legally entitled to enforce the distribution or division of the same, if dividend or distributed, whether divided or distributed or otherwise, and any such company, when requested by the Commissioner of Internal Revenue or any district collector of Internal Revenue, shall forward to him a correct statement of such profits and the names of the individuals who would be entitled to the same if distributed.

In response to questioning, Senator Williams tried to suggest that the provision was only designed to permit taxation of the part of the income the shareholder "would have the legal right to force the distribution of," but Senator Root pointed out that, in combination with the instructions to the Service to direct companies to supply names of stockholders who "would be entitled to the [profits] if distributed," it could have no other meaning than to permit pass-through taxation.

[66] "Attack new clause as double tax," *New York Times*, July 6, 1913, p. 5. One senator did object to the provision on the grounds that stockholders had no legal right to the money until it was distributed: see *Cong. Rec.*, vol. 50, p. 3774 (1913) (statement of Sen. Root), but this was more an argument about what is now known as the realization principle than about the separate personality of the corporation.

[67] *Cong. Rec.*, vol. 50, p. 3774 (1913).

[68] Revenue Act of 1913, ch. 16, § II(A)(2), 38 Stat. 114, 166–7 (1913).

[69] As evidenced, for example, by the fact that the corporation had accumulated earnings that were far in excess of the reasonable needs of the corporation's business. Ibid.

rata share of the earnings as if they had been distributed.[70] This meant that, in such corporations, the shareholders would effectively be taxed on corporate profits under the same terms as Civil War-era shareholders – "whether divided or otherwise."[71] The retention of such an aggregate feature should have been entirely inconsistent with an entity theory-inspired move to a corporate income tax if that had been the guiding principle.

One possible explanation for this seemingly wayward provision is that contemporary legislators believed the pass-through penalty tax would not apply to "real" corporations. In trying to allay opponents' fear that it would interfere with the sound business judgment of a corporation's directors, the bill's principal spokesman, Senator Parham Williams, explained that its "main purpose is to prevent holding companies. Here is a man, for example, with an income as large as Mr. Carnegie's income, let us say. There would be nothing to prevent him from organizing a holding company and passing his income from year to year up to undivided profits."[72] This suggests that it would only apply to corporations that were mere shams or the alter ego of their owners and therefore ineligible for the entity status normally attributable to corporations.

Although it would have been plausible to target the provision at sham entities, it was not drafted in such a limited way and its supporters explicitly acknowledged this point. During the debates, Senator William Borah asked for clarification on the breadth of the provision:

> Suppose that a corporation has been legitimately organized and it can not be said to be fraudulent or formed for the purpose of doing the specific thing of holding property and holding dividends; suppose it is a legitimate corporation and they do not distribute, then is there any way under this bill to tax or get at the dividends which a corporation might hold which has been legitimately organized?[73]

Senator Williams responded to this query by making clear that such legitimate corporations would also be covered by the undivided profits tax penalty.[74] In doing this, Williams conceded that "[i]t is a very difficult problem because there is no right to anybody to have a dividend unless the directors declare a dividend."[75] This response foreshadowed the difficulties the United States would face in applying an aggregate

---

[70] Ibid.   [71] Act of June 30, 1864, ch. 173, § 117, 13 Stat. at 282 (1864).
[72] *Cong. Rec.*, vol. 50, p. 4380 (1913) (statement of Sen. Williams).
[73] Ibid., p. 5318 (statement of Sen. Borah).   [74] Ibid., p. 5318 (statement of Sen. Williams).
[75] Ibid., p. 5319 (statement of Sen. Williams).

perspective to a business entity that was rapidly developing in a fashion that distinguished it from corporations in the UK.

5.2   The divergence in the nature of the corporation

Notwithstanding the weaknesses of formal entity theory as an explanation for the divergence in how the USA and the UK taxed corporations, there is a kernel of truth to the observations that underlie it. The differing contemporary descriptions of the corporation and the differences that developed in the fundamental nature of the respective corporate tax systems are connected. Rather than relying on the varying legal and popular perceptions in the two countries, though, which suggests that this can be explained as an intellectual or cultural divide, it is more valuable to examine the divergence in the development of the corporation itself that occurred between the turn of the century and the onset of World War II. This includes legal and practical differences in the position of shareholders and the *locus* of power as a result of the varying degree to which ownership separated from control in the two countries over this period. Although the development of the US and UK stock markets and the rise of companies with widely dispersed public owners occurred roughly on a parallel path, the continued dominance of family blockholders and shareholder-friendly practices delayed the onset of a true outsider/arm's-length system of corporate governance in the UK until after World War II. As will be further explained in section 5.3 below, this affected the way the corporation was treated for tax purposes, although not in a way that was so rigid as to preclude deviations from the respective approaches when conditions dictated it.

5.2.1   Ownership dispersion

USA

An important factor in the development of corporations in America was the increasing public ownership of corporate enterprises. Prior to the 1880s, most industrial or manufacturing companies other than the large transportation concerns were small, privately held (often by members of the same family), and frequently unincorporated.[76] This soon changed.

---

[76] See Walter Werner, "Corporation Law in Search of its Future," *Columbia Law Review* 81 (1981): 1640; Jonathan Barron Baskin and Paul J. Miranti, Jr., *A History of Corporate Finance* (Cambridge University Press, 1997), p. 193.

Prompted in large part by a turn-of-the-century merger movement, companies began to go to the public market to raise capital for acquisitions rather than rely upon the private offerings that had sustained most corporations throughout the nineteenth century.

As a consequence of this move to take companies public, the New York Stock Exchange (NYSE) experienced significant growth. In 1885, 151 companies had stocks traded on the NYSE, more than 80 percent of which were railroads. In the ensuing two decades, the total number of traded stocks more than doubled to 341, with railroads making up less than half of the public companies by 1905.[77] Industrial companies, which had made up a mere 16 percent of the Exchange in 1885, had grown to 41 percent in 1905.[78] To accommodate this growth, between 1901 and 1903 the Exchange constructed a massive new facility at a cost of more than $4 million.[79] By 1930, the total number of traded stocks had reached 1,273, more than 80 percent of which were industrials.[80] This rise in the number and diversity of companies with traded stocks helped trigger a significant increase in the volume of shares traded as well. Between 1896 and 1907, the number of shares changing hands annually more than quadrupled from 57 million to 260 million.[81]

The number of companies with traded stock is even larger when the inquiry is broadened to include companies that were not eligible for listing under the NYSE's strict rules.[82] To accommodate these ineligible firms and thwart potential competitors, the NYSE created an "Unlisted Department." According to the NYSE's economist, J. Edward Meeker, "the new industrial shares which could not altogether meet the increasingly strict requirements of the Committee on Stock List could nevertheless be admitted for trading purposes."[83] By the turn of the century

[77] Mary O'Sullivan, "The Expansion of the US Stock Market, 1885–1930: Historical Facts and Theoretical Fashions," *Enterprise and Society* 8 (2007): 499, tbl. 2.

[78] Ibid., 499; see Thomas R. Navin and Marian V. Sears, "The Rise of a Market for Industrial Securities, 1887–1902," *The Business History Review* 29 (1955): 136.

[79] Robert Sobel, *Inside Wall Street: Continuity and Change in the Financial District* (New York: Norton, 1977), pp. 45–6.

[80] Ibid.

[81] Morton J. Horwitz, *The Transformation of American Law, 1870–1960: The Crisis of Legal Orthodoxy* (Oxford University Press, 1992), p. 95.

[82] Those skeptical of the extent of ownership dispersion among early twentieth-century American companies, such as Leslie Hannah, have omitted to consider companies beyond those listed on the NYSE. See Leslie Hannah, "The Divorce of Ownership from Control from 1900: Recalibrating Imagined Global Historical Trends," *Business History* 49 (2007): 406, 423.

[83] O'Sullivan, "The Expansion of the US Stock Market," 497.

trading volume for these unlisted securities was between 20 and 40 percent of the volume for listed securities and there were more than twice as many unlisted companies as listed companies.[84] Furthermore, stocks that were neither listed nor unlisted were traded on the New York Curb Market, which traded outside the Exchange building. By 1908, there were 157 companies traded on the Curb Exchange. Finally, none of these figures includes the companies traded on the various regional exchanges operating during the period in places such as Baltimore, Boston, Chicago, Cincinnati, Cleveland, Los Angeles, Philadelphia, Pittsburgh, and San Francisco. In 1900, there were 682 listed companies on these regional exchanges and by 1930 the number had grown to 2,659.[85]

Not only did the number of companies with traded stock grow, but the number of individuals holding shares of common stock in corporations increased dramatically in the early twentieth century. One source suggested it rose from a half-million in 1900 to 2 million in 1920 and 10 million in 1930.[86] Other estimates vary considerably due to the difficulty in ascertaining individual holdings through tax return and company data, with one pegging the total number of shareholders as high as 15 million by 1926 and another indicating that there were only 3 million by 1929; but all found the same upward trajectory.[87]

Firm-level data and other, more fine-grained analyses confirm the rise in the number of shareholders in public corporations. In an unpublished study of the shareholder rolls for seventy-five large corporations between 1901 and 1913, the National Civic Federation's Distribution of Ownership in Investments Subcommittee, which was chaired by economist E. R. A. Seligman, found that the aggregate number of shareholders in these companies nearly tripled, increasing from 140,072 to 414,945, over the period.[88] Lawrence Mitchell noted in his review of the National Civic Federation study that "[t]he data show a significant spread in share ownership across the population from the turn of the century on, both directly, in holdings of less than one hundred shares, and indirectly, in the form of increased stock ownership by insurance companies and

[84] Ibid., p. 501.   [85] Ibid., p. 523, tbl. 9.
[86] Baskin and Miranti, Jr., *A History of Corporate Finance*, p. 190.
[87] See Lewis Corey, "How is Ownership Distributed?," *The New Republic* 46 (1926): 322; Gardiner Means, "The Diffusion of Stock Ownership in the United States," *The Quarterly Journal of Economics* 44 (1930): 595; Sobel, *Inside Wall Street*, p. 203.
[88] Lawrence E. Mitchell, *The Speculation Economy: How Finance Triumphed Over Industry* (San Francisco: Berrett-Koehler Publishers, 2007), pp. 202–3.

savings banks."[89] Even corporations that already had widely dispersed ownership had significant increases in their shareholder bases. In one particularly striking example cited by Berle and Means, the number of shareholders in A.T. & T. increased from 7,500 in 1900 to 642,000 by 1931.[90]

Perhaps more significantly, for the first time there were many shareholders of moderate means.[91] The high individual income tax rates imposed during World War I, in the words of Gardiner Means, had made "the rich man a poor market for corporate securities."[92] At the same time, the successful Liberty Bond campaigns launched during the war had introduced the common man to investing and had created an infrastructure in the financial world designed to induce him to buy common stocks once his bonds matured after the war.[93] A report in *The New Republic*, which reminded readers that "the multiplication of stockholders is not equivalent to the democratization of corporate ownership," conceded that "real gains have been scored by the middle class."[94]

Quite apart from the reality of this transition to the widely owned corporation, the phenomenon had entered the popular consciousness at the same time that the corporate income tax was in its infancy. Utility magnate Samuel Insull commented in 1924 that

> [w]e are witnessing the passing of an age and the coming of another in the ownership of industrial America. Herbert Hoover was right when he said

---

[89] Ibid., p. 202.

[90] Adolf Berle and Gardiner Means, *The Modern Corporation and Private Property* (New York: The Macmillan Co., 1933), pp. 55, 108; Christopher Schmitz, *The Growth of Big Business in the United States and Western Europe, 1850–1939* (Basingstoke: Macmillan, 1993), p. 18.

[91] Victor De Villiers, "The growing army of 'small investors'," *The Magazine of Wall Street* 27 (1920): 30.

[92] Means, "The Diffusion of Stock Ownership," 586.

[93] H. T. Warshow, "The Distribution of Corporate Ownership in the United States," *The Quarterly Journal of Economics* 39 (1924): 35; Sobel, *Inside Wall Street*, p. 203; Charles Geisst, *Wall Street: A History* (Oxford University Press, 1997), p. 157. For at least a short time during the economic downturn in 1920–21, the Liberty Bond experience may have produced the opposite effect. One observer commented that "[f]or the past year, visiting around the Street, I have seldom been out of earshot of the dolorous charge, 'The public got stung on Liberty Bonds and became soured on all investments'." The observer called such complaints "drivel!" arguing that it was the lack of effective advertising that hurt those brokers. John Read, "Bringing Wall Street to the people," *The Magazine of Wall Street* 28 (1921): 212.

[94] Corey, "How is Ownership Distributed?," 325.

that a silent revolution is transferring ownership to the public. The great fortunes are retiring from the command of industry. The small fortunes, the moderate and small incomes are taking their place.[95]

John W. Prentiss, president of the Investment Bankers Association reportedly estimated that "there are twenty-five million individuals in this country who own stocks or bonds, or one stockholder to each family in the country."[96]

UK

In the UK, the evidence of dispersed ownership is a bit less clear, although it is probable that some ownership dispersion did occur during this period and that the dispersion started at an earlier point. During the middle of the nineteenth century, there were legal and customary obstacles to ownership dispersion, with the nature of business practice constituting the most significant impediment.[97] As Brian Cheffins explained, "between the 1720s and the 1840s the legal environment was not particularly congenial for corporate enterprise."[98] "Nevertheless," Cheffins continued, "even if the law had provided a congenial platform for corporate activity, the outcome would have been little different. Because industrial enterprises were low in the pecking order for investors and their proprietors generally had little inclination to carry out public offerings of shares, the industrial revolution was not destined to generate large, widely held industrial companies."[99]

By the middle of the nineteenth century, matters appeared to be more favorable for ownership dispersion. For instance, limited liability under the 1855 act was only available to those who signed a deed of settlement, which "shall be executed by shareholders not less than 25 in number, holding shares to the amount in the aggregate of at least three-fourths of the nominal capital of the company."[100] This necessarily encouraged share dispersion, although not necessarily to a wider segment of society. According to James Jefferys, this provision, which was continued in practice even after it was removed from subsequent acts, had the effect

---

[95] Theodore M. Knappen, "The silent revolution in American finance," *The Magazine of Wall Street* 35 (1934): 316.

[96] Barnard Powers, "Who are the real owners of Wall Street?," *The Magazine of Wall Street* 33 (1924): 1106.

[97] Cheffins, *Corporate Ownership and Control*, pp. 152–7.   [98] Ibid. at p. 157.   [99] Ibid.

[100] James B. Jefferys, *Business Organisation in Great Britain, 1856–1914* (New York: Arno Press, 1977), p. 383 (quoting Section 9 I.(4) of 18 and 19 Vict. c. 133).

of "keep[ing] out of the investment market all those who had not a substantial sum to invest for a long period."[101]

Much as in the USA, the UK experienced a stock market explosion around the turn of the century. A mere 70 industrial companies were listed on the London Stock Exchange (LSE) in 1885, but by 1907 this had jumped to 571 companies and the LSE was considered the top stock market globally.[102] In 1930, there were 1,700 industrial companies listed on the LSE, almost 500 more than on the NYSE.[103] This may have been due, in part, to the more lax listing standards on the LSE, which permitted companies to list any financial instruments.[104] Nevertheless, an official with the NYSE noted in 1914 that turnover on the LSE was ten times greater than turnover on his exchange, while another American observed in 1911 that "[t]he London Stock Exchange is the only really international market of the world. Its interests branch over all parts of our globe."[105] Indeed, almost twenty years before the NYSE expanded its space to accommodate increased trading activity, the LSE had more than doubled the size of its building and further expansions followed in 1896 and 1905.[106]

As in the United States, the LSE numbers undercount the growth in public companies. Part of this is because of the popularity of listing a company's shares for trading through a system of "special settlement" rather than full quotation, prior to the abolition of that procedure during World War I.[107] In 1910, one member of the LSE claimed that "99 per cent of the dealings in the shares of new companies were for the special settlement."[108] Another reason the LSE numbers understate the true magnitude of the growth in public companies is that, for much of the nineteenth century, it was common practice to list the company's securities on the exchange closest to the company's headquarters or

---

[101] Jefferys, *Business Organisation in Great Britain*, pp. 383–4.
[102] Julian Franks, Colin Mayer, and Stefano Rossi, "Spending Less Time with the Family: the Decline of Family Ownership in the United Kingdom," in Randall K. Morck (ed.), *A History of Corporate Governance around the World: Family Business Groups to Professional Managers* (University of Chicago Press, 2005), p. 588, tbl. 10.1; Cheffins, *Corporate Ownership and Control*, p. 57.
[103] Franks, Mayer, and Rossi, "Spending Less Time with the Family," p. 588, tbl. 10.1.
[104] Brian R. Cheffins and Steven A. Bank, "Is Berle and Means really a Myth?," *The Business History Review* 83 (2009): 443, 446.
[105] Ranald C. Michie, *The London Stock Exchange: A History* (Oxford University Press, 1999), p. 70.
[106] Ibid., p. 77.   [107] Cheffins, *Corporate Ownership and Control*, p. 196.   [108] Ibid.

operations.[109] In the case of industrial concerns, this was more likely to be located in Northern England or Scotland than in London. Insurance companies dominated the stock exchanges in Liverpool and Edinburgh.[110] Companies did move their securities to London as they sought more of a global market, but the provincial exchanges grew as well. For example, the number of companies quoted on the Manchester Stock Exchange grew from 70 in 1885 to almost 220 by 1906 and there were similar increases in the Glasgow and Edinburgh Stock Exchanges.[111] More generally, the total number of provincial stock exchanges doubled from 11 to 22 between 1882 and 1914 and the total number of companies listed on all exchanges that had their share information tracked in *Investor's Monthly Manual* jumped from 520 in 1870 to 1,100 in 1913.[112] Taken as a whole, the provincial exchanges were as large as the LSE and were likely more important for domestic securities than the London exchange, which quoted many foreign securities.[113]

There is little reliable data about the total number or the average income level of shareholders in early twentieth-century British corporations. According to one estimate, the number of individuals holding securities increased from 250,000 in 1870 to 1 million in 1914, but this includes securities of any kind such as debt and preferred stock.[114] The average value of stock held by shareholders in the mid 1920s was a mere £301, which suggests that ownership had become at least partially dispersed by this point although it does not exclude the possibility of a controlling shareholder.[115] Even the relatively modest average value of shareholdings does not speak to whether owning shares in public companies had become more of a middle class phenomenon. According to several reports, the new investors frequently came from the same social and economic circles as the company's founders, often merchants or landowners seeking to diversify their investments in light of declining

---

[109] Michie, *The London Stock Exchange*, p. 93.   [110] Ibid., p. 94.
[111] William Thomas, *The Provincial Stock Exchanges* (London: Cass, 1973), p. 133; Cheffins, *Corporate Ownership and Control*, p. 176.
[112] Cheffins, *Corporate Ownership and Control*, pp. 176–7. The latter is less reliable because it included all companies with listed securities, including foreign companies. Richard S. Grossman, "New Indices of British Equity Prices, 1870–1913," *The Journal of Economic History* 62 (2002): 124.
[113] Julian Franks, Colin Mayer, and Stefano Rossi, "Ownership: Evolution and Regulation," *The Review of Financial Studies* 22 (2009): 4017.
[114] Michie, *The London Stock Exchange*, p. 72.
[115] Schmitz, *The Growth of Big Business*, p. 18.

rental income.[116] Nevertheless, none of this should discount the reality that at least some measure of dispersion was occurring in the UK at this time, although some modern observers claim that "share dispersal was not as complete in England as it was in the United States at the time of *The Modern Corporation*."[117]

5.2.2   Familial capitalism and the presence of blockholders

Although the USA and the UK were more or less on parallel tracks in the growth and dispersion of their shareholder populations, the real area where the countries diverged was in the existence of blockholder control. This had two dimensions. First, families maintained controlling stakes in British public corporations, at least in the industrial and manufacturing sectors, to a relatively high extent. Second, American corporations more quickly developed a management structure that ceded control to individuals who were not directly associated with or controlled by the shareholders. The combination meant that even amidst the growth in public corporations and the expansion of stock ownership in both countries, different patterns emerged. While the USA was moving closer to the outsider/arm's-length structure of corporate governance, the UK continued to adhere to the insider/control-oriented model.

Blockholders

During the early twentieth century in both the UK and the USA, the founding families of newly public corporations often maintained control of their organizations by retaining ownership of a block of stock sufficient to affect voting. In the UK, for instance, Imperial Tobacco continued to be dominated by the Wills family even after a 1901 merger of seventeen UK tobacco companies and an ensuing public offering in 1902 designed to finance the merger. At the time, the Wills family owned 68 percent of the resulting company's ordinary shares and it still held 55 percent in 1911 after the death of William Henry Wills, the founding chairman of Imperial.[118] One commentator later described Imperial as a

[116] P. L. Cottrell, *Industrial Finance, 1830–1914: The Finance and Organization of English Manufacturing Industry* (London: Methuen, 1979), pp. 153–4; Brian R. Cheffins and Steven A. Bank, "Corporate Ownership and Control in the UK: the Tax Dimension," *Modern Law Review* 70 (2007): 780.

[117] Lorraine E. Talbot, "Enumerating Old Themes? Berle's Concept of Ownership and the Historical Development of English Company Law in Context," *Seattle University Law Review* 33 (2010): 1218–19.

[118] Cheffins, *Corporate Ownership and Control*, p. 244; B. W. E. Alford, *W. D. & H. O. Wills and the Development of the UK Tobacco Industry, 1786–1965* (London: Methuen, 1973), pp. 184–5, 240–41.

"glorified family firm."[119] This phenomenon was true even for very large firms with widely dispersed shareholders. Lever Brothers, a British soap manufacturer and the forerunner of the modern conglomerate Unilever, had 187,000 shareholders but "remained firmly under the thumb" of its founder, William Lever, until his death in 1925, through the family's control over the voting stock and the management structure.[120] To avoid diluting family control, the company only issued debentures and non-voting preferred stock, and other stock with limited or no voting rights, in connection with their aggressive acquisition campaigns.[121]

British companies were not unique in this regard in the early twentieth century. In the USA, large companies such as Ford Motor Company, the Mellon family's Gulf Petroleum and Aluminum Company of America, and the Duke family's American Tobacco Company were all heavily dominated by family ownership and control.[122] According to studies of corporations during the first several decades of the twentieth century, in the USA as in the UK, families or other shareholder groups maintained control over a significant percentage of corporations. As of 1929 in Berle and Means' study, 23 percent of the largest 200 American corporations were controlled by minority blockholders such as families.[123] Likewise, Leslie Hannah found that 55 percent of the largest 200 British corporations had family members on the board of directors in 1919, with that percentage rising to 70 by 1930.[124]

The difference between the USA and the UK was not in the presence of family control in the early 1900s, but rather in the extent to which it continued through the twentieth century. The development of a true outsider/arm's-length form of corporate governance in the UK was delayed in large part by the persistence of family control.[125] According

---

[119] T. R. Gourvish, "British Business and the Transition to a Corporate Economy: Entrepreneurship and Management Structures," *Business History* 29 (1987): 25.

[120] Charles Wilson, *The History of Unilever: A Study of Economic Growth and Social Change*, 2 vols., vol. I (London: Cassell, 1954), pp. 46–8, 290; John Micklethwait and Adrian Wooldridge, *The Company: A Short History of a Revolutionary Idea* (New York: The Modern Library, 2003), p. 89.

[121] Cheffins, *Corporate Ownership and Control*, pp. 71–2.

[122] Allan Nevins and Frank E. Hill, *Ford*, 2 vols., vol. I (New York: Scribner's, 1954), pp. 331, 572–3; Berle and Means, *The Modern Corporation and Private Property*, p. 95; Alfred Chandler, *The Visible Hand: The Managerial Revolution in American Business* (Cambridge, Mass.: Belknap Press, 1977), pp. 381–402.

[123] Berle and Means, *The Modern Corporation and Private Property*, p. 115.

[124] Schmitz, *The Growth of Big Business*, p. 18 (citing Hannah in Alfred Chandler, Jr. and Herman Daems (eds.), *Managerial Hierarchies: Comparative Perspectives on the Rise of the Modern Industrial Enterprise* (Cambridge, Mass.: Harvard University Press, 1980)).

[125] See Brian R. Cheffins, "History and the Global Corporate Governance Revolution: the UK Perspective," *Business History* 43 (2001): 90.

to Brian Cheffins, "[o]nly after World War II would the transformation to outsider/arm's-length corporate governance become complete."[126] Even considering the 1950s and 1960s as the demarcation point, there was still substantial evidence in the UK as late as the 1970s of the type of familial capitalism and blockholder control characteristic of an earlier generation.[127] Mary Rose distinguishes this from the experience in America, noting that "in contrast to the experience in the United States, where from the 1880s onwards ownership and control became increasingly divorced, in Britain personal capitalism persisted well into the twentieth century."[128]

Part of the reason family insiders were able to maintain control in many UK companies at such a high rate is because they frequently retained some or all of the voting equity after listing the company's other securities. As P. L. Cottrell observed, "[a]lthough the number of public companies grew, this development did not lead to 'outside' share-holders gaining control of their assets. The equity, which carried voting rights, remained generally in the hands of their vendors whereas extra funds were raised at the time of conversions, or subsequently, by the issues of either preference shares or debentures."[129] According to Cottrell, "[i]n the years before 1914 domestic public joint-stock companies issued more than 75 percent of their new capital in fixed-charge securities ... Ordinary shares remained generally with the original proprietors, who took them in payment for fixed assets and goodwill that they made over to the new limited concerns."[130] A. R. Hall confirms this, stating that "a large number of the 'disposals', probably the major-ity, did not involve the sale of ordinary shares but only preference shares and debentures."[131]

Although non-voting preferred stock and securities, voting trusts, and other legal devices to retain control were present in US corporations as well, they were often used by other corporations or financiers rather than by families. Thus, for example, many utility companies used a pyramid structure for stock interests to leverage small investments into control of

---

[126] Cheffins, *Corporate Ownership and Control*, p. 252.
[127] See Cheffins, "History and the Global Corporate Governance Revolution," 89–90.
[128] Mary B. Rose, "The Family Firm in British Business, 1780–1914," in Maurice W. Kirby and Mary B. Rose (eds.), *Business Enterprise in Modern Britain: From the Eighteenth to the Twentieth Century* (London, New York: Routledge, 1994), pp. 61, 67–8.
[129] Cottrell, *Industrial Finance*, p. 164.   [130] Ibid., p. 167.
[131] A. Rupert Hall, "The English Capital Market before 1914 – a Reply," *Economica* 25 (1958): 342.

large empires.[132] Similarly, the investment firm Dillon Read and Company was able to control Dodge Brothers, Inc. in the mid-1920s because the preferred stock and four-fifths of the common stock was non-voting, leaving Dillon Read's common stock as the only voting shares.[133] The Pennsylvania Railroad management used a voting trust to accomplish a similar measure of control in the reorganization of the Pennroad Corporation.[134] Many of these control mechanisms, though, were shut down by legislative developments during the New Deal, including the Public Utility Holding Company Act of 1935.[135]

Hannah has disputed this whole line of argument, arguing that it was actually British firms that took the lead in separating ownership from control and moving away from familial capitalism.[136] In light of the paucity of hard data on aggregate numbers, Hannah has asserted that LSE listing requirements necessarily meant that the rise in the number of listed companies must have been accompanied by a dramatic explosion in the number of shareholders.[137] His evidence for this is that, starting in at least the 1850s and continuing throughout this period, the LSE prohibited a company's securities from being listed unless at least two-thirds were available for subscription by the general public.[138]

This two-thirds rule is not very effective evidence for the dispersion of family control. As far back as 1885, *The Economist* called the rule "ineffectual and misleading," noting that "this condition is constantly evaded, and always can be when the necessity is sufficient to stimulate the inventive faculty."[139] Brian Cheffins explained that companies could sidestep the rule through stock buybacks, issuance of preference shares rather than common stock, and by arranging to have their shares traded through special settlement rather than full quotation or by raising additional capital privately or on regional exchanges.[140] In fact, the practice of retaining control by issuing non-voting stock or securities was reinforced by the two-thirds rule cited by Hannah as evidence of ownership dispersion. While two-thirds of a company's securities may have been

---

[132] Steven A. Bank and Brian R. Cheffins, "The Corporate Pyramid Fable," *Business History Review* 84 (2010): 453.
[133] Berle and Means, *The Modern Corporation and Private Property*, p. 75.   [134] Ibid., p. 77.
[135] Public Utility Holding Company Act of 1935, 49 Stat. 803 (1935).
[136] Hannah, "The Divorce of Ownership from Control," 425.   [137] Ibid., 404.
[138] Cheffins, *Corporate Ownership and Control*, p. 76.
[139] "Unmarketable securities and official quotations," *The Economist*, May 30, 1885, pp. 657, 658.
[140] Cheffins, *Corporate Ownership and Control*, pp. 226–30.

available for purchase by widely-dispersed shareholders on the LSE, this meant that ownership of one-third of the company's securities could be maintained by the original owners, thereby effectively creating an ownership block for control purposes.[141] According to Cheffins, "the two-thirds rule does not provide a sufficient factual foundation to support Hannah's contention that prior to World War I dispersed ownership was the norm in larger UK companies."[142]

Cheffins performed his own study to test Hannah's conclusions. Hannah had compiled a list of the world's largest one-hundred industrial companies as of 1912 and Cheffins examined the ownership structures of the fifteen that were based in the UK.[143] Cheffins found that "contrary to Hannah's argument, a separation of ownership and control was the exception to the rule in the 15 companies. In only one instance (Consolidated Gold Fields of South Africa) is there no evidence of a sizeable concentrated block of shares on the eve of World War I."[144] Given that a large firm was more likely to have diffuse ownership and manager control than a small firm, Cheffins concluded that "[t]his implies, in turn, a divorce of ownership and control was generally rare in the industrial sector."[145]

This does not mean that separation of ownership and control had not spread to any British industries. An early example of such separation occurring was in the railroads. In 1872, a Joint Select Parliamentary Committee noted that

> [o]n railways there is a powerful bureaucracy of directors and officials. The real managers are far removed from the influence of the shareholders and the latter are to a great extent a fluctuating and helpless body. The history of railway enterprise shows how frequently their interests have been sacrificed to the policy, the speculations, and the passions of the real managers.[146]

As Cheffins explained, "[o]wnership was divorced from control in large UK railway companies as far back as the mid-19th century and the situation remained unchanged up to World War I."[147] Nevertheless, in the British industrial sector, where businesses were often local and may have had a disproportionate influence on popular thinking about the

---

[141] Ibid., p. 227. [142] Ibid., p. 230. [143] Ibid., p. 243. [144] Ibid. [145] Ibid.
[146] Report of the Joint Select Committee (1872), pp. xxix–xxx, quoted in A. W. Currie, "British Attitudes toward Investment in North American Railroads," *Business History Review* 34 (1960): 214.
[147] Cheffins, *Corporate Ownership and Control*, p. 230.

nature of the firm, familial and personal capitalism continued to be dominant.[148]

Managers

Between 1880 and 1930, the small, privately held, family-controlled US business appeared to gradually give way to the large, publicly traded, manager-controlled corporation.[149] According to Alfred Chandler, this transformation primarily occurred before World War I, with US companies developing independent and sophisticated management structures quite distinct from their shareholders.[150] This phenomenon was repeatedly emphasized by contemporary observers. F. Edson White, the president of meatpacking firm Armour and Company, reported in a 1924 interview that "[b]ig business is rapidly becoming decentralized in ownership – and it desires to be."[151] The *New York Times* noted the following year that "a widespread diffusion of corporate ownership is unquestionably now in full swing."[152] By 1927, economist William Ripley noted that "[t]he prime fact confronting us as a nation is the progressive diffusion of ownership on the one hand and of the ever-increasing concentration of managerial power on the other."[153]

The rise of the manager-led corporation was considered dangerous for both shareholders and the corporation. Thorstein Veblen complained about the shift to "absentee ownership," lamenting the decline of "these time-worn principles of ownership and control."[154] Of General Motors, which itself had relatively concentrated ownership despite the fact that 40 percent of its shares were held by a widely dispersed group of 70,000 shareholders, the corporation's president wrote in 1927,

> there is a point beyond which diffusion of stock ownership must enfeeble the corporation by depriving it of virile interest in management upon the part of some one man or group of men to whom its success is a matter of

---

[148] Ibid., pp. 242–51.   [149] Werner, "Corporation Law in Search of its Future," 1641.
[150] Alfred D. Chandler, Jr., "The United States: Seedbed of Managerial Capitalism," in Chandler, Jr. and Daems (eds.), *Managerial Hierarchies*, p. 9; Alfred D. Chandler, Jr., *Scale and Scope: The Dynamics of Industrial Capitalism* (Cambridge, Mass.: Belknap Press, 1990), pp. 52, 84–5.
[151] Knappen, "The silent revolution in American finance," 263.
[152] Evans Clark, "15,000,000 Americans hold corporation stock," *New York Times*, November 22, 1925, p. XX5.
[153] William Z. Ripley, *Main Street and Wall Street* (Boston: Little, Brown, and Co., 1927), p. 131.
[154] Thorstein Veblen, *Absentee Ownership and Business Enterprise in Recent Times: The Case of America* (New York: B. W. Heubsch, Inc., 1923), p. 5.

personal and vital interest. And conversely at the same point the public interest becomes involved when the public can no longer locate some tangible personality within the ownership which it may hold responsible for the corporation's conduct.[155]

One economist observed in 1933 that "[t]he separation of ownership and management has left the stockholders, i.e., the owners, with hardly any influence on the investment of corporate savings. How is management to overcome the temptation of ploughing earnings back into the institution, even if retrenchment were wiser than expansion?"[156] This was more than a merely hypothetical problem. William Ripley wrote that "for many of the [prospering companies during the Twenties] the rebuilding of the plant from earnings, undertaking very expensive extensions through charges to operation, the accumulation of all sorts of reserves, has gone on seemingly without regard to the right of the present generation of shareholders to the immediate enjoyment of the income of the business."[157]

Adolf Berle and Gardiner Means offered empirical data to buttress these contemporary observations of the transformation to a manager-led corporation. In their famous 1932 study,[158] Berle and Means documented that in 1930 a substantial majority of the 200 largest corporations were controlled by management rather than by an individual or family.[159] They wrote "[w]e have reached a condition in which the individual interest of the shareholder is definitely subservient to the will of a controlling group of managers even though the capital is made up of the aggregated contributions of perhaps many thousands of individuals."[160] Although their conclusion was not as clearly supported by their data as they asserted,[161] other studies soon followed to confirm that many of the largest corporations in the USA were indeed controlled by managers. Thus, in 1938, Robert Gordon examined newly available filings with the Securities and Exchange Commission for 155 of the 200 corporations in the Berle and Means study and concluded that "[i]n these very large corporations the separation of both management

---

[155] Ripley, *Main Street and Wall Street*, pp. 131–2.
[156] Robert Weidenhammer, "Causes and repercussions of the Faulty Investment of Corporate Savings," *The American Economic Review* 23 (1933): 40.
[157] Ripley, *Main Street and Wall Street*, p. 150.
[158] Berle and Means, *The Modern Corporation and Private Property*, p. 94.
[159] Ibid.   [160] Ibid., p. 244.
[161] Cheffins and Bank, "Is Berle and Means really a Myth?," 453.

and control from ownership has proceeded far."[162] Two years later, the Temporary National Economic Committee, a joint committee of Congress and the President formed to investigate economic concentration in the USA, cast doubt on these findings,[163] but a subsequent re-examination of the data by Gordon once again reaffirmed the belief that during the 1930s the largest US corporations were primarily controlled by managers.[164] Citing Gordon's work, Robert Larner wrote, "[t]he evidence of the late 1920s and 1930s, then, seemed to indicate that management control existed to an important extent among America's largest nonfinancial corporations."[165] This does not mean that blockholders were uncommon among large American corporations. Indeed, they could be found as late as the 1960s in many corporations;[166] there has never been what might be called a "total" or "complete" divorce of ownership from control in the USA and studies have offered conflicting conclusions over the years.[167] Nevertheless, the available evidence suggests that the typical pattern among large firms became one in which managers were dominant.

In the UK, this transformation to a manager-controlled corporation appeared to take place much later than in the USA. John Micklethwait and Adrian Wooldridge, in their history of the company, described this divergence:

> British entrepreneurs clung to the personal approach to management long after their American cousins had embraced professionalism. As late as the Second World War, a remarkable number of British firms were managed by members of the founding families. These founders kept the big decisions firmly within the company, only calling on the help of professional managers *in extremis*. Family-run firms had no need for

---

[162] Robert A. Gordon, "Ownership by Management and Control Groups in the Large Corporation," *The Quarterly Journal of Economics* 52 (1938): 395–6.

[163] Raymond Goldsmith *et al.*, *The Distribution of Ownership in the Two Hundred Largest Nonfinancial Corporations*, TNEC Investigation of Concentration of Economic Power, Monograph No. 29 (Washington, DC, 1940), p. 15.

[164] Robert A. Gordon, *Business Leadership in the Large Corporation* (Washington, DC: The Brookings Institution, 1945), p. 42. See Robert J. Larner, *Management Control and the Large Corporation* (New York: Dunellen Publishing Co., 1970), p. 7.

[165] Larner, *Management Control*, p. 7.

[166] This depends to some extent upon how you define blockholders. Many of the most dubious studies on the Berle and Means conclusions, published in the 1960s and 1970s, used a 5 percent threshold for defining control. A 10 percent threshold, which is the reporting standard the Securities and Exchange Commission originally adopted in 1935, would have likely reduced the number of blockholders considerably. Cheffins and Bank, "Is Berle and Means really a Myth?," 458.

[167] Ibid. at 467.

the detailed organizational charts and manuals that had become com-
monplace in large American companies. They relied instead on personal
relations and family traditions.[168]

During the 1930s, some British commentators asserted that the management revolution had arrived in UK companies. One observer wrote in 1934
that "to-day the divorce of ownership from management is almost complete," while two others indicated that "ownership is divorced from active
participation in industry, except in agriculture and certain sectors of distribution."[169] Still another wrote that "[i]t is now impossible for the shareholders to exercise effective control in their corporate capacity, so that a
huge amount of capital remains in the uncontrolled hands of management,
in which such management may itself have little at stake."[170] The explanation appeared to be that the shareholders that had invested in corporate
stock during the interwar years were primarily passive, thereby permitting
managers to run the companies free from interference.[171]

As it turns out, such conclusions were, in the view of Brian Cheffins,
"premature."[172] For example, a study by Phillip Sargant Florence of
eighty-two of the largest industrial and commercial firms in Britain as
of 1936 found that the vast majority had a dominant owner.[173] Although
Florence conducted a similar test on very large industrial and commercial companies as of 1951 and found far fewer dominant shareholders,
Cheffins concluded that "[t]he limitations with Florence's research,
combined with some other empirical data, suggest blockholders had
not been fully marginalized at the beginning of the 1950s."[174] In a recent
study of fifty-five listed UK firms as of 1950 by Julian Franks, Colin
Mayer, and Stefano Rossi, the authors reported that the ten largest
shareholders held an average of almost 49 percent of the shares.[175] The
real transition appeared to occur during the 1960s. In 1961, Anthony

[168] Micklethwait and Wooldridge, *The Company*, p. 82.
[169] David Finnie, *Capital Underwriting: An Account of the Principles and Practice of Underwriting Capital Issues, Together with a Critical Analysis of the Main Underwriting and Sub-Underwriting Agreements* (London: Sir Isaac Pitman & Sons, 1934), p. 28; M. Compton and E. H. Bott, *British Industry: Its Changing Structure in Peace and War* (London: L. Drummond, 1940), p. 128.
[170] Robert Ashworth, "The bulletin of the Federation of British Industries" (1934), in Jefferys, *Business Organisation in Great Britain*, p. 382.
[171] Cheffins, *Corporate Ownership and Control*, pp. 293–6.   [172] Ibid., p. 297.
[173] P. Sargant Florence, *Ownership, Control and Success of Large Companies: An Analysis of English Industrial Structure and Policy, 1936–1951* (London: Sweet & Maxwell, 1961).
[174] Cheffins, *Corporate Ownership and Control*, pp. 304–5.
[175] Franks, Mayer, and Rossi, "Ownership," 4025, tbl. 2.

Sampson analyzed twenty-three of the largest UK companies by asset value and concluded that among these firms "there is still often a family or an individual with a dominating influence on the board."[176] A decade later, in 1971, Sampson concluded that "the big corporations are left, like perpetual clocks, to run themselves; and the effective power resides not with the shareholders but with the boards of directors."[177]

5.2.3 Corporate governance

Even if the formal separation of ownership and control had occurred at roughly the same time in the two countries, shareholders maintained a degree of influence over corporate governance in British companies that did not exist in the USA. This may have had long-standing roots. Lorraine Talbot attributes the British conception of shareholders to the survival of legal protections that emerged during the dominance of quasi-partnership companies in the post-Bubble Act era, noting that even after shares in widely dispersed companies were reconceptualized as personal property rather than taking on the character of the firm's assets, "[s]hareholders were still conceived as owners with the entitlement of owners, which seems to be more extensive than mere ownership of shares."[178] This concept is evident in a number of specific areas, most notably dividend policy and in the policies and practices regarding shareholder presence and participation at a corporation's annual meetings. Beyond those formal differences, though, this sense of influence appears to have pervaded the dealings between shareholders and companies in a way that helped to reinforce the different levels of shareholder control in the two countries. Talbot even suggests that this persists to the modern day, although this may be an overstatement: "In the United Kingdom, shareholders continue to be considered the owners of companies and the proper recipients of corporate activity, regardless of the level of share dispersal."[179]

One area where the difference in shareholder rights was particularly stark, at least on the face of it, was in dividend policy. From the middle of the nineteenth century, British shareholders in most companies were accorded the right to vote on the Board's recommendation to declare a dividend. This right was incorporated in Table A of the UK's Companies Acts, which set forth a number of default rules that companies could adopt

---

[176] Anthony Sampson, *The Anatomy of Britain* (London: Hodder & Stoughton, 1961), p. 478.
[177] Anthony Sampson, *The New Anatomy of Britain* (London: Hodder & Stoughton, 1971), pp. 599, 602.
[178] Talbot, "Enumerating Old Themes?," 1217.   [179] Ibid.

in constructing their charters.[180] According to paragraph 72 of Table A, "[t]he Directors may, with the Sanction of the Company in General Meeting, declare a Dividend to be paid to the Members in proportion to their shares."[181] Many companies' articles of association borrowed liberally from Table A, including the provision for shareholder vote on dividends.[182] According to Professor Colleen Dunlavy's forthcoming database on corporate charters, which describes dividend and other provisions in a series of UK charters adopted between 1845 and 1865, two-thirds of those included provisions requiring shareholder approval for declaration of a dividend.[183] Although shareholders generally could not vote to change the amount of a board's recommended dividend, and neither could they initiate a dividend,[184] they could veto a dividend recommendation.

By contrast, US shareholders have never held any power, even in the form of a veto right, over the dividend decision. The board of directors had the sole discretion to determine dividend policy. There were early instances in which the dividend decision was delegated to stockholders under the corporation's bylaws,[185] but by the end of the century the rule

---

[180] *Fisher* v. *Black and White Publishing Co.*, [1901] Law Reports 174 [Ch. 1900]; Cheffins, *Corporate Ownership and Control*, p. 33.

[181] IX Companies Act 1862, Cap. 89, First Schedule, Table A, para. 72 (Eng.).

[182] Cheffins, *Corporate Ownership and Control*, p. 33.

[183] For a description of the database, *see* http://history.wisc.edu/dunlavy/Corporations/ c_database.htm.

[184] II Companies Act 1929, 19 & 20 Geo. 5, ch. 23, Reg. 89 (Eng.) ("The company in general meeting may declare dividends, but no dividend shall exceed the amount recommended by the directors."). *Cf.* Companies Act 1985, ch. 6, Reg. 102 (Eng.) ("Subject to the provisions of the Act, the company may by ordinary resolution declare dividends in accordance with the respective rights of the members, but no dividend shall exceed the amount recommended by the directors.")

[185] See Arthur Stone Dewing, *The Financial Policy of Corporations*, 2 vols., vol. I (New York: Ronald Press Co., 5th edn., 1953), p. 91, n. dd ("In rare cases the dividends are declared by the stockholders, in accordance with a provision of the bylaws. Among early corporations the stockholders' control over dividend disbursement was quite usual. Such a reservation of power is now very rare; it runs counter to the generally accepted theory of the powers and responsibilities of directors.") Some charters went so far as to specify the dividend payments required, rather than leaving this to stockholders, although this often functioned as a method of repaying the initial investors before resuming the normal pattern of entrusting the decision to the directors. See John Cadman, Jr., *The Corporation in New Jersey: Business and Politics, 1791–1875* (Cambridge, Mass.: Harvard University Press, 1949), 321 (The 1791 charter of the Society for Establishing Useful Manufacturers provided "[t]here shall be a yearly Dividend for the first Five Years immediately ensuing the last Day of December next, and thenceforth a half-yearly Dividend, of so much of the Profits of the said Society as to the Directors thereof shall seem expedient.").

was firmly established that "[t]he directors, being the agents of the corporation, alone have the power to determine the amount and to declare a dividend from earnings – a power resting in their honest discretion, uncontrollable by the courts."[186] Stockholders had a mere "inchoate right" in the profits of the corporation until a dividend was declared by the directors.[187] Thomas Cooley elaborated, writing in an opinion for the Michigan Supreme Court that "until the dividend is declared . . . the dividend is only something that may possibly come into existence."[188]

The established norm of shared or at least quasi-shared responsibility for the dividend decision in British companies may have perpetuated their high dividend payout ratios, especially since the depressed profits of British firms during the 1920s made maintaining level dividend payments more difficult.[189] For example, Charles H. Grinling, writing in 1903, attributed this liberal dividend practice to the shareholder-oriented corporate governance structure in British railroads:

> [O]wing to the predominance of shareholders' influence upon British railway policy, it has been the custom to divide the profits of each half-year "up to the hilt," subject only to a more or less liberal current expenditure for the maintenance of the property. Then the net profits are divided up amongst the shareholders as far as they will go, an amount being "carried forward" to next half-year, usually because it was not possible to squeeze out another ¼ percent.[190]

This shareholder influence over dividend policy continued at least up until World War II. Economist Norman Buchanan wrote in 1938 that "[t]he tendency to distribute a larger share of the total annual earnings as dividends in Great Britain may, however, be partially explained by the rather common practice of having the shareholders vote upon the question in meeting, rather than leaving the dividends to be determined by

---

[186] Cyrus LaRue Munson, "Dividends," *Yale Law Journal* 1 (1891): 196.

[187] H.W.R., "Dividends," *Central Law Journal* 9 (1879): 163.

[188] *Lockhart* v. *Van Alstyne*, 31 Mich 76, 78 (1874).

[189] See A. James Arnold, "Profitability and capital accumulation in British industry during the Transwar Period, 1913–1924," *The Economic History Review* 52 (1999): 48. The vast majority of investors preferred current income rather than capital appreciation. See Horace B. Samuel, *Shareholders' Money* (London: Sir Isaac Pitman and Sons, 1933), p. 145 ("Excluding that comparatively small number of persons who buy for capital appreciation, the majority of investors in this country purchase securities in the hope of enjoying the dividends that they anticipate will be paid.")

[190] Charles H. Grinling, "British Railways as Business Enterprises," in William J. Ashley (ed.), *British Industries* (New York: Longmans, Green & Co., 1903), p. 166.

the directors as in American corporations."[191] Notwithstanding that shareholder power over dividends was limited to the right to vote on a proposal by directors, the requirement that directors submit a proposal to a shareholder vote was a reflection of shareholder power and influence. As Benjamin Graham and David Dodd observed, "the mere fact that the dividend policy is submitted to the stockholders for their specific approval or criticism carries an exceedingly valuable reminder to the management of its responsibilities, and to the owners of their rights, on this important question."[192]

In addition to dividend policy, the differential influence of US and UK shareholders over corporate governance is also reflected in the location and nature of the corporate annual meeting. While British managers often moved their annual meetings to facilitate shareholder attendance, US managers did the exact opposite, "preferring to hold annual general meetings far from where shareholders lived or worked."[193] In 1947, the Investors' League cited the examples of a paper company that held its annual meeting at an abandoned paper mill that could only be reached by a special train and a meeting of the American Can Company in an upstate New York town that was not accessible by rail at all.[194] Even where meetings were held in cities accessible to most shareholders, they were held on the same day as meetings of other corporations in different cities, effectively preventing a shareholder from attending meetings of more than one of the corporations in which it held shares.[195]

Part of the explanation for this difference in approach to annual and special meetings was structural differences in the corporate law governing UK and US companies. As Janette Rutterford has explained, the federal system in the USA permitted businesses to be headquartered in one state, but incorporated in an entirely different and often far-off state. Because the choice to incorporate in a state was often a product of a competition among states to offer the most favorable laws for business and its managers, this meant that the protections for shareholders and the disclosure requirements were often quite minimal. The USA did not

---

[191] Norman S. Buchanan, "Theory and Practice in Dividend Distribution," *The Quarterly Journal of Economics* 53 (1938): 83, n. 7.
[192] Benjamin Graham and David L. Dodd, *Security Analysis: Principle and Techniques* (New York, London: Whittlesey House; McGraw-Hill Book Co., Inc, 2d edn. 1940), p. 383, n. 1.
[193] Janette Rutterford, "The Shareholder Voice: British and American Accents, 1890 to 1965" (forthcoming) *Enterprise and Society* 15–16.
[194] Ibid., 16.   [195] Ibid.

provide uniform disclosure requirements until the 1930s with the creation of the Securities Exchange Commission. The difference between the
business home and legal home of a corporation also meant that annual
meetings held near the registered office were more ceremonial than
substantive, since they could be located quite a distance from any natural
shareholding population surrounding the actual business operation of
the company.[196] By contrast, in the UK, with all English and Welsh
companies filing documents and information to the Registrar of
Companies in London starting in 1900, there was no advantage to locate
far from a company's base of operations and its natural shareholder and
employee constituency.[197] Disclosure was also more complete in the
early twentieth-century UK firm, with the Companies Act of 1900 even
requiring the publication of shareholder lists.[198] In a legal environment
in which disclosure was required more broadly, the annual meeting
might have the chance of actually being informative rather than merely
ceremonial.

Even apart from the logistical obstacles to attending annual meetings
in the USA, average shareholders had little incentive to attend.
Frequently, their questions were ignored if there was even time reserved
for questions at all.[199] Corporate management was highly suspicious of
shareholder motives in this context. One railroad chief executive officer,
James J. Hill of the Great Northern Railroad, reportedly testified before
the Pujo Committee in 1913 that in thirty years "no stockholder so far as
he could remember had attended the meetings ... unless he wanted to
make trouble."[200] John Broderick, in his book, *A Small Stockholder*,
offered a colorful explanation for why the lack of any chance to influence
the corporation led people to ignore annual meetings:

> What I am trying to calculate at the moment is the measure of interest
> that there is for me in any meeting of corporation stockholders which I
> am entitled to attend. In fact, while I am usually at ease in the presence of
> death in any form, if I were obligated to choose between hying to one of
> these corporate powwows, with its arid ceremonial, and going to a
> funeral, with its moving solemnity, there is no doubt that I would pick
> the funeral. At a friend's obsequies one may at least speak a consoling
> word to the widow, if he knows how, and possibly serve as a pallbearer.[201]

---

[196] Ibid., 13.   [197] Ibid.   [198] Ibid., 18.   [199] Ibid., 24.

[200] John H. Sears, *The New Place of the Stockholder* (New York: Harper & Brothers
Publishers, 1929), pp. 148–9.

[201] Ibid., p. 151 (quoting John T. Broderick, *A Small Stockholder*).

As a result, John Sears of the Corporation Trust Company noted that "[i]t has become ... customary for stockholders' meetings to be ... devoid of personal attendance or participation in discussions."[202]

There was reportedly a very different scene at annual meetings of British corporations, where annual meeting attendance had a long tradition. Indeed, while there were some instances of non-attendance and proxy voting, it "should not be assumed that it was very widespread."[203] In 1886 a Royal Commission found that "the directors are as a rule well looked after, meetings are frequent: generally they are held quarterly."[204] This general practice continued in the twentieth century, although by then proxy voting had gained a foothold, leading to dire predictions of the decline of the importance of the meeting.[205] Such predictions did not prove true. Sears noted that "[i]n contrast with our American experience we hear frequent reference to the large attendance, real discussions, and results secured at stockholders' meetings in England."[206] The *Wall Street Journal* marveled that

> [s]tockholders' meetings are held in London in a hall that accommodates two thousand people and it is frequently crowded. There is always a good attendance. The directors sit on the platform, with their chairman, and answer questions after the report has been read. The questions are usually shrewd and searching, and woe betide the director who tries to evade them. Such meetings are well reported in the newspapers, especially if the company is a prominent one. The result of this publicity is that the will of the stockholder tends to prevail.[207]

This does not mean, of course, that shareholders in the UK agreed with their American counterparts in concluding that British shareholder meetings were productive and useful or that shareholders in the USA were ineffective in imposing their will on directors. The popularity and significance of the shareholder meeting does suggest why a British shareholder might feel more involved in the governance of the corporation than a comparable American shareholder.

Company law provided further encouragement to the annual meeting function of British corporations. Shareholders in the UK were afforded some legal entitlements that were absent under most state corporate law

[202] Sears, *The New Place of the Stockholder*, p. 153.
[203] Jefferys, *Business Organisation in Great Britain*, p. 399.
[204] Royal Commission on the Depression (1886), p. 4592, quoted in ibid., p. 400.
[205] Jefferys, *Business Organisation in Great Britain*, p. 429.
[206] Sears, *The New Place of the Stockholder*, p. 150.
[207] Ibid., p. 150 (quoting the *Wall Street Journal*).

statutes in the USA. In the UK, for example, starting in 1900, share-holders collectively holding 10 percent or more of the stock had the right to call a meeting of the company.[208] The situation before 1900 was only somewhat less favorable. The default rule under Table A of the Companies Act of 1862 was that a general meeting could be called by 20 percent of the shareholders.[209] As Richard Nolan has explained, these rules reflected the basic assumption "that shareholders would make decisions at face-to-face meetings."[210] Even if the discussions at such meetings did not result in real changes,[211] they afforded the shareholders fairly significant power. According to Nolan, "the shareholders could require a meeting whether or not they had the power to do so under the company's articles, and whether or not the company's directors were willing to use their powers to call a meeting."[212] Given these background rules and the actual custom of participation, it therefore would not be surprising if the public conceived of the UK company as an aggregation of individual shareholders.

5.3   The effect on corporate tax design

The real differences in the nature of at least the large public industrial corporation in the USA and the UK during the first third of the twentieth century appeared to have an effect upon the development of the respec-tive corporate tax systems. In the UK, for instance, where large corpo-rations were often controlled by families or individual shareholders, tax measures often favored shareholders. During periods of concern about excessive distributions, though, tax measures were targeted at wealthy shareholders who were suspected of draining the corporate coffers at the expense of both labor and the economic community at large. By contrast, in the USA, where large corporations were often controlled by managers, tax measures often served to protect the corporation from the high

---

[208] Companies Act 1900, 63 & 64 Vict. c. 48, sec. 13; Cheffins, *Corporate Ownership and Control*, pp. 129–30. This right continues under modern law, but the threshold was lowered in 2009 to permit stockholders possessing 5 percent or more of the vote to call the meeting. See Christopher M. Bruner, "Power and Purpose in the 'Anglo-American' Corporation," *Virginia Journal of International Law* 50 (2010): 604.

[209] Companies Act 1862, 25 & 26 Vict. c. 89, Sch. 1, Table A, Art. 32; Cheffins, *Corporate Ownership and Control*, p. 130, n. 214.

[210] R. C. Nolan, "The Continuing Evolution of Shareholder Governance," *The Cambridge Law Journal* 65 (2006): 103.

[211] Cheffins, *Corporate Ownership and Control*, pp. 127–9.

[212] Nolan, "The Continuing Evolution of Shareholder Governance," 103.

graduated marginal rates applicable to individuals. During periods of concern about excessive retentions, though, tax measures were targeted at the entity level to limit the ability of managers to drain the corporate coffers at the expense of shareholders and the economic community at large. In other words, although both countries were worried about the problem of governmental expropriation or a tax burden that was too excessive for business to continue to thrive, the UK also worried about shareholder expropriation while the USA worried about managerial expropriation. Since laws and attitudes linger long after the facts supporting them have dissipated, tax policy continued to be animated by these concerns at least through the post-World War II period, and in some cases through to the current day.

5.3.1   UK focus on the shareholders

The most obvious evidence that the UK targeted the shareholder rather than the entity in its approach to corporate taxation was its use of an integrated system. Under the form of company taxation in effect in the early twentieth century, corporations were entitled to deduct from dividends the amount necessary to pay tax at the standard rate. Shareholders then received a credit for taxes paid on their behalf, effectively wiping out any standard-rate liability on that income. Although General Rule 20, adopted as part of the consolidation of the revenue laws in 1918, was held to merely authorize corporations to deduct the tax paid from dividends and did not require such deduction,[213] the effect was to leave the corporations and their shareholders free to arrange their affairs as they saw fit rather than impose a scheme that might not have conformed to custom.

Despite nominally imposing a tax on the corporation as a separate entity, the British system was considered to be consistent with the aggregate theory of corporations. In a memorandum submitted to the Royal Commission on the Taxation of Profits and Income in 1951, the Association of British Chambers of Commerce viewed the shareholder credit system as "broadly satisfactory," noting that "[a] company should be regarded as an association of individuals acting in common. While the income earned by the company is in the possession of the company, it should be regarded as being impersonal and be taxed at a flat rate. When the income comes into the possession of the individual members, it

[213] See Chapter 2.

should then be re-assessed in accordance with their total income."[214] The notion was that the corporation was treated as if it was a separate entity when the tax was imposed, but an adjustment was made when the money was distributed to shareholders.

Even when the British began to differentiate between corporations and other business vehicles, they did so in a way that suggested the true target was wealthy shareholders. Thus, as discussed in Chapter 2, when the super-tax was adopted under the Finance Act of 1910, it meant that the corporate and shareholder income taxes were not completely integrated in the sense that the shareholder credit did not cover any additional taxes due on the dividend received by shareholders.[215] Nevertheless, the super-tax was imposed at the shareholder level and only applied to those shareholders subject to the higher rates. Therefore, even if it burdened corporate income given the demographics of the typical shareholder, it was targeted at the shareholder rather than the entity itself. Similarly, corporate income was indirectly taxed at a higher rate than most individual income under the Finance Act of 1907,[216] but in a way that was focused at the shareholder-level. Since corporate income was classified as unearned because shareholders did not actively participate in the management and operation of a company, at least not in their shareholder capacity, then income from corporations (i.e. dividend payments) was effectively taxed at a higher rate. Under the integrated system, though, this was simply added to the shareholder's other sources of unearned income and collectively taxed at the higher rate for such income.

An obvious response to any attempt to characterize the UK company tax schemes as shareholder-focused is the adoption of various profits taxes during the twentieth century. The Corporation Profits Tax in place from 1920 to 1924 suggests that the British were not incapable of viewing the corporation as a separate entity, but, as discussed in Chapter 2, this was frequently characterized as an additional levy on shareholders. Indeed, the Profits Tax was adopted after the rejection of a proposal to subject corporations to the individual surtax as a means of checking avoidance of the surtax.[217] Part of the reason the tax was repealed after such a short lifespan was that the Labour party determined that it offered

---

[214] Association of British Chambers of Commerce to the Royal Commission on the Taxation of Profits and Income (see note 3 above), p. 108.
[215] See Chapter 2, above.   [216] See Chapter 2, above.
[217] Harold M. Groves, *Postwar Taxation and Economic Progress* (New York: McGraw-Hill Book Co., 1946), p. 69.

little aid in their quest to reach wealthy shareholders.[218] Moreover, Labour's Hugh Dalton pointed out that the tax disproportionately harmed ordinary shareholders since, unlike the preferred shareholders and fixed-income holders, their income fluctuated with the corporation's profits.[219]

The Differential Profits Tax enacted after World War II was even more clearly focused on wealthy shareholders than its predecessor. By taxing distributed profits at a higher rate than undistributed profits, the UK took an approach opposite to the Undistributed Profits Tax in use by the USA prior to the war. The Differential Profits Tax was aimed at dividends under the theory that profits were being drained by the wealthy shareholders through dividends rather than being reinvested in the company, and by extension, the economic community. Although shareholders had no formal power to declare dividends, the shareholder influence over dividends in corporate meetings and under the default provisions of British company law, even in the absence of effective shareholder control through family management or blockholding, gave credence to the idea that shareholders were responsible for dividend policy and taxation was a means of punishing shareholders. As Richard Whiting wrote in his book on the Labour Party's tax strategy, "Labour ministers gave strong support to the [differential profits] tax for the way it served the movement's general hostility to shareholders as much for its function in the management of demand. There was a good deal of feeling against the distribution of profits as dividends to 'non-producers' and a greater acceptance of them being ploughed back into the company to help 'the producers'."[220] Thus, the tax potentially served the dual function of punishing wealthy shareholders and either making more money available to pay the working class or, in the face of inflationary pressures, helping to rationalize wage limits.

The adoption of a classical corporate double tax in 1965, while seemingly marking a sharp departure from the integrated system of corporate taxation that it replaced, was in many ways an extension of the function and underlying rationale of the Differential Profits Tax.[221] The primary

[218] Richard C. Whiting, *The Labour Party and Taxation: Party Identity and Political Purpose in Twentieth-Century Britain* (Cambridge University Press, 2000), pp. 17–18.

[219] Ibid.; Martin J. Daunton, "How to Pay for the War: State, Society, and Taxation in Britain, 1917–24," *The English Historical Review* 111 (1996): 896.

[220] Whiting, *The Labour Party and Taxation*, p. 85.

[221] Daunton, *Just Taxes*, p. 290 ("The change implied a return to Dalton's differential profits tax of 1947 by another route.")

justification was once again the ability to restrain dividends, primarily as an anti-inflationary device, but also as a means of controlling wealthy shareholders and keeping the profits invested in the economy. According to Whiting, the double taxation of corporate income under the classical system was an aspect of its "political appeal . . . as a means of showing the trade unions [Labour] was serious about taxing dividends."[222] Indeed, part of the reason the adoption of a classical corporate income tax in 1965 was paired with the introduction for the first time of a Capital Gains Tax, was "to reassure the unions that dividend restraint would not simply lead to capital gains. The capital gains tax would 'provide a background of equity and fair play' for the government's wage policy."[223]

The adoption of a classical corporate tax, to the extent it reflects a shift in the conception of the corporation, also reflects the changing composition of British shareholders and the growing separation of ownership and control. By the 1960s, family control was on the wane and institutional investors had become much more prominent among equity investors. The percentage of shares owned by pension funds grew from 1 percent in 1957 to 17 percent in 1975, while insurance companies likewise extended their holdings from 8 percent in 1957 to 16 percent in 1975.[224] By the end of the 1970s, family ownership had been largely unwound in most British companies.[225] If the shareholder imputation system of corporate taxation had been influenced by the dominant presence of individual and family control, the transition to institutional control may have made the move to a classical corporate tax less troublesome. The British corporation and the American corporation had effectively converged.

5.3.2   US focus on the managers

Although the separate corporate tax in the USA operated to protect corporations from the high individual income tax rates so as to allow corporations to expand and flourish, there has been a counterbalancing concern that this offered managers too much power. As described in Chapter 3, a variety of provisions have been enacted to guard against managerial abuse

---

[222] Whiting, *The Labour Party and Taxation*, p. 159.   [223] Daunton, *Just Taxes*, p. 292.
[224] Cheffins and Bank, "Corporate Ownership and Control in the UK," 802.
[225] Geoffrey Jones and Keetie Sluyterman, "British and Dutch Business History," in Franco Amatori and Geoffrey Jones (eds.), *Business History Around the World* (Cambridge University Press, 2003), pp. 111, 116–18.

of the corporate form to retain earnings. This helps explain why, unlike in the UK, the corporate income tax has been more frequently focused at the entity level rather than at the shareholder level.

In the early days of the income tax, the push to separate the corporate and individual income taxes was motivated in part by a desire to help managers without allowing the corporation to serve as a vehicle for indefinite deferral. Initially, there were proposals to combat this indefinite deferral through accumulated earnings taxes such as the ones pushed by Senator Andrieus Jones starting in 1917.[226] When those proposals were defeated or amended to make them ineffective against all but the most egregious abuses, Congress raised the corporate normal tax rate above the individual income tax rate, transforming the exemption from the normal rate for dividends from nearly full to partial integration. This differential, which was supposed to provide a revenue stream similar to if the income had been distributed and subject to the individual surtax rates, thus permitted corporate managers to retain earnings free from shareholder pressure. Thus, the classical corporate income tax has its roots in a pro-manager policy.

There were a variety of New Deal tax measures aimed at corporate bigness and managerial power,[227] but the most prominent example was the Undistributed Profits Tax enacted in 1936. This responded to a deep-seated concern about managerial power over retained earnings during the 1920s. Rex Tugwell, a member of President Franklin D. Roosevelt's "Brain Trust" and a Columbia economics professor,[228] had argued that, because of managerial control over retained earnings, corporations "grow overconfident of the future and expand their own activities beyond all reason."[229] This dovetailed nicely with fellow Brain Truster Adolf Berle's conclusion that because of a growing separation between ownership and control managers increasingly became interested in using retained earnings to fund expansion plans or further their own job security, rather than to support dividends to stockholders.[230]

[226] See Chapter 3, above, at notes 23–26.

[227] Steven A. Bank, "Tax, Corporate Governance, and Norms," *Washington & Lee Law Review* 61 (2004): 1164.

[228] Daniel Fusfeld, *The Economic Thought of Franklin D. Roosevelt and the Origins of the New Deal* (New York: Columbia University Press, 1954), pp. 207–10. The other key academics in the Brain Trust were Adolf Berle and Raymond Moley.

[229] Rexford G. Tugwell, *The Industrial Discipline and the Governmental Arts* (New York: Columbia University Press, 1933), p. 205.

[230] Berle and Means, *The Modern Corporation and Private Property*, pp. 349–50.

Such concerns were not merely academic. One *New York Times* columnist wrote in 1936 that,

> [f]or a long time Washington has received complaints against managers of large corporations who, exercising minority control, decided to pile up large surpluses instead of passing them out in the form of dividends. This was done without consulting the scattered stockholding majorities, under powers granted by the charters of the corporation. But, however legal, and, in numerous instances, however wise, the policy has irritated many stockholders with the need or the wish for accessions to income.[231]

A letter to the *Wall Street Journal* echoed such sentiments, complaining about "the flippant and often insulting replies made by corporation presidents to stockholders who ask why they do not receive dividends when the aforesaid officials are drawing down enormous salaries" and suggesting that "[t]hese 'brass collars' are riding for a fall just the same as the old time railroad man."[232] The imposition of a tax of up to 27 percent on undistributed profits was specifically targeted at the abuse of retained earnings by corporate managers. Tugwell had suggested that government needed to "drive corporate surpluses into the open investment market" and out of the hands of managers through "a tax . . . imposed on funds, over and above replacement, which are kept for expansion purposes."[233] This reflected the US focus on the entity level during a period of concern about managerial expropriation.

---

[231] Arthur Krock, "Opposition is divided over President's tax proposal," *New York Times*, March 4, 1936, pp. 20, 22.

[232] W. R. Draper, Letter to the Editor, "Salaries, taxes, and dividends," *Wall Street Journal*, April 30, 1936, p. 4.

[233] Tugwell, *The Industrial Discipline*, p. 206.

6

Politics

The previous chapters have discussed the influence of profits and power in the development of the corporate income tax in the United Kingdom and the United States, but those explanations cannot possibly tell the whole story. After all, the British corporate tax system, in particular, underwent radical changes during the twentieth century, from an integrated approach to a classical approach and back again in less than a decade, while changes in dividend policy and corporate power have been much more gradual and less volatile over the same time period. The missing ingredient is the effect of politics on the approach to corporate taxation.

Because of structural differences between the legislative process in the USA and the UK, one might expect that politics would be less of a factor in the latter than the former. In the UK, the tax policymaking process has been described as "closed" or shrouded in "secrecy, with a strong emphasis on the exclusion of interest groups."[1] Tax measures are decided by British officials and voted upon in Parliament, with little room offered for amendment.[2] John Tiley observed that "[o]pposition parties can propose amendments, and sensible (such as technically helpful and zero-cost) ones will often be adopted by the government, but only on the basis that it does the drafting."[3] As a result, Michael Keen noted, tax

---

[1] Stephanie Hunter McMahon, "London Calling: Does the UK's Experience with Individual Taxation Clash with the US's Expectations?," 54 *St. Louis University Law Journal* (forthcoming 2011); Martin J. Daunton, *Just Taxes: The Politics of Taxation in Britain, 1914–1979* (Cambridge University Press, 2002), p. 18.

[2] Daunton, *Just Taxes*, pp. 18–20. See David W. Williams, "Taxing Statutes are Taxing Statutes: The Interpretation of Revenue Legislation," *Modern Law Review* 41 (1978): 404, 406 ("The power of the House of Lords to amend a Finance Bill is almost non-existent. The Commons regard it as a breach of their privileges if the Lords attempt to interfere with financial legislation . . . Finance Bills are therefore creatures of Treasury Ministers and their Revenue advisers.").

[3] John Tiley, "The United Kingdom," in *Comparative Income Taxation: A Structural Analysis*, 3rd edn. (Boston: Aspen Publishers, 2010), p. 157.

provisions "are commonly announced in the annual Budget speech of the Chancellor of the Exchequer as, in effect, *fait accompli*."[4] By contrast, in the USA, while the President may propose tax measures on his own or as part of the administrative process, bills themselves originate in and are negotiated by the legislative branch, with special interest groups afforded generous access to politicians who vote on proposed legislation and their staffers who advise them how to vote on the legislation.

Historically, special interests have had some access to the lawmaking process in the UK, but Martin Daunton suggests that this has been very limited.

> Officials and ministers might receive deputations or written submissions from the Federation (later Confederation) of British Industries (FBI), the TUC [Trades Union Congress] and other associations, but there was not a dialogue. These associations expressed their views and concerns, and would at most receive bland general assurances or statements of principle. The officials and ministers would not share their concerns or hint at any proposals for change in the tax system.[5]

This does not mean that British tax policymakers were "immune to special pleading,"[6] but it does suggest that this was much more difficult to achieve in the UK than in the USA.

Notwithstanding such structural obstacles to the politicization of the British corporate tax system, it appears that political influences affected the direction of reform in the latter half of the twentieth century. When Labour was in power, the focus was on taxing shareholders and other individuals perceived to be the beneficiaries of unearned income, rather than on taxing the company itself. The party targeted dividends for heavier taxation so as to reach wealthy shareholders and encourage corporations to plow their earnings back into the business and, indirectly, the workers. Accordingly, Labour pushed through the enactment of differential profits taxation and the adoption of the classical corporate income tax. By contrast, when Conservatives were in power, the focus was on allowing dividends to flow freely so as to encourage market forces to direct the flow of investment. Accordingly, that party repealed the differentiation feature of the profits tax and ushered in the return of a shareholder imputation approach.

---

[4] Michael Keen, "Peculiar Institutions: A British Perspective on Tax Policy in the United States," *Fiscal Studies* 18 (1997): 371, 392.

[5] Daunton, *Just Taxes*, p. 20.   [6] Keen, "Peculiar Institutions," 393.

Moreover, even if special interests did not actively participate in a discussion on the merits of proposed legislation in the UK, various groups interacted with these political parties to exercise behind-the-scenes influence on the development of their respective tax positions. Thus, the Trades Union Congress ("TUC") was often influential in the Labour Party, sometimes involved quite directly in Labour's budget preparations directly or through its representatives on Labour's National Executive Council,[7] even though the two groups did not always see eye-to-eye on the appropriate focus of taxation.[8] Similarly, although the Federation of British Industry ("FBI") and other business trade groups were not as connected with the Conservative Party as the TUC was with Labour, they were viewed as counterweights to the TUC and were often sought out as a source of business views on an issue.[9]

In the USA, the influence of politics and special interest groups is clearly evident in the development of the corporate income tax, but more for preventing fundamental change than for promoting it. Although rates have changed over the years and corporate tax preference items have proliferated, significant reform has been elusive. Some of the more radical corporate tax proposals to be seriously considered during the early to mid twentieth century, such as the Undistributed Profits Tax during the New Deal and the dividend tax cut during Dwight D. Eisenhower's first term in office, were watered down in the final legislation and were ultimately scaled back and repealed. In part, this is because the business community, which has been the most involved in discussions over corporate taxation generally, has never reached a consensus about its interest in altering the current system. It is also due to the fact that unions and other progressive groups, while stymied by their own disagreements, served as a practical counter-weight to many proposals that appeared to favor corporations over low- and middle-income individuals in the interwar period and after World War II. Only on smaller or more technical issues, involving very specialized interests, was reform possible.

---

[7] Richard Whiting, *The Labour Party and Taxation: Party Identity and Political Purpose in Twentieth-Century Britain* (Cambridge University Press, 2000), p. 254; Ann Robinson and Cedric Sandford, *Tax Policy-Making in the United Kingdom: A Study of Rationality, Ideology and Politics* (London: Heinemann Educational Books, 1983), pp. 67–8. According to Robinson and Sandford, "[a]lthough almost half of the membership of the NEC consists of trade unionists elected by trade unionists, the TUC has preferred a more direct approach in its dealings with the Labour Party since 1974 through the TUC Labour Party Liaison Committee." Ibid.

[8] Whiting, *The Labour Party and Taxation*, p. 231.

[9] Daunton, *Just Taxes*, p. 22; Robinson and Sandford, *Tax Policy-Making in the UK*, p. 76.

6.1   United Kingdom

In the UK, politics played an important role in the development of corporate taxation. This did not mean that each party always got its way when it had control over Parliament, but the views of the parties and their allies were fundamental in shaping the compromises that emerged.

6.1.1   World War I and the 1920s

In the early twentieth century, politics were particularly evident in the UK as the country struggled to finance wartime expenses. Beginning in World War I and continuing in its immediate aftermath, there was substantial agitation from the Labour Party and the TUC for the imposition of a one-time "capital levy" as a means of paying down the war debt.[10] According to Labour leader Hugh Dalton, "[t]he Capital Levy, as proposed by the Labour Party, would be a special emergency payment by all individuals owning more than a certain amount of wealth. This payment would be graduated according to individual ability to pay."[11] As early as 1916, the TUC adopted a resolution in favor of the "conscript [ion] . . . of the accumulated wealth of the country" and it was a central plank of the Labour Party's platform in 1922 and 1923.[12]

It is not surprising that the Labour Party would be concerned about the allocation of the tax burden as between individual wage earners and the owners of accumulated wealth. The members of the working class that Labour presumed to represent had cause to feel burdened not only because they bore a higher brunt of the physical sacrifice of fighting the war as compared with the wealthy, but also because they bore a non-trivial part of the burden from the rise in fiscal sacrifice through higher income tax rates. Although the wealthy saw the highest increases in rates,[13] the tax burden on wage earners increased by 3.7 times.[14] Even

---

[10] M. J. Daunton, "How to Pay for the War: State, Society and Taxation in Britain, 1917–24," *The English Historical Review* 111 (1996): 882, 890.

[11] Hugh Dalton, *The Capital Levy Explained* (London: The Labour Publishing Company, Ltd., 1923), p. 29.

[12] Daunton, *Just Taxes*, p. 890 (quoting TUC Resolution, Birmingham, September 1916), 896.

[13] Individuals earning £50,000 per year paid at an 8.4 percent rate at the outset of the war and at a 50.6 percent rate at the conclusion of the war. Hew Strachan, *Financing the First World War* (Oxford University Press, 2004), p. 78.

[14] Ibid.

wage earners in the lowest tax bracket saw their tax levy double.[15] The capital levy was designed to shift some of the burden to wealthy shareholders drawing their income from stocks and securities.

What may be surprising is that, even though a healthy percentage of the country's accumulated wealth remained in companies,[16] in proposing the capital levy Labour's focus was to target wealthy shareholders and not the corporations themselves. As Dalton explained, "[i]t is a point of fundamental importance, which is not always understood, that the basis of assessment would be individual and not corporate. No Company would be liable to the Levy, though its individual shareholders would be liable, if their total net wealth, including their shares in the Company, exceeded a certain figure."[17]

This was not merely a semantic or administrative choice to focus on shareholders. Although J. A. Hobson, a future member of the Labour Party's Advisory Committee on Trade and Finance, was one of the first to push for profits taxation,[18] initially this was not favored by the Labour Party itself. Indeed, Labour was considered "hostile to taxation of company profits," with Dalton arguing that it was "especially objectionable, discriminating against ordinary shareholders in joint-stock companies as compared with other property owners, and discouraging, in a specially high degree, the taking of business risks."[19] Martin Daunton explained that "[c]ompany taxation contradicted Labour's strategy of taxing 'unearned' income and instead seemed to place a tax on enterprise. A tax on an aggregate body was also criticized as a departure from the basic principle of taxing individuals on their ability to pay," presumably because the shareholders would bear the burden of the tax regardless of whether and at what rate they actually owed tax.[20]

Nevertheless, Labour leaders began to recognize that support for a capital levy was becoming counterproductive in political terms. The TUC and the Labour Party's joint research group had come to believe that the net revenues from the levy would be lower than originally predicted. As Daunton explained, "continued support of the levy became less a matter of fiscal pragmatism and more a device for creating public

---

[15] Ibid.

[16] Estimates for the percentage of retained profits in 1922 and 1923 range from 15 percent to 30 percent. William A. Thomas, *The Finance of British Industry 1918–1976* (London: Methuen & Co. Ltd., 1978), p. 94, tbl. 4.5.

[17] Dalton, *The Capital Levy Explained*, p. 30.

[18] Whiting, *The Labour Party and Taxation*, p. 17.

[19] Daunton, "How to Pay for the War," 914.   [20] Ibid.

ownership and changing the social structure. It was becoming more difficult to deny that the Trojan horse of debt redemption hid a socialist menace."[21] Thus, Daunton concluded, "[t]he leadership of the Labour party found it expedient to retreat" on the question of the capital levy, referring it for more study.[22]

Thus, the Treasury was able to push through the more politically acceptable Corporation Profits Tax in 1920, which would for the first time add a classical system-style tax on corporate profits to the existing imputation tax on shareholders. This was hardly an endorsement of the classical system, though. Indeed, from the perspective of its proponents, the Corporation Profits Tax was forwarded to "block more radical proposals from Labour for 100 per cent EPD or a capital levy."[23] Although Labour did believe that the Corporation Profits Tax could serve as "a device to construct a producers' alliance between workers, small shopkeepers, and businessmen with moderate incomes against *rentiers* 'who can live in idleness on the productive work of others',"[24] it proceeded to abolish the tax in the first Labour budget in 1924.[25]

6.1.2   World War II and the postwar era

During World War II, Labour remained focused on shareholder wealth. In 1940, the Labour Party's Home Policy Committee "reiterated the old nostrum of an attack on unearned wealth through death duties, an increase in the graduation of the income tax and a capital levy in order to break 'that ugly tradition which binds poverty in one generation to poverty in the next, and perpetuates great fortunes by unearned inheritance'."[26] According to the policy statement, which was unanimously adopted at the Labour Party's Annual Convention, "[t]he Labour Party does not seek to treat harshly those who have profited by an outworn and unjust system. But we are convinced that the existing vast differences in wealth poison the relation between classes in a way that is incompatible with the achievement of a common good."[27] Unearned income was viewed as an obstacle to egalitarianism and reinvested profits were an acceptable and efficient step toward supply-side economic planning and even nationalized

---

[21] Ibid., 895.   [22] Ibid., 896.   [23] Ibid., 900.   [24] Ibid., 891.
[25] Daunton, *Just Taxes*, p. 93.   [26] Ibid., p. 190.
[27] *Labour's Home Policy*, unanimously adopted by the Annual Conference of the Labour Party, May 1940, at 7.

production.[28] Accordingly, Labour recommended "a bold capital levy" and "other taxes falling on . . . forms of unearned increment."[29]

One specific area where Labour's focus on unearned income was particularly sharp was the relationship between dividend policy and wages. Because of concerns about runaway inflation, governments had been pressuring unions to accept wage limits in the late 1940s and early 1950s. From the perspectives of trade union leaders, though, there was an intimate connection between union wage demands and corporate dividend policy. The president of the Union of Shop, Distributive, and Allied Workers reportedly told the participants in a conference of professional and industrial workers held in the spring of 1950 that although "wage restraint was an irksome necessity if workers' living standards were to be maintained . . . they had the right to demand more stringent measures with regard to dividends, inflated salaries, and directors' fees."[30] At the same conference, a top official of the Clerical and Administrative Workers' Union recommended conditioning wage restraints on an agreement "that incomes from management, profits, and interest should be restrained as well."[31] A few months later, the president of the Amalgamated Engineering Union suggested at the union's annual meeting that there be a legal limit imposed on dividends and "any surplus earned by companies over and above the legal limit should be shared in agreed proportions between workers and employers."[32]

Related to this was a concern that corporations were manipulating financial accounting statements and keeping dividends high to siphon money away from labor and toward wealthy shareholders through dividends. This was a long-standing issue. As far back as the 1920s, Labour had been concerned about the use of "hidden reserves" in financial accounting by many companies. Such reserves were purportedly designed to allow the company to pay a stable dividend without appearing too profitable and thereby attract the attention of workers seeking higher wages. Labour leader Ernest Bevin, reflecting his party's perception of this practice, stated that: "reserves . . . are really the unpaid wages of industry."[33]

---

[28] See Daunton, *Just Taxes*, pp. 201–2.   [29] *Labour's Home Policy*, 7.
[30] "Limits of Wage Restraint," *The Times* (London), April 10, 1950.   [31] Ibid.
[32] "Limitation of Dividends," *The Times* (London), June 13, 1950.
[33] Janette Rutterford, "From Dividend Yield to Discounted Cash Flow: A History of UK and US Equity Valuation Techniques," *Accounting, Business & Financial History* 14 (2004): 115, 130.

Regardless of the origins of this concern about dividends, it was clear that they had become a political fixation for the Labour Party. *The Times* wrote in 1950 that "[i]t is almost unnecessary now to recall that the original undertaking to limit dividends was given on political and psychological rather than economic grounds."[34] Thus, it was not surprising that union groups supported the Differential Profits Tax enacted after World War II. In a memorandum submitted to the Royal Commission on the Taxation of Profits and Income, the TUC wrote that

> [o]ur support of the Profits Tax in principle is based mainly on the grounds that the community as a whole (through the Government) is entitled to share in the additional profits which accrue to companies on conditions of full employment. As we have already pointed out, full employment increases demand and reduces risk: thus the high profits earned in times of full employment cannot be regarded merely as the reward of efficiency and enterprise but as, at least in recent part, the result of exploiting conditions not created by the business community.[35]

The TUC specifically endorsed the differential higher rate on distributed profits, responding to a question on this point that "[w]e think that the existence of a differential . . . has encouraged firms to plough back profits into their businesses with a consequent increase in efficiency and the level of production and productivity, so the existence of a differential there, we are satisfied, is a desirable thing."[36]

These sentiments were consistent with Labour leaders' statements on the necessity of a Differential Profits Tax. As Whiting pointed out, "Labour ministers gave strong support to the tax for the way it served the movement's general hostility to shareholders as much as for its function in the management of demand. There was a good deal of feeling against the distribution of profits as dividends to 'non-producers' and a greater acceptance of them being ploughed back into the company to help 'the producers'."[37] Thus, for example, in his Budget statement at the end of the war, Labour's Chancellor of the Exchequer, Hugh Dalton, had urged dividend restraint on the grounds that the money needed to be reinvested in companies rather than put into shareholders' pockets:

> Last autumn I expressed the view that post-war development should come before increased dividends, and I invited industry to plough back

---

[34] "Dividend Policy Next Year," *The Times* (London), December 18, 1950, p. 10.
[35] Memorandum submitted by the Trades Union Congress to the Royal Commission on the Taxation of Profits and Income (London, 1952), p. 237.
[36] Ibid., 247.   [37] Whiting, *The Labour Party and Taxation*, p. 85.

increased profits rather than distribute them to shareholders. The
response to this invitation has been very patchy. Many of the most
efficient and up-to-date concerns have responded very well, but others
have shown a tendency to chuck money about among the shareholders
rather than to strengthen their reserves and buy up the latest
equipment.[38]

According to Dalton, this lack of voluntary self-restraint had led him to
consider whether "it would be in the general interests to introduce a new
tax designed to check these . . . unfortunate practices."[39]

Dalton subsequently supported the profits tax in his Budget speech in
1947 by explaining that "these increased dividends are a case of paying more
money for no work at all."[40] He tied together the anti-inflation rationale for
the tax with Labour's anti-shareholder rationale by noting that

> the cheap money policy has reduced . . . the income of many *rentiers* or
> other persons living on redeemable fixed-interest-bearing securities. The
> equity stockholder has suffered no such disadvantage, and in some cases,
> may have actually gained through capital reconstructions which have
> improved his relative position . . . An increased Profits Tax, therefore,
> whatever may be said about it generally, has a special justification in these
> days of cheap money, in order to do justice as between one section and
> another of those who receive income from investments.[41]

This does not mean, though, that Labour leaders were altogether
unanimous in their disdain for dividends. Martin Daunton has explained
that even many advocates of differential profits taxation in the Labour
Party acknowledged that retained earnings were not altogether a positive
if they simply permitted the payment of higher dividends at a later date
or if they acted to increase the value of the stock and thereby further
enrich the shareholders.[42] Even Dalton himself had criticized profits
taxation when it had been employed earlier after World War I, a point
which opponents raised during the debates in Parliament.[43]
Nevertheless, Dalton maintained that the combination of inflation and
the disproportionate effect it had on certain kinds of investment justified
pursuing profits taxation and adding the differential feature in the wake
of World War II.[44] Trying to placate the unions, particularly when he

[38] "The Budget," *The Times* (London), April 10, 1946, p. 6. See also *Hansard*, HC, vol. 414,
ser. 5, cols. 1896–7 (1945).
[39] "The Budget," *The Times* (London), April 10, 1946, p. 6.
[40] *Hansard*, HC, vol. 436, ser. 5, col. 84 (1947).   [41] Ibid., cols. 84–5.
[42] Daunton, *Just Taxes*, p. 205.   [43] *Hansard*, HC, vol. 436, ser. 5, col. 1117 (1947).
[44] Ibid., col. 1130.

was also pressing for wage controls, Dalton soon doubled the rate on dividends, explaining "I have noticed, with regret, a continuing and persistent inclination on the part of many concerns to declare increased dividends. This is contrary to advice which I have ventured to offer from time to time; it is inflationary, because it puts more purchasing power in circulation; and it is very disturbing to industrial relations."[45]

In contrast to Labour, business groups were generally opposed to profits taxation, although they focused more on the entity-level Undistributed Profits Tax than the higher rate imposed on distributed profits. The FBI opposed the Profits Tax in part because it objected to the double taxation of company income.[46] In the Federation's 1952 memorandum on the Royal Commission on the Taxation of Profits and Income, it declared that

> so far as the Profits Tax is concerned the Federation has consistently held the view that there is no justification of any kind for the discrimination against companies which this tax represents. The tax is imposed in addition to income tax and is a deduction in arriving at the profit chargeable to income tax. This double-layered taxation of corporate profits has the effect of obscuring the true rate of taxation upon those profits which is, of course, a higher rate than either the income tax rate or the Profits tax rate taken separately.[47]

As Sir Paul Chambers of the FBI pleaded, "every time there is an additional profits tax on distributed profits there appears to be the inference that the payment of dividends is a bad and an improper thing; that, from the point of view of British industry, we regard as unsound."[48] When pressed, though, Chambers conceded that "in so far as there may be a question of reducing the profits tax, there is much to be said for reducing it on undistributed profits before you reduce it on distributed

---

[45] *Hansard*, HC, vol. 444, ser. 5, col. 401 (1947).

[46] See Daunton, *Just Taxes*, p. 320. It also may have represented either an extension of the hostility to any entity-level tax, whether a profits tax or a corporation tax, that characterized their opposition in the 1950s (see text accompanying notes 79–81), or a concern for the instability that the new measures would bring. See Stephen Blank, *Industry and Government in Britain: The Federation of British Industries in Politics, 1945–65* (Westmead/Lexington: Saxon House/Lexington Books, 1973), p. 224.

[47] Federation of British Industries, Memorandum submitted to the Royal Commission on the Taxation of Profits and Income (London, 1952), p. 82.

[48] Minutes of Evidence Taken before the Royal Commission on the Taxation of Profits and Income (November 1, 1951), p. 84 (testimony of Mr. S. P. Chambers, Federation of British Industries).

profits."[49] The FBI's focus was clearly on the entity-level tax rather than on the differential rate on dividends.

The National Union of Manufacturers opposed profits taxation generally, but it too reserved its greatest displeasure for the tax on undistributed profits. In a 1951 letter to the Chancellor of the Exchequer, it declared that "present circumstances establish an overwhelming case for the abolition of the profits tax on undistributed profits."[50] Later that year, in its opening memorandum submitted to the Royal Commission on the Taxation of Profits and Income, the group indicated that it took "special exception [to] the Profits Tax on undistributed profits."[51] When asked whether this opposition carried over to the tax on distributed profits, W. R. Clemens, representing the group, said "at the present time I think there must be some business tax on profits in addition to the normal income tax; therefore tax on the distribution of those profits is fair, but not on the undistributed profits, because that is what is required for the business to endeavour to assist the working capital of which there is a tremendous dearth at the present time, particularly among our members of the smaller calibre."[52]

Similarly, during the same hearings before the Royal Commission, the Association of British Chambers of Commerce also focused on the need for business to accumulate retained earnings as a means of financing corporate growth and expansion. In its memorandum, the Association explained that "[s]elf-financing is the best kind of investment from the national aspect because it is discriminating and the money is the most economically used. It is bad for the State to expropriate these savings by means of the Profits Tax because the State cannot invest them as profitably as the business can."[53]

Some have suggested that business groups were not merely ambivalent about the higher rate on distributed profits, but actually welcomed it for two reasons. First, it may have aided them in their negotiations with unions over wages. In his 1951 Budget message, Chancellor of the

---

[49] Ibid.

[50] "Tax on Undistributed Profits, Manufacturers' Call for Abolition," *The Times* (London), April 2, 1951, p. 3.

[51] The National Union of Manufacturers, Memorandum submitted to the Royal Commission on the Taxation of Profits and Income (November 2, 1951), p. 125.

[52] Minutes of Evidence, Royal Commission on the Taxation of Profits and Income (London, 1952), p. 128.

[53] Memorandum submitted by the Association of British Chambers of Commerce to the Royal Commission on the Taxation of Profits and Income (London, 1952), p. 108.

Exchequer Hugh Gaitskell claimed that business trade groups did not object to the heavier tax on distributions in part because they believed that higher dividends led to demand for higher wages and subjecting dividends to an external constraint would allow them to reduce dividends without drawing the ire of shareholders.[54] Second, some businesses, especially larger ones with dispersed ownership in the period after World War II, may have viewed a higher tax on dividends as an ally in their quest to retain a higher percentage of their earnings. This was reported during the debates over the imposition of a classical corporate income tax during the mid 1960s. According to *The Economist*, "a good few company chairmen" applauded the proposed adoption of a tax disincentive to distributions because they saw "dividends as an extravagance and retained profits as the real source of expansion."[55] Malcolm Crawford explained, "companies in industry and commerce here prefer financing from retentions, treating external finance as a residual source, for meeting peaks in investment programmes, or when forced into the market by a credit squeeze."[56] As evidence of the residual nature of capital market financing, Crawford noted that large dividend distributions were not matched by large public offerings of additional stock.[57] There was some suggestion that stockholder pressure would counterbalance business's temptation to use the new tax as justification to increase retained earnings,[58] but others thought that the tax would "widen the gulf between modern and contemporary industrial management and the shareholders" so as to increase the power of the former to ignore the demands of the latter.[59]

The combination of Labour's focus on targeting shareholders and the absence of significant business opposition was the perfect political recipe for the adoption of the differential rate on distributed profits. Although the two groups had different aims and neither was satisfied with the other, this uneasy and implicit coalition helped maintain the profits tax

---

[54] See A. Rubner, "The Irrelevancy of the British Differential Profits Tax," *Economic Journal* 74 (1964): 347, 352.

[55] "Labour's Tax Imprint," *The Economist* 738 (1964).

[56] Malcolm Crawford, "The 1965 Reforms in the British Tax System," *Moorgate and Wall Street*, Autumn (1965): 38, 42.

[57] Ibid.

[58] See *Hansard*, HC, vol. 712, ser. 5, cols. 131–2 (1965) (statement of Mr. Duffy) ("We know, and some hon. Members opposite know better than we do, how many directors are so concerned for their standing in the markets that they will be tempted to cut back retentions to preserve dividends.").

[59] *Hansard*, HC, vol. 713, ser. 5, col. 1829 (1965) (statement of Mr. Biffen).

for more than a decade. It survived even the ascendency of the Conservative Party in 1951, in part because of the paralysis suffered by the party over fiscal policy. As Martin Daunton explained, "[b]etween 1951 and 1964, chancellors were cautious, fearing the political conse-quences of radical change. There was a sense of being trapped by the existing institutional structures and trade-offs."[60] Robert Hall, a top Treasury official and academic, despaired that it was unlikely that "we could make new Ministers, if they are Conservative, take painful deci-sions. They are very nearly pledged to do little about social services, they certainly do not want to produce more unemployment, and they cannot really start by making taxes much more regressive."[61]

Notwithstanding the distaste for radical change, Conservatives did manage to reduce the bite of the Differential Profits Tax. As described in Chapter 2, the rate on distributed profits was cut in half and the rate on undistributed profits was lowered even further.[62] For a short time in the mid-1950s, the Conservatives accepted the recommendations of the minority report from the Royal Commission on the Taxation of Profits and Income and reversed course, raising the differential rate on distrib-uted profits. By 1958, however, Conservatives declared the experiment a failure and omitted the differential rates entirely from the Budget pro-posal for that year. Perhaps sensing that its argument that the rise in dividends would have been greater in the absence of the preferential rates lacked rhetorical force, "the Labour Party did not mount a concerted attack" against this omission.[63]

6.1.3   1960s and 1970s

The classical corporate income tax

Labour's return to power in 1964 led directly to a shift toward a classical corporate income tax. Just as about the Differential Profits Tax, the Labour Party and the Conservative Party had very different views about the appropriate use of corporate profits. As Conservative member Terrence Higgins pointed out during the 1965 debates over the Corporation Tax, "there is a fundamental difference between the two

---

[60] Daunton, *Just Taxes*, p. 233.
[61] Ibid. (quoting *The Robert Hall Diaries, 1947–1953* (A. Cairncross, ed.) (London, 1989), p. 174).
[62] See Chapter 2.
[63] Rubner, "The Irrelevancy of the British Differential Profits Tax," 347, 354.

parties; whether we believe profits should be ploughed back into companies and taxes should encourage this, or whether we should encourage the distribution of profits and the operation of the capital market in such a way that capital is attracted into new uses by market forces."[64] Labour not only anticipated that the imposition of a double tax would have a potential adverse effect on dividends, but welcomed this. *The Economist* stated that "this discrimination against distributed income is among the attractions of a corporation tax for Labour, which (like a few good company chairmen) sees dividends as an extravagance and retained profits as the real source of expansion."[65] Richard Whiting pointed out that the Corporation Tax, like its predecessor the Differential Profits Tax, was connected to demands for wage restraint and to concerns about shareholder wealth:

> Using a tax to squeeze dividend receivers, which was the most "political" aspect of the 1965 corporation tax, had already been tried in the 1947 profits tax, which differentiated in favour of retained rather than distributed profits. This has been devised to encourage trade union support for pay restraint, and observed a long-held radical distinction between producers and non-producers. It was the distribution of the "surplus" to non-producing shareholders which aroused trade union anger, rather than the creation of profits themselves.[66]

Effectively, it was not some sudden change in the underlying economic or organizational circumstances that prompted this switch to the classical corporate double tax system, although the gradual changes on both fronts helped lay the groundwork for this reform, but rather the change in the party in control of government.

This political effect was well understood. Business had anticipated that Labour's victory would likely translate into a reversal in corporate tax policy. Indeed, the idea of a corporation tax had "been on the Labour Party's drawing board for ten years."[67] Nicholas Kaldor's memorandum of dissent to the Royal Commission report had provided the blueprint for the corporation tax and Kaldor had assumed a forceful leadership role for Labour on tax matters, which "was clearly attractive to Labour at a time when their 'in-house' talent, Hugh Dalton, was coming to the end

---

[64] *Hansard*, HC, vol. 710, ser. 5, col. 105 (1965).
[65] "Hitting Dividends, Sideways," *The Economist*, November 14, 1964, p. 738.
[66] R. C. Whiting, "Ideology and Reform in Labour's Tax Strategy, 1964–1970," *The Historical Journal* 41 (1998): 1121, 1125.
[67] A. R. Prest, "The Corporation Tax," *District Bank Review* (1965): 3, 24.

of his career."[68] The Federation of British Industries wrote in its in-house journal in 1964 that "[i]t is common knowledge that the Labour Party would wish to relieve the tax burden on individual taxpayers at the expense of corporate bodies, and that this would almost certainly be accompanied by revival of the dual rate profits tax; and that some form of capital taxation, probably by increasing the impact of the tax on capital gains is likely."[69]

Notwithstanding the advance warning, business groups did not offer significant opposition to this move to a classical corporate income tax. There were reports that "British companies [were] complaining bitterly about the new tax proposals," but either such protests did not lead to active opposition or that opposition was not particularly effective.[70] As discussed previously, in part this may have been because of the general indifference of some businesses to higher dividends. According to a report from London in the *New York Times* in the fall of 1966, "the dividend curbs have not sparked any great outcry in the business community because the outlook for corporate profits is rather grim in an economy now swinging into recession."[71] The business community may have decided to defer a battle on this issue until profits returned to normal levels.

One additional factor that may have limited business influence at this point is that there had not been a single voice for business issues during major policy debates. Up until 1960, the Federation of British Industries had been "viewed as the voice of British industry" on a variety of issues, although it perhaps would be better to characterize it as a somewhat reluctant spokesman.[72] With a broad and diverse membership, the Federation preferred to react to legislative matters as they arose, fostering a "reputation for political neutrality and technical competence."[73] According to Stephen Blank, this ad hoc approach "thus minimized in terms of its own internal politics the whole notion of policy... It also

---

[68] Whiting, "Ideology and Reform," 1125.

[69] "Taxation Notes: Second Thoughts," *FBI Review* 170 (1964): 53.

[70] Clyde H. Farnsworth, "Tax Battle of Britain," *New York Times*, May 1, 1965, p. 34; "Foreboding over Finance Bill," *The Times* (London), June 2, 1965, p. 18.

[71] Clyde H. Farnsworth, "Freeze on dividends working in Britain with no big outcry," *New York Times*, October 12, 1966, p. 57; "Britain expects firms to avoid increases in dividends this year," *Wall Street Journal*, October 6, 1966, p. 2.

[72] See John Sheail, "Business and the Environment: An Inter-War Perspective on the Federation of British Industries," *Contemporary British History* 11 (1997): 21.

[73] Blank, *Industry and Government in Britain*, p. 213.

helped the leaders of the Federation deal with a problem they so deeply feared, of dividing the organization's membership."[74]

Moreover, the Federation was often at odds with similar organizations, which diminished the effectiveness of all groups. As Blank observed, "[t]he representation of industry's interests at the national level was made more difficult in Britain between 1916 and 1965 by the existence of competing peak associations."[75] For example, distrust of Federation leaders after World War I led to the formation of a separate organization, called the British Employers' Confederation (BEC), to handle labor issues.[76] This new group reportedly "posed recurring problems for the FBI,"[77] in part because it was much more decentralized than the Federation and it was far more secret about its activities.[78] Sir Norman Kipping, the Federation's Director General between 1946 and 1965, reported "I cannot pretend that we in the FBI found our relations with the BEC either easy or particularly congenial."[79] Thus, even if the Federation had been a spokesperson during the mid to late 1950s, this was no longer true a few years later. "By 1961, however, when Britain first applied to join the EEC, the FBI was far more circumspect and less influential and two years later was simply relieved that the negotiations had broken down as this ended a period of uncertainty for business."[80] In some respects, the FBI had become a bit of an outlier. For example, the Conservative government had established the National Economic Development Council, or "Neddy," as it was called, in 1961 to work with industry toward the development of national economic policy.[81] One of the first issues Neddy grappled with, a proposal for a profits tax regulator that would cause a profits tax to rise if aggregate profits increased more than aggregate wages, was accepted by the BEC, the National Association of British Manufacturers (NABM), and the Association of British Chambers of Commerce, but the FBI refused to support it and the issue ultimately died until Labour resumed power.[82]

[74] Ibid., pp. 213–14.   [75] Ibid., p. 199.
[76] Wyn Grant and David Marsh, *The Confederation of British Industry* (London: Hodder and Stoughton, 1977), p. 20.
[77] Ibid., p. 20.   [78] Blank, *Industry and Government in Britain*, p. 18.
[79] Grant and Marsh, *The Confederation of British Industry*, p. 20.
[80] Alan McKinlay, Helen Mercer, and Neil Rollings, "Reluctant Europeans? The Federation of British Industries and European Integration, 1945–63," *Business History* 42 (2000): 91, 92.
[81] Blank, *Industry and Government in Britain*, p. 5.   [82] Ibid., p. 187.

It soon became apparent that this arrangement for discussion of matters of interest to business was unacceptable. Wyn Grant and David Marsh noted that "[i]n the context of the renewed interest in economic planning after 1960, the need for more effective arrangements for the representation of industrial opinion became more pressing."[83] At the encouragement of the government, the FBI, the BEC, and the NABM began talks toward merging the three organizations that ultimately resulted in the creation of the Confederation of British Industry (CBI) in 1965.[84] For the first time, one industry group represented both trade groups and employers groups and this allowed it to attain much greater influence than its predecessors.[85] Nevertheless, this united voice quickly broke down. According to Stephen Blank, "[t]he weakening of the original consensus on economic policy and the rise of new and contentious issues . . . encouraged a growing divisiveness within the organization," culminating in a near "revolt" within the Confederation in the fall of 1967.[86] By 1970, observers were openly questioning the power of the CBI, with *The Times* asking in a headline, "just how influential is the CBI?"[87]

Regardless of the reason, it was clear that trade unions directly and indirectly affected tax policy more than business groups during this period. This was true even when Conservatives were in power. According to Richard Whiting,

> Conservatives adopted [a capital gains tax in 1962] because they thought it was a necessary part of any agreement which they might strike with the trade unions over incomes policy . . . As they tried to contain demand through incomes policies, the Conservatives felt that their best chance with the trade unions lay in convincing them that the government was being "fair," in that all forms of economic reward would be under some kind of control.[88]

Finally, in addition to the domestic political change that led to the adoption of a classical corporate income tax, there were external political factors that helped shape this change. As the FBI explained, there was significant pressure for tax reform designed to harmonize British and European laws preceding the entry of the UK into the European

---

[83] Grant and Marsh, *The Confederation of British Industry*, p. 25.   [84] Ibid., pp. 25–6.
[85] Blank, *Industry and Government in Britain*, p. 228.   [86] Ibid., pp. 233–4.
[87] Maurice Corina, "Just how influential is the CBI?," *The Times* (London), March 10, 1970, p. 26.
[88] Whiting, "Ideology and Reform," 1128.

Economic Community.[89] More specifically, the Brussels committee considering the future tax structure of the EEC "recommend[ed] the introduction of a separate corporation income tax."[90] It did not advocate imposing double taxation; instead, it suggested "that profits ploughed back should be taxed more heavily than the profits distributed to shareholders. This would ensure that taxpayers would not be taxed twice on their dividends."[91] Not surprisingly, the FBI disfavored this approach. The group cited with some measure of approval or interest a paper by the chairman of the Fiscal and Financial Committee of the EEC, which had recommended a flat corporate rate and a second corporate tax "which would be graduated according to 'the proportion of profits to the working capital of the company'."[92] This was similar to the German system, which subjected retained earnings to a higher tax than distributions, with the combined corporate and shareholder rate on dividends equaling the rate on retentions. According to Daunton, many businesses did not want to "plough back earnings into reserves and expos[e] them to the discipline of the market."[93] The trend in Europe was to follow the EEC and German approach, but the UK was moving in the opposite direction.[94]

The return to shareholder imputation

Not surprisingly, the government ended the experiment with a classical corporate tax and returned to the shareholder imputation system soon after the Conservatives returned to power in 1970. In his first Budget statement of the new Parliament, Chancellor of the Exchequer Anthony Barber announced that he intended "to reform the structure" of the Corporation Tax after giving "adequate time for consideration and consultation" and "regard to the developments in company taxation within the EEC."[95] According to Barber, the Conservative Party "are and always have been opposed to the substantial discrimination which it [the Corporation Tax] entails in favour of retained as opposed to distributed profits. This discrimination distorts the working of market forces and so tends towards the misallocation of scarce investment

---

[89] "Taxation Notes: Capital Allowances," *FBI Review* 152 (1963): 59, 61.   [90] Ibid.
[91] Ibid.
[92] Ibid. (citing a paper by Prof. Neumark printed in *The Accountant*, December 1, 1962).
[93] Daunton, *Just Taxes*, p. 320.   [94] Prest, "The Corporation Tax," 3, 7.
[95] *Hansard*, HC, vol. 814, ser. 5, col. 1383 (1971). See *Reform of Corporation Tax, presented to Parliament by the Chancellor of the Exchequer* (March 1971), which was released immediately following the Budget statement.

resources."[96] Although Barber acknowledged that they were still considering possible alternatives, he stated that "the conclusion we have reached is
that the present system of corporation tax should be replaced by one which
would be neutral as between distributed and undistributed profits."[97]

When Labour regained power in 1974, they did not seek a revival of
the Corporation Tax. Instead of focusing on corporate shareholders, the
party focused on wealthy individuals more generally. Thus, Denis
Healey, Labour's new Chancellor of the Exchequer, proposed an annual
wealth tax on the rich.[98] Ultimately, though, a Select Committee could
not reach agreement on the nature of such a levy and it was never
formally introduced.[99] In part, this broadened focus was because of
the decline in direct individual investment. Every year between 1963
and 1977 individuals sold more shares than they bought even though
equities generally outperformed debt over the same period.[100] Overall,
the percentage of shares owned by individual investors dropped from
66 percent in 1957 to 20 percent in 1991.[101] As discussed in chapter 5,
institutional investors filled this gap, becoming major equity holders
during this period. The percentage of equity shares that were owned by
pension funds increased from 1 percent in 1957 to 17 percent in 1975,
while the percentage owned by insurance companies increased from 8
percent in 1957 to 16 percent in 1975.[102] Some of this was driven by the
flight of wealthy investors to refuge in tax-favored investment vehicles,
but it was also fueled by a dramatic growth in pension assets invested for
the benefit of an expanding workforce.[103] This made it more difficult to
muster an attack on shareholders as "parasitical plutocrats" and the
politics of taxation took a different turn.[104]

6.2   United States

Politics in the USA were important in the aftermath of World War I, but
unlike in the UK where political change frequently led to corporate tax
reform, such change had a conservative effect in America. Political
movements tended to cancel each other out in the corporate tax arena

---

[96] *Hansard*, HC, vol. 814, ser. 5, col. 1383 (1971).   [97] Ibid., col. 1384.
[98] Daunton, *Just Taxes*, p. 331.   [99] Ibid.
[100] Brian R. Cheffins and Steven A. Bank, "Corporate Ownership and Control in the UK:
The Tax Dimension," *Modern Law Review* 70 (2007): 778, 805.
[101] Ibid., 781.   [102] Ibid., 778, 802.
[103] John Littlewood, *The Stock Market: 50 Years of Capitalism at Work* (London: Financial
Times/Pitman Publishing, 1998), pp. 254–5.
[104] Daunton, *Just Taxes*, p. 336.

and thereby helped to maintain the status quo for much of the twentieth century.

6.2.1   1920s

The political equilibrium in the USA was particularly evident during the 1920s when Congress debated whether to continue the income tax in any form and whether to make permanent the profits tax enacted during the war. The end of World War I brought demand for radical reform of the tax system. Although the income tax had helped to meet wartime revenue demands, the cessation of hostilities revealed its defects. As Thomas S. Adams, a Yale economics professor and special advisor to the Treasury, wrote in August of 1921, "[p]lainly there is 'something the matter with the income tax.' About the necessity of thoroly [*sic*] revising the income tax law at this session of Congress there is general agreement."[105] Both Democrats and Republicans called for tax reform, perhaps in part motivated by the widespread dissatisfaction with the tax among businesses and the public.[106] The House Ways and Means and the Senate Finance Committees each "received thousands of letters" expressing "a demand for revision."[107]

In this call for tax reform, there was substantial pressure to repeal the excess profits tax and the high surtaxes on individual income.[108] A variety of groups supported the sales tax concept as a replacement, including the Business Men's National Tax Committee, the Tax League of America, and the New York Board of Trade, and prominent business leaders such as Otto Kahn, Jules Bache, and Charles E. Lord joined them in their efforts.[109] Sales tax proponents understood the need for the

---

[105] Thomas S. Adams, "Fundamental Problems of Federal Income Taxation," *Quarterly Journal of Economics* 35 (1921): 527, 528. See *Brief of the Trades Council of the Manufacturers' Club of Philadelphia in Internal-Revenue Hearings on the Proposed Revenue Act of 1921 before the Sen. Fin. Committee*, 67th Cong., 1st Sess. 44, 45 (1921) ("*1921 Senate Hearings*").

[106] Roy G. Blakey and Gladys C. Blakey, *The Federal Income Tax* (New York: Longman, Green & Co., Ltd, 1940), p. 190.

[107] James A. Emery, "Address," in *Proceedings of the National Industrial Tax Conference, Special Report No. 9* (1920): 4, 5; *1921 Senate Hearings*, 22 (statement of Sen. Boies Penrose, Chair).

[108] In 1920, income and excess profits taxes brought in $4.5 billion in revenues, compared with excise taxes, which brought in $1.5 billion. Steven A. Bank, Kirk J Stark, and Joseph J. Thorndike, *War and Taxes* (Washington, DC: Urban Institute Press, 2008).

[109] See Blakey and Blakey, *The Federal Income Tax*, p. 190; Randolph E. Paul, *Taxation in the United States* (Boston: Little, Brown & Co., 1954), p. 128.

income tax and the excess profits tax during the war, but as Lord explained in a speech to the National Industrial Conference Board, "[t]he emergency . . . is past and we should promptly discard a theory of taxation which is both so uncertain and working so many evil results, and should seek a method which will be surer in its incidence, more equitable in its operation [and] simpler in its collection . . . Can such a way be found? Certainly; as soon as we commence to tax what people spend instead of what they save, we are on the right road."[110]

Unions occupied the other side of the debate, taking the position that the high rates on corporations should be maintained rather than replacing them with a sales tax. During consideration of the Revenue Act of 1921, the American Federation of Labor (AFL), led by Samuel Gompers, specifically advocated retaining the excess profits tax. At a conference of the AFL and affiliated organizations, labor leaders released a statement calling the proposal to end the excess profits tax and reduce surtax rates "clearly devised to favor the rich and powerful corporations."[111]

Labor's support for high corporate tax rates was not affected by the separation of ownership and control and the spread of stock ownership among the middle classes during this period. In large part this was because union workers did not participate in the spread of stockholding. Despite the growth of employee stock ownership during the 1920s, it was largely centered outside union membership. In 1927, the New York *Herald Tribune* noted that "[t]he biggest corporations, all of them non-union, have drawn the biggest share of the workers' investment capital. It is noteworthy, too, that the railroads which have a long history of union relationship are low in employee stock ownership."[112]

The relatively lower stock ownership among union members was not accidental. Unions were suspicious of the dispersion of corporation ownership in the early part of the twentieth century and they typically counseled their members against acquiring stock in the companies that employed them. According to John Sears, attorney for the Corporation Trust Company in New York, "labor union opposition [to employee stock ownership] is outspoken. It is feared by many that in periods of financial depression losses in income return and in market value of

---

[110] Charles E. Lord, "Address," in *Proceedings of the National Industrial Tax Conference, Special Report No. 9* (1920): 45, 49.

[111] "Labor denounces Fordney Tax Bill," *New York Times*, August 20, 1921, p. 1.

[112] Quoted in John H. Sears, *The New Place of the Stockholder* (New York: Harper & Brothers Publishers, 1929), pp. 50–51.

shares held will create more discontent than all the good that can possibly be accomplished in times of corporate prosperity."[113]

In theory, unions should have supported the growth of stock ownership. Because the spread of ownership included an increase in employee stock ownership, workers could participate in the governance of the corporation more directly than they could through union activism alone. Thomas Nixon Carver, an economist at Harvard, wrote that "where the workers in an industry actually own it or a considerable share in it they automatically acquire a place in its councils. The participation of labor in management does not then have to be artificially promoted."[114] Such union gains from employee stock ownership, however, were considered merely theoretical. As the *New York Times* pointed out, "so far, however, there is no record of the election of employees to the boards of directors of any of the companies which have taken the lead in employee ownership."[115] Sears wrote that "[r]epresentation in management by employee stock is thus far unusual."[116] All of this led Donald Richberg, chief counsel for the railway brotherhoods, to conclude in a speech before the Academy of Political Science that the growth of shareholders, even among employees, was "merely an improvement in the mechanism of minority control."[117]

Labor's suspicion about stock ownership may have been warranted. During the 1920s, business leaders actively referred to ownership dispersion as a means of aligning the interests of voters and stockholders. Sears wrote that "[w]ide distribution is of considerable interest. As distribution increases so that the number of stockholders approaches the number of political voters, stock control and political control will perhaps coincide. When this point is reached many expect that legislators will cease to pass ill-considered and unjustly adverse legislation against corporations, and will advance the interest of their stock-owning constituency."[118] Thus, throughout the 1920s labor evidenced little support for proposals to substantially reduce the tax burden on corporations.

This stand-off between unions and business interests, as well as opposition from merchants and retail establishments, helped to defeat the sales tax proposal. Republican Senator Reed Smoot of Utah had

---

[113] Ibid., p. 51.
[114] Evans Clark, "15,000,000 Americans hold corporation stock," *New York Times*, Nov. 22, 1925, p. XX5.
[115] Ibid.   [116] Sears, *The New Place of the Stockholder*, p. 52.   [117] Ibid.   [118] Ibid., p. 35.

introduced a measure for a temporary sales tax in the spring of 1921,[119] but the controversial nature of this proposal was immediately evident during the ensuing hearings. Almost fifty individuals or groups, nearly evenly divided for and against, testified on the general concept of a sales tax. Their testimony consumed more than 450 pages of the official record and took place over several weeks.[120] Proponents argued that a general sales tax was simpler to administer and relieved the inequitable burden imposed upon higher incomes under the income tax.[121] While opponents generally conceded the need for reform, they argued that the sales tax was a regressive levy imposed not in accordance with an individual's ability to pay.[122] In a vote divided along party and regional lines, Smoot's proposal was eventually defeated by a single vote.[123] An alternative proposal from Representative Ogden Mills for a graduated spending tax never even made it out of the House Ways and Means Committee.[124]

The campaign for reform was not a complete failure, but the result was a compromise between business and labor interests. On one hand, the excess profits tax was indeed repealed and the high surtax rates were reduced. The top rates of income tax dropped from their wartime high of 77 percent to a more modest 25 percent by the middle of the 1920s. On the other hand, corporate tax rates increased from 12 percent to just below 14 percent over the decade. More importantly, a differential developed between the corporate and individual normal rates. Under the Revenue Act of 1921, the corporate tax rate increased beyond the

---

[119] Cong. Rec., vol. 61, p. 151 (1921) (statement of Sen. Smoot). A companion bill authored by Rep. Isaac Bacharach of New Jersey was introduced in the House. See "Prepare to press for tax on sales," New York Times, April 11, 1921, p. 1.

[120] See 1921 Senate Hearings.

[121] See ibid., 56 (statement of C. H. Smith, Tax Committee, National Association of Manufacturers) (urging a sales tax on grounds of simplicity and convenience); ibid., 77 (brief of Tax League of America) (the sales tax "is characterized by simplicity, equity, capacity to produce the needed revenue, economy of administration, and the very essential quality of honesty.").

[122] See ibid., 360 (statement of Walter W. Liggett, Committee of Manufacturers and Merchants of Chicago) ("we consider the proposed Smoot sales-tax bill one of the most iniquitous measures that has ever been devised. We consider that the Smoot sales tax is a step backward to the days of the Roman empire . . ."); ibid., 412 ("I am fearful, therefore, lest we find ourselves saddled with a great new tax machine, a tax which is inherently unjust in that it is a tax on consumption, a tax which bears more heavily on the poor than on the rich.").

[123] See John F. Witte, The Politics and Development of the Federal Income Tax (Madison: University of Wisconsin Press, 1985), p. 90.

[124] See Steven A. Bank, "The Progressive Consumption Tax Revisited," Michigan Law Review 101 (2003): 2238, 2244–5.

individual normal tax rate by two percentage points, with a 4.5 percent differential scheduled to take effect the following year as corporate rates increased and individual rates dropped or remained stagnant.[125] In effect, business interests had traded the excess profits tax for the beginnings of the double taxation of corporate income.

Although trade unions were not strong lobbyists for double taxation *per se*, they may have encouraged this development. As in the UK, unions initially attempted to link dividends and wages. In 1930, the AFL argued that reserve funds should be established for wages, just as they existed for dividends. According to Edward F. McGrady, the legislative representative of the AFL, "[t]he wage earner has the same right to security of employment that the stockholder has to the security of dividend payments."[126] William Green, president of the AFL, repeated this view, stating at its annual meeting in 1931 that "[t]he wage standard must be built up ... The earnings of industry are most inequitably distributed. Instead of corporations declaring a 40 percent dividend to stockholders, they should divide the profits with the workers who have earned it."[127] Green threatened to back tax measures if industry failed to act on its own: "If they refuse to listen, then we will go to the sovereign people through the ballot and bring about a distribution of these large fortunes back to the people through the power of taxation."[128]

6.2.2 The Undistributed Profits Tax

The controversy over the enactment of an Undistributed Profits Tax in 1936 is a particularly vivid example of the political stalemate that has historically gripped the USA on the question of corporate tax reform. As described in Chapter 3, President Roosevelt's proposal for a tax on retained earnings was a radical approach to corporate taxation. The original plan was to repeal the corporate income tax in its entirety. Corporations would only be subject to a tax that was graduated according to the amount of earnings retained. So that corporate income would not escape tax entirely, the exemption from the individual normal tax for dividends would be repealed. Thus, if a corporation distributed all of its earnings each year, the income would be subject to the individual normal

---

[125] Revenue Act of 1921, ch. 136, sec. 210, 230(a)–(b), 42 Stat. 227.

[126] "A.F. of L. official urges wage reserve funds, making employment as secure as dividends," *New York Times*, December 22, 1930, p. 4.

[127] "Green assails high dividends," *Los Angeles Times*, October 6, 1931, p. 6.   [128] Ibid.

tax, and the surtax, if applicable, and no entity-level tax would be imposed at all.

Initial reaction to Roosevelt's proposal was quite positive. Many of his supporters in Congress and the press hailed the Undistributed Profits Tax idea as a "master political stroke," a "natural," and "politically painless" because of its ability to raise the necessary revenues by imposing a tax on a small, generally wealthy, segment of the population.[129] A *New York Times* editorial noted that the proposal already had "strengthened public confidence in the integrity of the Government's credit" as evidenced by "the prompt oversubscription in a single day of the enormous issue of bonds and notes offered by the Treasury."[130] *The Nation* boldly concluded that "[n]o tax could be devised which would be less likely to alienate the voters."[131]

Despite such rosy predictions, the Undistributed Profits Tax scheme strayed mightily from its original blueprint when finally enacted. The corporate income tax was retained rather than repealed and the Undistributed Profits Tax was levied in addition to it as a form of penalty tax. Notwithstanding the fact that this ended the rationale for removing the dividend exemption from the normal tax, dividends remained taxable under the final act for managers to use as a counterweight to the distributive pressure of the tax on undistributed profits. Moreover, within two years the top Undistributed Profits Tax rate was slashed from 27 percent to 2.5 percent and the levy itself was gone within a year.

---

[129] Alfred G. Buehler, *The Undistributed Profits Tax* (New York: McGraw-Hill Book Co., 1937), p. 23; George B. Bryant, Jr., "Reform motive in tax program," *Barron's*, March 30, 1936, p. 13; Arthur Krock, "House is finding new problems as tax bill is studied," *New York Times*, March 18, 1936, p. 22. See also "A sound tax," 142 *The Nation* 337 (March 18, 1936) ("[T]he President's proposed tax on undivided corporation profits represents masterly strategy . . . he has saved Congress from the painful necessity of imposing an income or sales impost on the eve of a national election"); "Taxing Corporate Surplus," 86 *The New Republic* 153 (March 18, 1936) ("[The Undistributed Profits Tax proposal] is thought by many commentators to be merely an ingenious way of escaping the wrath that would follow an increase of income-tax rates in an election year.").

[130] Editorial, "The President's Message," *New York Times*, March 4, 1936, p. 20.

[131] "A Sound Tax," 142 *The Nation* 337 (March 18, 1936). See also "Robinson urges speed on Tax Bill," *New York Times*, March 4, 1936, p. 3 (quoting the reaction of numerous members of Congress, including that of the Speaker of the House, who said that "it will meet with the approval of the majority of people"). As one commentator pointed out in describing the political virtues of the tax, "[i]t seems to avoid any tax upon 99 per cent of the voters. It raises the tax upon the remaining 1 per cent, who in the opinion of the aforementioned 99 per cent should pay higher taxes anyway." Joseph Stagg Lawrence, "A Death Sentence for Thrift," 93 *Review of Reviews*, May 1936, at 450, 451.

   This about-face was a result of what Senator Robert La Follette called "the most widely organized and most successful propaganda campaigns in the history of tax legislation" and the virtual absence of any support from labor or other progressive groups.[132] According to Mark Leff, "[t]he US Chamber of Commerce, overseeing the details of tax legislation, served as a prime information source for many congressmen, even drafting major Republican amendments."[133] As Treasury Secretary Henry Morgenthau later recalled, "[t]he opposition from the conservative press and big business, and their influence in both parties on the Hill, made a terrific impact."[134] It was only the force of President Roosevelt's will and the loyalty of his Democratic colleagues in Congress that pushed through some semblance of the legislation and kept it alive for one more year as part of a "face-saving compromise" for Roosevelt in 1938.[135]

   Furthermore, the failure to restore the dividend exemption from the individual normal tax after the demise of the Undistributed Profits Tax reflects the ambivalence of business on the issue. On one hand, the end of the Undistributed Profits Tax levy helped to realign manager–shareholder interests. With double taxation no longer necessary to offset the distributive pressure of the profits tax, corporate managers acknowledged the negative effect that double taxation had on investment in corporations. As one executive wrote in a letter to the Ways and Means Committee, "since in recent years all corporate dividends were made subject not only to the graduated surtax but also to normal tax upon the stockholder receiving the dividend the corporation tax on income has been nothing but a penalty tax upon the corporate form of doing business."[136]

   On the other hand, business groups had higher tax priorities than removing double taxation. The main focus was to expedite a business tax aid program negotiated by Congressional leaders and officials from Treasury and the Administration.[137] Under this program, business

---

[132] *Cong. Rec.*, vol. 83, p. 4932 (1938).
[133] Mark Leff, *The Limits of Symbolic Reform: The New Deal and Taxation 1933–1939* (Cambridge University Press, 1984), p. 275.
[134] See John Morton Blum, *From the Morgenthau Diaries: Years of Crisis, 1928–1938* (Boston: Houghton Mifflin, 1959), p. 319 (quoting from the Diaries).
[135] "Profits tax looms as election issue," *New York Times*, April 24, 1938, p. 4.
[136] *Revenue Revision – 1939: Hearing Before the House Committee on Ways & Means*, 76th Cong., 1st Sess. 190–91 (1939) (statement of D. P. Larsen, Shevlin, Carpents & Clarke Co.).
[137] See "Congress leaders plan to expedite tax aid legislation," *Wall Street Journal*, May 17, 1939, p. 1; "Leaders to push business tax aid at present session," *Wall Street Journal*, May 16, 1939, p. 1.

would receive four major tax benefits: (1) Replace the Undistributed Profits Tax and corporate income tax at rates ranging from 16.5 percent to 19 percent with a flat 18 percent corporate income tax; (2) Permit an annual revaluation of capital stock for purposes of the capital stock tax; (3) Eliminate the limit on capital loss deductions for corporations; and (4) Permit corporations to carry forward losses for two or three years.[138] Unlike the relief of double taxation, these measures were designed to increase managers' flexibility and independence. As the *Wall Street Journal* pointed out with respect to the capital loss provision, "[r]emoval . . . of the $2,000 limitation on the deduction of capital losses from taxable income would do something to encourage corporation managements to venture more freely for the development of new lines of business, greater volume in old lines and wider employment in both."[139] A similar view was expressed with respect to the loss carry-forward provision, with one expert opining "the provision might also encourage some corporate investment, inasmuch as a considerable portion of entrepreneur investing in the past has been done by corporations."[140] In effect, business interests opted for less visible, but still meaningful change rather than pursuing radical reform.

6.2.3   World War II and the postwar decade

Just prior to World War II, there were signs that some labor leaders had started to reverse course on the question of business taxation. Stung by the loss of jobs during the Great Depression, labor was "awakening to the danger of the tax problem because taxes which keep business from expanding or from profiting reduce employment opportunities and lower the standard of living for the workers."[141] In a speech before the Republican-dominated New York Union League Club, Matthew Woll, the vice president of the AFL, "urged business to cooperate with organized labor to save private enterprise from the danger of destruction

---

[138] Alfred F. Flynn, "Four point plan for tax revision being considered," *Wall Street Journal*, May 13, 1939, p. 1. The latter provision was eventually extended to individuals and partnerships in the final House bill. See "Two new concessions to business included in house tax bill," *Wall Street Journal*, June 17, 1939, p. 1; "House passes tax revision bill; Approval by Senate likely," *Wall Street Journal*, June 20, 1939, p. 2.

[139] Editorial, "Promising changes in tax laws," *Wall Street Journal*, May 26, 1939, p. 4.

[140] William J. Enright, "Losses provision in Tax Bill hailed," *New York Times*, June 25, 1939, § III, p. 7 (citing J. M. Finke, of Klein, Hind & Finke, CPA).

[141] "Woll urges business to pull with labor; Asks team-work to bar destructive taxes," *New York Times*, November 8, 1940, p. 13.

through excessive taxation."[142] Although Woll acknowledged that "some groups in labor were hostile to private enterprise," likely referring to the Congress of Industrial Organizations (CIO), he promised the cooperation of the AFL if the olive branch he extended were accepted.[143]

Any possibility of a united front between business and labor on the question of taxation was cut short by the onset of World War II. Union leaders resumed their crusade for taxing accumulated wealth in the form of high surtax rates and excess profits taxes.[144] They also focused on defeating efforts to finance the war through "soak the poor" measures, such as by broadening the individual income tax base and lowering the exemptions, or by instituting a national sales tax.[145] In 1942, Phillip Murray, the president of the CIO was particularly emphatic in criticizing the latter proposal, noting that "[i]n peacetime, a sales tax is vicious enough, but in wartime, when we are trying to assure our war workers of sufficient funds to maintain themselves, the proposed sales tax levy would be the equivalent of military defeat."[146]

Business leaders, by contrast, were more muted than unions in their approach to tax policy. They did not want to appear unpatriotic by openly resisting proposals to force them to bear their fair share of the tax burden. Thus, on the excess profits tax, tax lawyer George Douglas reported that "[t]o the best of my knowledge, no business executive opposes the principle of an excess profits tax which seeks to return to government exorbitant profits arising directly or indirectly from the war effort."[147] That did not mean that business lobbying was non-existent during the war, but it was focused on the under-the-radar details and exemptions in an excess profits tax rather than on its existence.[148]

Labor might have seized this opportunity to impose its own tax program as a source of financing for the huge war costs, but the various unions disagreed about the right approach. While the AFL was not willing "to put up a last-ditch fight against a levy which was confined

---

[142] Ibid.   [143] Ibid.

[144] "Substitute plan for joint return slated in House," *New York Times*, August 4, 1941, p. 1; "AFL tax program stresses heavy levy on surplus income," *New York Times*, March 20, 1942, p. 15.

[145] Thomas J. Hamilton, "Unions, industry criticize Tax Bill," *New York Times*, July 30, 1942, p. 1; Turner Catledge, "CIO condemns wider tax base," *New York Times*, August 14, 1941, p. 10; "Unions fight US sales tax," *Los Angeles Times*, August 24, 1941, p. 3.

[146] Committee on Ways and Means, *Revenue Revision of 1942*, 77th Congress, 2nd Sess. (1942), p. 913.

[147] George Douglas, "Excess Profits Taxation and the Taxpayer," *Law and Contemporary Problems* 10 (1943): 140, 143.

[148] Bank, Stark, and Thorndike, Jr., *War and Taxes*, p. 89.

to luxury articles," the CIO opposed "any kind of sales tax."[149] Similarly, the two union associations differed in their view of President Roosevelt's proposed $25,000 limit on individual income, with the AFL opposing it and the CIO welcoming the measure.[150] Such disagreements limited their collective influence in shaping the wartime tax program.

In part because of these obstacles for both business and labor, neither group emerged unscathed. During the war, Congress enacted an excess profits tax with rates reaching as high as 95 percent and effective rates exceeding 70 percent for many firms. This was imposed in addition to the normal corporate income tax, which itself was made more burdensome by an increase in its top rate from 24 to 31 percent in 1941 and again to 40 percent in 1942.[151] At the same time, Congress broadened the income tax base considerably by reducing the exemption limit, which had been as high as $3,500 for married couples in 1931, to $1,200 in 1942.[152] Consequently, the number of taxpayers subject to the income tax grew sevenfold during the war, so that by 1945 more than 90 percent of the labor force were required to file tax returns.[153]

After the war, the respective political and special interest groups returned to their traditional positions, including many of their traditional disagreements and divisions over the appropriate postwar tax program. Among progressive groups, the CIO led the charge against corporations, supporting retention of the excess profits tax and a revival of the Undistributed Profits Tax.[154] The AFL, which would merge with the CIO in a decade,[155] endorsed the same basic package of tax reforms even though it was more focused on reducing the burden on lower-income individuals than on increasing it on corporations. Matthew Woll of the AFL argued that the biggest concern from an economic

---

[149] Thomas J. Hamilton, "10 billion increase in Tax Bill urged," *New York Times*, August 13, 1942, p. 10.

[150] Ibid.

[151] Internal Revenue Service, *Corporate Income Tax Brackets and Rates, 1909–2002*, available at www.irs.gov/pub/irs-soi/02corate.pdf.

[152] Bank, Stark, and Thorndike, *War and Taxes*, p. 97.

[153] Ibid., p. 84.

[154] "CIO tax bill would retain Excess Profits Levy, limit relief to low-income individuals," *Wall Street Journal*, October 1, 1945, p. 3; C. P. Trussell, "CIO proposes cut of $6,675,000,000 in personal taxes," *New York Times*, October 17, 1945, p. 1; "CIO charges large corporations try to camouflage profits," *Wall Street Journal*, December 22, 1947, p. 2; "CIO asks tax rise for high incomes," *New York Times*, February 15, 1950, p. 21.

[155] The merger took place in December 1955. Harold G. Vatter, *The US Economy in the 1950s: An Economic History* (New York: W. W. Norton & Co., Inc., 1963), p. 241.

perspective was not the high taxes on business, but the relatively high taxes on those least able to bear them, because of the "great danger that our post-war recovery will hit a sudden snag through a drastic reduction in effective purchasing power."[156] Others in the labor movement, however, sought much more radical changes. The United Electrical, Radio, and Machine Workers of America, which had been expelled from the CIO because of "Communistic influences," urged "drastic taxation of excess profits [and] proposed a $25,000 ceiling on individual incomes."[157]

Business groups were just as active in the postwar tax policy discussion, but fared no better in reaching a consensus as to the appropriate path for reform. During the two years following the conclusion of the war, more than sixty proposals were forwarded to reform the taxation of corporate income.[158] In fact, during the summer of 1944 alone, three different business groups released prominent tax reform proposals within weeks of each other, each radically different from the others in approach. The first, which was prepared on behalf of the National Planning Association by Beardsley Ruml, the chairman of the Federal Reserve Bank of New York and the treasurer of R. H. Macy & Co., and Hans Christian Sonne, an investment banker, proposed replacing the corporate income tax with a 5 percent franchise tax and a form of undistributed profits tax.[159] The second proposal, which was prepared by a group of twenty-two businessmen from the Minneapolis/St. Paul area, proposed to continue the corporate tax at 1942 rates, while repealing the excess profits tax and cutting individual surtax and capital gains tax rates.[160] Finally, the third proposal, which was prepared by the business-influenced Committee for Economic Development, proposed to reduce corporate and individual income tax rates and provide shareholders with a refundable credit for taxes paid on their behalf at the corporate level.[161] Moreover, most of the most prominent business trade

---

[156] "Tax reform seen as complex task," *New York Times*, December 7, 1946, p. 29.
[157] John D. Morris, "CIO would raise Profits Tax to 85%," *New York Times*, November 18, 1950, p. 1.
[158] "Tax Report," *Wall Street Journal*, January 30, 1946, p. 1.
[159] Beardsley Ruml and H. Chr. Sonne, *Fiscal and Monetary Policy* (Washington, DC: National Planning Association, July 1944), p. 9.
[160] *The Twin Cities Plan: Postwar Taxes. A Realistic Approach to the Problem of Federal Taxation* (St. Paul, Minn.: Twin Cities Research Bureau, 1944), pp. 12–13.
[161] *A Postwar Federal Tax Plan for High Employment* (Committee for Economic Development, August 1944), p. 30; "Business body asks corporate tax end as way to job peak," *New York Times*, September 6, 1944, p. 1.

groups – including the National Association of Manufacturers, the US Chamber of Commerce, and the National Retail Dry Goods Association – proposed large drops in individual and corporate tax rates and repeal of the excess profits tax.[162]

Instead of adopting these or any of the other proposals forwarded for radical reform of the corporate income tax, Congress confined itself to repealing the excess profits tax. In part, this was because of the constraints of the budget and the higher priority accorded to repealing the excess profits tax among the possible reform options.[163] In part, however, this was because of the lack of unity among business groups. According to the *Wall Street Journal*, "[b]usiness itself is far from agreed as to what it wants . . . Sixty relief plans to cure this one evil are evidence of the widely divergent views on how to reduce double taxation."[164] Reaching consensus was particularly difficult for interest groups given the uncertainty regarding the incidence of the corporate tax or of any of the other possible alternatives.[165] Furthermore, with the easing of the equity crunch that had led some businesses to advocate dividend tax reform,[166] leaders were able to focus on other things.

Politics did appear to play a part in the eventual adoption of a corporate tax reform plan in 1954, but not as large as one might assume. Dwight D. Eisenhower was the first Republican President in two decades and many members of his party likely expected that his election in 1952 would usher in changes in tax policies. In some respects, this expectation was realized. Congress did enact corporate tax reform in 1954, adopting a $50 exclusion for dividends and a 4 percent shareholder credit. This reform fell short of the original proposal of a 15 percent shareholder credit,[167] however, and was a far cry from the radical reform discussed after World War II.

Part of the reason that in the 1950s political change in the USA did not lead to fundamental corporate tax reform like it did in the UK is that the

---

[162] C. P. Trussell, "George forecasts 5 billion tax cut," *New York Times*, October 18, 1945, p. 15; *Revenue Act of 1945, Hearings before the Finance Committee*, U.S. Senate, 79th Cong., 1st Sess. (October 16, 1945), pp. 171, 202, 206.

[163] Steven A. Bank, *From Sword to Shield: The Transformation of the Corporate Income Tax, 1861 to Present* (Oxford University Press, 2010), pp. 201–3.

[164] "Tax Report," *Wall Street Journal*, January 30, 1946, p. 1.

[165] "Tax reform seen as complex task," *New York Times*, December 6, 1946, p. 29.

[166] Richard B. Goode, U.S. Treasury Department, *The Postwar Corporation Tax Structure* (1946), p. 4.

[167] Alan L. Otten, "President asks Congress to put corporate income taxes partially on a pay-as-you-go basis, starting in 1955," *Wall Street Journal*, January 22, 1954, p. 5.

change in the party of the President did not translate to a change in the party in control of government. Eisenhower was elected in part because of support from committed independents and Democrats who continued to be loyal to their party in lower-office elections. As one commentator explained, Eisenhower was "more popular than his political party ... It was clear that Eisenhower put the Republican Party in power and not the reverse."[168] The Republicans had only a slim plurality in the House in 1952 and Democrats regained control of both chambers of Congress in the mid-term elections of 1954 and maintained it in 1956.[169]

Moreover, Eisenhower did not even have the unanimous backing of the Republican Party on tax issues. In fact, many Republican congressmen complained that Eisenhower's tax program was largely identical to that of President Truman before the Korean War, especially given its focus on balancing the budget and his initial moves to extend the life of the excess profits tax by six months and to rescind a scheduled 5 percentage point drop in the corporate income tax rate.[170] There were several major confrontations with Senate Republican leader Robert Taft and newly-installed House Ways and Means Committee chairman Daniel Reed over his deferral of tax cuts, with Reed even threatening to resign over it.[171] As Gary Reichard observed, "[t]o many congressional Republicans, the President's failure to espouse immediate tax cuts was heresy. Consequently, there ensued a struggle between Republican advocates of instant tax reductions and an administration which believed in the principle of such reductions, but wanted to reduce spending first. The battle consumed a major part of the energy of both sides throughout the first session of the Eighty-third Congress."[172]

Given this tenuous political resolution, it is not surprising that the modest relief for dividend taxation failed to endure. As described in Chapter 3, the shareholder credit was repealed in 1964 as part of

[168] John W. Sloan, *Eisenhower and the Management of Prosperity* (Lawrence: University Press of Kansas, 1991), p. 54.
[169] Ibid., pp. 56–7 (Tbl. 3.1).
[170] Aaron L. Friedberg, *In the Shadow of the Garrison State* (Princeton, NJ: Princeton University Press, 2000), pp. 131–2; Dan T. Smith, "Two Years of Republican Tax Policy: An Economic Appraisal," *National Tax Journal* 8 (1955): 2; "Text of President Eisenhower's Message to Congress on Taxation," *New York Times*, May 21, 1953, p. 27.
[171] Raymond J. Saulnier, *Constructive Years: The US Economy Under Eisenhower* (Lanham, Md.: University Press of America, 1991), pp. 46–8.
[172] Gary W. Reichard, *The Reaffirmation of Republicanism: Eisenhower and the Eighty-Third Congress* (Knoxville: University of Tennessee Press, 1975), p. 98.

President Kennedy's base-broadening move to permit tax rate cuts, although the exemption remained because of its apparent aid for small shareholders. Initially, at the House Ways and Means Committee hearing in 1961, this proposal "ran into a barrage of criticism from business and investment interests. A union leader was the lone supporter."[173] Nevertheless, an Advisory Committee on Labor-Management Policy comprising business and labor leaders to provide Kennedy with "their advice on fiscal and monetary policy," agreed that a reduction in individual and corporate income tax rates took higher precedence than preference items such as the dividend tax credit.[174] Although Kennedy returned the presidency to Democratic hands and therefore might have been expected to roll back Republican gains on the integration front, the actual story reflects the more complex balance between political interests over taxation. The fact that the credit was repealed, but the small exemption continued illustrates the resulting compromise.

[173] "Business attacks Kennedy plan to tighten dividend taxation; Labor backs proposal," *Wall Street Journal*, May 12, 1961, p. 3.

[174] Richard E. Mooney, "10-billion tax cut urged by labor–business panel," *New York Times*, November 10, 1962, p. 1.

PART III

Conclusion

7

1970s to Present – A Time of Convergence?

The three themes discussed in the previous chapters – profits, power, and politics – have each continued to influence the modern debate over corporate tax reform in the United Kingdom and the United States during the last twenty years. American politicians have maintained their focus on the paucity of dividends and the actions of managers while their British counterparts revived their concern about shareholder expropriation and inadequate retained earnings. Moreover, political changes have ushered in dramatic reforms in both countries, although in the case of the USA the modification to the tax treatment of dividends that was ultimately enacted in 2003 was once again less radical than the original proposal and fell short of the goal of full integration. In the latest round of reforms, these common themes seem to be pushing the two systems toward convergence rather than divergence, which seems predictable in light of the growth of multinational corporations and the globalization of commerce. What is uncertain, however, is the effect of developments outside of each country, such as the growing power of the European Union, the European Court of Justice, and other countries, in dictating whether convergence is inevitable or even possible.

7.1   United Kingdom

In the mid 1990s, the UK once again became concerned with dividends and firm investment. A 1995 study published by the Institute for Fiscal Studies ("IFS") announced that there had been a dramatic rise in the percentage of profits paid out as dividends during the previous decade.[1] In a press release accompanying this announcement, the IFS noted that "[t]he dividend payout ratio ... is higher in the UK than in any other major economy. There is a danger that these high dividend payouts are

---

[1] See Stephen Bond et al., "Company Dividends and Taxes in the UK," *Fiscal Studies* 16 (1996): 3.

having an adverse effect on business investment."[2] Other studies reached similar conclusions regarding the dangers of increased dividends.[3] By 1997, with dividends continuing to rise and Labour poised to retake power for the first time in eighteen years,[4] the corporate tax system appeared to be headed for another revision.[5]

In his July 2, 1997 Budget Message, Chancellor Gordon Brown noted that "[s]ince 1980 the UK has invested a lower share of GDP than most other industrialised countries . . . For every £100 invested per worker in the UK, Germany has invested over £140, the US and France around £150, and Japan over £160 per worker."[6] Brown announced that, while the Labour Party had been studying the system for the past two years with an eye toward redressing this investment deficiency, "this point in the recovery is . . . the right time to make changes in corporation tax to encourage more long term investment."[7] The bill for reform was passed in less than a month.[8]

Labour revised the Corporation Tax in two phases. Effective immediately in 1997, it reduced the corporate tax rate by two percentage points from 33 to 31 percent and abolished the refundable shareholder dividend tax credit for tax-exempt institutional investors such as pension funds.[9] Prior to this latter reform, a dividend of £80 to a tax-exempt investor was worth £100 because of the refund of the 20 percent tax credit then provided for under the partial imputation system.[10] As Brown emphasized in his Budget Message, subsidizing dividend payments to pension funds, which owned more than half of all public stock at the time,[11]

---

[2] See Press Release, "Company Dividends and Taxes in the UK (August 31, 1995)," available at http://www.ifs.org.uk/press/fsdivs.shtml, last visited on August 21, 2002.

[3] See David Wighton, "Labour tax shake-up likely to highlight investment," *Financial Times* (London), April 1, 1997, p. 10 (citing a study by the Commission on Public Policy and British Business).

[4] See Malcolm Gammie, "The End of Imputation: Changes in UK Dividend Taxation," *Intertax* 25 (1997): 333.

[5] See Barry Riley, "Reaping Tory dividends," *Financial Times* (London), April 19, 1997, p. 1; Robert Peston, "Brown may scrap dividend credit," *Financial Times* (London), June 16, 1997, p. 1; Jim Kelly, "Under fire for 'victimless' tax increase: Brown may defy critics over dividend credits," *Financial Times* (London), June 16, 1997, p. 11; The Lex Column, "Taxing times," *Financial Times* (London), June 16, 1997, p. 22; Philip Coggan, "Not the easy option," *Financial Times* (London), June 21, 1997, p. 8.

[6] The Chancellor's 1997 Budget Speech at para. 59, available at http://archive.treasury. gov.uk/pub/html/budget97/chxstat2.html (last visited February 5, 2003) ("1997 Budget Message").

[7] Ibid. at paras. 60, 62.   [8] See Gammie, "The End of Imputation," 333.

[9] Finance (No. 2) Act 1997, s. 19.   [10] See Gammie, "The End of Imputation," 335.

[11] Ibid.

"encourage[d] companies to pay out dividends rather than reinvest their profits."[12]

The parallel with Labour's previous reform proposals was not lost on commentators. As *The Times* noted, "[t]he agenda is an old Labour one. It dates back to the revolution in company tax made in Lord Callaghan's comparable first Labour Budget of 1965 . . . Essentially, Mr. Brown aims to reinstate the reforms proposed by the late old Labour Lord Kaldor a generation ago."[13] This time, however, it did not have the support of business trade groups. Adair Turner, director general of the Confederation of British Industry (CBI), reported that "one measure – the radical change to the corporation tax regime – we do not support . . . The CBI is disappointed that such a major change in corporate taxation was introduced without proper prior consultation."[14]

In the second phase of the revision to the Corporation Tax, effective April 6, 1999, the elimination of the refundable shareholder tax credit for tax-exempt investors was extended to taxable shareholders.[15] The shareholder tax credit on dividends was also reduced from 20 percent to 10 percent.[16] In an additional reform enacted in 1998, but implemented at the same time as the second phase of the 1997 reform, the advance corporation tax was abolished altogether.[17] The combined effect of the 1997 and 1999 reforms has been to drastically scale back, if not repeal outright, the UK's shareholder imputation system and push it ever closer to a classical double tax.[18] As John Tiley has described it, the resulting hybrid corporate tax system "is a very odd beast, at least in theoretical terms."[19]

---

[12] 1997 Budget Message, at para. 72.

[13] See Graham Searjeant, "Dividend grab is economic nonsense," *The Times* (London), July 24, 1997.

[14] See "Brown's first Budget – business and market reaction," *Financial Times* (London), July 3, 1997, p. 3.

[15] Finance (No. 2) Act 1997, s. 30.   [16] Ibid.   [17] Finance Act 1998, s. 31.

[18] See Peter Casson, "International Aspects of the UK Imputation System of Corporate Taxation," *British Tax Review* 5 (1998): 493 ("the abolition of advance corporation tax (ACT) with effect from April 1999 will mark the end of the imputation system of corporation tax introduced a quarter of a century ago"); Reuven Avi-Yonah, "Back to the 1930s? The Shaky Case for Exempting Dividends," *Tax Notes* 97 (2002): 1599 (noting that "[i]ntegration has been cut back severely in . . . the UK"); Andreas Tontsch, "Corporation Tax Systems and Fiscal Neutrality: The UK and German Systems and their Recent Changes," *Intertax* 30 (2002): 178 ("With the abolition of ACT, the only link between the corporation tax paid by the company and the tax credit for the shareholder has been eliminated. The tax credit is granted regardless of whether any corporation tax has been paid on the profit at all. Consequently, it cannot be said that corporation tax is imputed to the shareholder.").

[19] John Tiley, "The United Kingdom," in *Comparative Income Taxation: A Structural Analysis*, 3rd edn. (Hugh J. Ault and Brian J. Arnold, eds) (New York: Aspen Publishers, 2010), p. 147.

In some respects, these reforms recall Labour's historic antagonism toward unearned income received from passive investments. The problem was that the shift from individual stockholders to institutional investors had altered the nature of this argument for taxing dividends more heavily. Not only were pensions affected by the repeal of the refundable shareholder credit, but pensioners with annual incomes not subject to tax because they were too low were also destined to lose their credit in the reform.[20] This latter effect was particularly controversial, with small shareholders accusing the government of having "stolen" part of their income.[21] One said "[t]he Government has run roughshod over people on lowish incomes for whom the tax credits could be a significant sum of money."[22] Pensioners' groups "expressed dismay," but were unable to reverse the reform.[23]

In recent years, there are signs that these reforms may be temporary. Conservatives have promised to "investigate the possibility of reversing the abolition of the dividend tax credit for pension funds."[24] Part of the concern is the effect that the elimination of the refundable feature had on both pension coffers and on the value of equity investment. According to one study, the higher tax burden on dividends to pension funds under the current rules has caused pensions to demand higher returns to invest in corporations.[25] This has raised the cost of capital for corporations, which is blamed for slowing the rate of new corporate investment during the post-1997 period. Although the measure was touted as a means of boosting business investment and reducing the pressure to pay dividends, dividends continued to rise. As a result, there was less capacity for other things and business investment reportedly "slowed dramatically. In 1996 and 1997, it grew by an average 12.5 per cent a year. In the six following years it grew by an average of only 4.5 per cent. If the boom

[20] Caroline Mitchell, "Treasury urged to reprieve tax credit for poor," *The Times* (London), May 15, 1998.

[21] Peter Benton, Letter, "Pensioners' income hit by double whammy," *The Times* (London), September 17, 1998.

[22] Gavin Lumsden and Fran Littlewood, "Brown's tricks revealed," *The Times* (London), March 27, 1999.

[23] Gavin Lumsden, "Dismay over refusal to restore tax credits," *The Times* (London), December 12, 1998.

[24] James Charles, "Where the manifestos hit our wallets," *The Times* (London), May 1, 2010, p. 82. This was not the first time such a proposal was made.

[25] Leonie Bell and Tim Jenkinson, "New Evidence of the Impact of Dividend Taxation and on the Identity of the Marginal Investor," *Journal of Finance* 57 (2002): 1321.

year of 1998 is excluded, that falls to 2 per cent."[26] Moreover, "[t]here is a widespread belief in the City and the business community that the disintegration of the country's once-proud pensions industry has been mainly the fault of the Chancellor" and his tax policies, although others blame "regulation and litigation" rather than tax reform.[27] Regardless of the cause, the top 350 UK companies were estimated to have an aggregate pension fund deficit of £47 billion as of 2006.[28] Reversing the repeal of the refundable dividend tax credit for pension investors would provide as much as a £5 billion per year boost to the industry.[29]

7.2   United States

7.2.1   1970s to early 1990s

While the UK was moving away from integration by scaling back its shareholder imputation system, the USA was making efforts to move toward integration. Much like in the late 1930s and the early 1950s, however, business ambivalence helped to scale back, and in some cases reverse, the success of integration reform efforts. As mentioned briefly in Chapter 3, there were several corporate tax reform proposals advanced in the 1980s and early 1990s that failed to get traction in Congress or among the business community. Even before that, however, business interests demonstrated their indifference to tax reform efforts aimed at integrating the corporate and shareholder income taxes.

In the late 1970s, there were significant fears of an impending shortage of equity capital in which the corporate double tax was, if not the primary culprit, a contributing factor.[30] As one tax specialist observed, "[t]he [corporate tax reform] debate has become particularly heated in recent years because of the growing concern that US business faces a possible capital shortage in the near future."[31] Both the Treasury

---

[26] Graham Searjeant, "Seven years on, Brown's swoop on pensions looks less clever," *The Times* (London), October 15, 2004, p. 58.

[27] Anatole Kaletsky, "Regulations killed the pensions industry," *The Times* (London), October 16, 2006, p. 35; Philip Webster and Greg Hurst, "Brown slaps down claim that he wiped £1bn from pensions," *The Times* (London), April 18, 2007, p. 22.

[28] Graham Searjeant, "The unforeseen cost of putting a tax on dividends," *The Times* (London), September 28, 2006, p. 58.

[29] See Gabriel Rozenberg and Christine Seib, "Tories may restore tax credit for pensions," *The Times* (London), January 12, 2005, p. 41.

[30] Jacob T. Severiens, "Does a Dividend Tax Credit Work?," *Taxes* 54 (January 1976): 17.

[31] John H. Cox, "The Corporate Income Tax and Integration: A Summary of Positions and the Prospects for Change," *Taxes* 58 (January 1980): 10, 22.

Department and many economists were predicting "a $4.5 trillion capital 'gap' over the next decade."[32] Although this prediction was not uncontroversial, the USA did have the lowest rate of private investment increase among industrialized countries and as a percentage of gross national product US stock flotations ranked among the lowest at the time.[33] Treasury economists argued that "the nation must 'tilt' the share of gross national product that it saves for all private investment to 16% from the recent average of 15%, or roughly $15 billion for 1976."[34] To achieve that, net new investment needed to increase by almost 16 percent and there was a growing belief that integration offered a promising mechanism "by lessening the extra burden which presently falls on capital and the income from capital."[35]

Partly because of such concerns about a capital crunch, both President Ford and President Carter indicated an interest in considering integration proposals. Carter went so far as to release a draft proposal in 1977 to implement a shareholder credit, but he quickly abandoned it after "running into serious opposition."[36] According to observers, it was "denounced" by members of the Business Roundtable and the chairman of General Electric complained that the plan "benefits the individual, not the business itself."[37] Businessmen were described as "leery of the proposal."[38] As one prominent tax lawyer explained, "top industrial executives I've talked to have their staff combing out these integration ideas to see what the tradeoffs would be,"[39] especially in light of Treasury Secretary William Simon's suggestion that "integration would not be adopted unless business gave up some of the specialized tax preferences it now enjoys in partial exchange."[40]

When Carter's integration proposal was revived in 1978 by House Ways and Means Committee Chairman Al Ullman,[41] it was reported

---

[32] Ibid.   [33] Ibid.

[34] "The drive to revamp the corporate income tax," *Business Week*, July 28, 1975, p. 58.

[35] Frederic W. Hickman, "Tax Equity and the Need for Capital," *National Tax Journal* 28 (1975): 282, 283, 287.

[36] Art Pine, "Carter's dividend tax proposal is in trouble," *Washington Post*, October 25, 1977, p. D7.

[37] Ibid., Martin A. Sullivan, "Dividend *Déjà vu*: Will Double Tax Relief Get Canned – Again?," *Tax Notes* 98 (February 3, 2003): 647.

[38] "The drive to revamp the corporate tax," *Business Week*, July 28, 1975, p. 58.   [39] Ibid.

[40] H. Lawrence Fox, "Washington Tax Watch," *Journal of Corporate Taxation* 2 (Autumn 1975): 360, 365–6.

[41] H. Lawrence Fox and James K. Jackson, "Washington Tax Watch," *Journal of Corporate Taxation* 3 (Summer 1976): 176.

that "most businesses remained lukewarm" and it died in committee.[42] Donald Lubick, Assistant Treasury Secretary under Carter, explained that "corporate integration was ultimately killed by big business ... which wanted rate reduction instead."[43] As a 1978 Conference Board survey of 400 chief executive officers revealed, "[t]op-level business executives strongly favored a cut in the corporate tax rate over other tax relief measures being considered ... [including] partial relief from the double taxation of dividends."[44]

Ultimately, the only integration measure adopted was an increase in the dividend exemption from $100 for individuals and $200 for married couples filing jointly to $200 for individuals and $400 for married couples, brought in under the Crude Oil Windfall Profits Tax Act of 1980.[45] Not only did this fall far short of what Carter had proposed, but it was affirmatively repudiated by the White House, with administration officials calling it a "waste [of] $2 billion a year of tax money."[46] Moreover, this was only a temporary measure, as it was scheduled to be effective until 1982 under the legislation, at which point the original $100 exclusion for individuals and the $200 exclusion for married couples would remain.[47]

Under the Tax Reform Act of 1986, even the meager exclusion remaining from 1954 was repealed. According to the President's proposal to Congress on this provision, "[t]he $100 dividend exclusion narrows the base of income subject to tax without creating a proportionate incentive for investment in domestic corporations. The exclusion provides no marginal investment incentive for individuals with dividend income in excess of $100, and only a minor incentive for other individual taxpayers."[48] The Senate Finance Committee and the House Ways and Means Committee found the small exclusion inadequate on other grounds, with the former noting that "the dividend exclusion for individuals under present law provides little relief from the two-tier

---

[42] Sullivan, "Dividend *Déja vu*," p. 647.

[43] Sheryl Stratton, "Lubick Looks at Treasury Past and Treasury Present," *Tax Notes* 84 (1999): 1702, 1706.

[44] "Firms like tax rate cut," *Washington Post*, January 18, 1978, p. D12.

[45] James E. Smith, "The Dividend and Interest Exclusions: A Changing Scene," *Taxes* 60 (March 1982): 240, 241.

[46] "Tax reduction voted on interest and dividends," *Wall Street Journal*, February 21, 1980, p. 2.

[47] Ibid.

[48] *The President's Tax Proposals to the Congress for Fairness, Growth, and Simplicity* (May 1985): 130.

corporate income tax because of the low limitation. As an exclusion from income, it also tends to benefit high-bracket taxpayers more than low-bracket taxpayers."[49]

More significant integration efforts fared little better among business representatives during the 1986 Act and beyond. Treasury had initially proposed in 1984 to replace the dividend exclusion with a provision permitting corporations to deduct 50 percent of all dividends paid, which "would have gone a long way toward integrating the taxation of corporations and shareholders."[50] In 1985, when its first proposal failed to get support, Treasury offered a second proposal to provide corporations with a 10 percent dividends-paid deduction.[51] This proposal was included in the House Bill, but was eliminated from the final act.[52] Robert Leonard, the chair of the House Ways and Means Committee, blamed the defeat of the 1984 and 1985 Treasury proposals for a corporate dividend deduction largely on a "lack of enthusiasm in the business community."[53] According to Leonard, this ambivalence was due to a variety of factors, including (1) higher priorities for rate cuts and investment incentives, (2) concern that it would put pressure on managers to distribute profits as dividends, (3) it offered little benefit to growth companies and threatened their tax preferences as part of the package to make integration revenue-neutral, and (4) the difficulty of dealing with foreign shareholders.[54]

Perhaps the most significant structural corporate tax reform in the 1986 Act was the partial repeal of the so-called *General Utilities* doctrine, but this solidified the classical corporate tax rather than pushing it toward integration.[55] In 1935, in *General Utilities and Operating*

---

[49] "Tax Reform Act of 1986," *Report of the Committee on Finance, United States Senate*, 99th Cong., 2nd Sess. (1986): 222; "Tax Reform Bill of 1985," *Report of the Committee on Ways and Means, House of Representatives*, 99th Cong., 1st Sess. (1985): 247.

[50] James S. Eustice *et al.*, *The Tax Reform Act of 1986: Analysis and Commentary* (Boston: Warren, Gorham & Lamont, 1987), pp. 2–63; Treasury Department, *Tax Reform for Fairness, Simplicity, and Economic Growth* (November 27, 1984): 118–19.

[51] *The President's Tax Proposals*, 122.

[52] Eustice *et al.*, *The Tax Reform Act of 1986*, pp. 2–63.

[53] Robert J. Leonard, "A Pragmatic View of Corporate Integration," *Tax Notes* 35 (1987): 889, 895.

[54] Ibid.

[55] In a non-structural reform, the 1986 Act reduced the top corporate rate from 46 percent to 34 percent and reduced the top individual rate to 28 percent, thus inverting the rate structure to tax corporate income higher than individual income for the first time in American history. This situation was quickly reversed, though, when the individual income tax rate was increased to 39.6 percent in 1993.

Co. v. Helvering,[56] the Supreme Court treated a distribution of appreciated property as a nonrecognition event at the entity level. This meant
that if the corporation sold the property, the gain would be taxed once at
the entity level and a second time at the shareholder level upon distribution as a dividend. By contrast, under the *General Utilities* doctrine, if
the corporation first distributed the property as a dividend and then the
shareholders sold it, the only layer of tax would be at the shareholder
level. Over the years, the Internal Revenue Service had, with some
success, attempted to limit the doctrine by characterizing a shareholder
sale in form as a sale by the corporate entity in reality,[57] but Congress
ultimately codified it, broadened it, and enacted several rules that
harmonized the treatment of pre-distribution and post-distribution
sales of appreciated assets.[58] This provided a fairly large exception
permitting the bailout of profits without the imposition of two layers
of tax.

Under the 1986 Act, in one of its "most far-reaching changes" according to the accounting firm Arthur Andersen, Congress required the
recognition of gain on distributions of appreciated property.[59] This
repealed the *General Utilities* doctrine in most respects.[60] According to
the Joint Committee on Taxation's explanation, "the *General Utilities*
rule tended to undermine the corporate income tax" and "could create
significant distortions in business behavior."[61] In light of the repeal of
the dividend exclusion and the defeat of the dividend deduction, plus the
repeal of *General Utilities* and the ability to distribute appreciated property without corporate-level tax, one group of commentators observed
that the 1986 Act effectively "strengthen[ed] the two-tier regime for
taxing corporations and shareholders."[62]

---

[56] 296 US 200 (1935).
[57] Compare *Commissioner v. Court Holding Co.*, 324 US 331 (1945) with *United States v. Cumberland Pub. Serv. Co.*, 338 US 451 (1950).
[58] IRC § 311 (nonliquidating distributions), § 336 (liquidating distributions), § 337 (sales pursuant to a plan of complete liquidation). See Robert J. Peroni, Steven A. Bank, and Glenn E. Coven, *Taxation of Business Enterprises*, 3rd edn. (St. Paul, Minn.: Thomson/West, 2006), pp. 206–07, 359–61, 372.
[59] Arthur Andersen & Co., *Tax Reform 1986: Analysis and Planning* (1986): 99.
[60] It was only a partial repeal because it did not repeal the nonrecognition of losses on the distribution of property under Section 311(a).
[61] Staff of the Joint Committee on Taxation, *General Explanation of the Tax Reform Act of 1986* (1987): 336.
[62] Eustice *et al.*, *The Tax Reform Act of 1986*, pp. 2–63.

A later Treasury proposal, in 1991 during George H. W. Bush's presidency, suffered a similar fate. The proposal, which resulted from the additional investigation mandated as a part of the Tax Reform Act of 1986,[63] opted for dividend exclusion rather than a dividend deduction. According to R. Glenn Hubbard, the deputy assistant secretary for tax policy in 1986 and later the chairman of President George W. Bush's Council of Economic Advisers, "the recommendations in the Treasury Department's corporate integration study . . . have been resisted by some in the business community who would prefer to go the route of investment tax credits."[64]

7.2.2   2003

Soon after the UK passed legislation in the late 1990s to address the problem of excessive dividends, concern about excessive retained earnings in America helped prompt US legislators to revisit this issue early in the twenty-first century. According to US Commerce Department data, pretax profit among US companies more than doubled between 2001 and 2005.[65] During this period, cash and short-term investments skyrocketed.[66] Excluding financial services business,[67] S&P 500 firms retained $260 billion at the end of 1999.[68] By the same point in 2003, that number had almost doubled to just under $500 billion.[69] In percentage terms, cash on hand rose to close to 10 percent for non-financial companies, which was far above the historical average of 6 percent.[70]

---

[63] Section 634 of the Tax Reform Act of 1986 directed Treasury to study the possibility of reforming the taxation of corporate income under Subchapter C and report back to Congress by 1988. This appears to be a reference to the Senate Finance Committee staff's proposal to replace transactional electivity for nonrecognition treatment in reorganizations with a simpler, elective, nonrecognition system to opt for carryover basis treatment. Eustice et al., The Tax Reform Act of 1986, para. 2.08.

[64] Joanna Richardson, "Integration Faces 'Marketing Problem,' Says Treasury's Hubbard," Tax Notes Today 92 (September 23, 1992): 193–8.

[65] "Exxon, Dell, Pfizer, under pressure to spend, may spur economy," Bloomberg.com, August 22, 2005.

[66] Justin Lahart, "Cash-rich firms urged to spend," Wall Street Journal, November 21, 2005, p. C1 (citing Howard Silverblatt, equity market analyst at Standard & Poor's).

[67] Financial companies are excluded because they are required to maintain sizable reserves already.

[68] Jonathan Fuerbringer, "Companies with cash hoards don't necessarily pay it out," New York Times, July 22, 2004, p. 7.

[69] Ibid.

[70] Ibid. (citing Vadim Zlotnikov, chief investment strategist at Sanford C. Bernstein & Company).

Rather than resulting in a corresponding rise in dividends or share repurchases, there was a persistent concern about "disappearing dividends" and "the dividend deficit."[71] The average dividend yield – or the dividends paid as a percent of the stock price – of S&P 500 companies declined from 5.9 percent in 1940 to 1.1 percent in 2000, which one commentator described as "the lowest number since statistics were first collected in 1825."[72] While another commentator conceded that "dividends have been falling steadily since the 1950s,"[73] it was clear that "during the great bull market of the 1990s, dividends fell out of favor."[74] The dividend yield dropped "at the fairly constant rate of 2.5 basis points per year throughout the decade" from 1990 to 2000.[75] In fact, between 2000 and 2002, S&P 500 companies reportedly paid out 3.3 percent less in dividends, which amounted to "the largest decline since 1951" and combined with a 2.5 percent drop in 2000, "marked the first back-to-back dividend declines since 1970 and 1971."[76] Moreover, for the first time more than 25 percent of the S&P 500 firms paid no dividend at all in 2001.[77]

There was a significant outcry in the press and among academics for action in the tax arena to address the issue of burgeoning retained earnings and declining dividends. James Glassman of the *Washington Post* reported that "dividends are getting more scarce" and blamed this on heavy dividend taxation: "Double taxation encourages companies to hold on to most of what they earn, whether the companies really need the money or not."[78] Similarly, Wharton professor Jeremy Siegel wrote that "our tax system has played a crucial role ... [in contributing] to the sharp fall in the dividend yield."[79] According to the *Wall Street Journal*, "[t]here is, however, one big problem with dividends: The government taxes them twice ... Little wonder then that over the past decade or so, as investors become more sensitive to taxes, they start rewarding companies for retaining earnings instead of paying out dividends."[80]

---

[71] Steve Stein, "Taxes, Dividends, and Distortions," *Policy Review*, June–July 2002, p. 60; Jeremy Siegel, "The dividend deficit," *Wall Street Journal*, February 13, 2002, p. A20.
[72] James Glassman, "Liberate the Dividend," *The American Enterprise*, September 2002, p. 13; Siegel, "The dividend deficit," p. A20.
[73] Stein, "Taxes, Dividends, and Distortions," p. 60.
[74] Siegel, "The dividend deficit," p. A20.
[75] Stein, "Taxes, Dividends, and Distortions," p. 60.
[76] "Dividends of S&P companies shrink the most in five decades," *St. Louis Post-Dispatch*, January 9, 2002, p. C1.
[77] James K. Glassman, "Numbers you can trust," *Washington Post*, February 10, 2002, p. H1.
[78] Ibid.   [79] Siegel, "The dividend deficit," p. A20.
[80] Editorial, "Bring back dividends," *Wall Street Journal Online*, August 6, 2002.

Commentators opined that dividends would flow more freely if double taxation were removed. Thus, Siegel, along with economists Paul Gompers and Andrew Metrick, advised that "at the top of [Bush's] agenda should be the elimination of one of the most detrimental taxes in our economy – the corporate dividend tax. The sharp decline in cash dividends on common stocks over the past decade has been the major cause of the woes bedeviling the stock market."[81] Law professor Edward McCaffery went a step further, suggesting that "if we repealed the corporate income tax . . . [c]orporations would no longer have an excuse for growing large, or an incentive for hiding their gains from everyone to avoid taxation. They could instead pay dividends."[82]

On the heels of this controversy over retained earnings, President Bush announced in January of 2003 a proposal to eliminate the double taxation of corporate income.[83] Under his proposal, income would be subject to the corporate income tax as under the current regime, but dividends on that income would be exempt from the shareholder income tax. The Bush proposal was largely motivated by the perception that corporations were unnecessarily retaining earnings due to the tax disincentive for dividends and that this was harming the economy.[84] According to Treasury's Blue Book on Integration, which was released in connection with the Bush announcement, "double taxation of corporate profits encourages a corporation to retain its earnings rather than distribute them in the form of dividends."[85] Treasury explained that "[t]his lessens the pressure on corporate managers to undertake only the most productive investments because corporate investments funded by retained earnings may receive less scrutiny than investments funded by outside equity or debt financing."[86] Moreover, some asserted that reducing the bias against dividends would help prevent the corporate scandals of the 1990s. As one chief executive said "you need real cash to pay dividends. You can't pay them with Tyco or Enron accounting."[87]

---

[81] Paul Gompers, Andrew Metrick, and Jeremy Siegel, "This tax cut will pay dividends," *Wall Street Journal*, August 13, 2002, p. A20.

[82] Edward J. McCaffery, "Remove a major incentive to cheat," *Wall Street Journal*, July 9, 2002, p. B2.

[83] White House News Release, "President Bush Taking Action to Strengthen America's Economy," January 7, 2003.

[84] Stein, "Taxes, Dividends, and Distortions," p. 59.

[85] See U.S. Treasury, Blue Book on Integration 1 (2003), *available at* http://www.ustreas. gov/press/releases/docs/bluebook.pdf (visited on January 11, 2003).

[86] Ibid.

[87] David Leonhardt and Claudia H. Deutsch, "Few officials at companies expect surge in dividends," *Nytimes.com*, January 8, 2003.

Senator Don Nickles stated in introducing the President's proposal that "[p]resent law encourages a lot of corporate shenanigans and corporate games trying to get around taxes."[88] The Council of Economic Advisers concluded that the President's proposal might resolve this issue by increasing the percentage of corporate profits paid out as dividends by as many as four percentage points.[89]

Much like during the period after World War II, the President's proposal was rejected in favor of more modest integration of the corporate and shareholder income taxes. Under the Jobs and Growth Tax Reconciliation Act of 2003, "qualified dividend income" was taxed at the same rate as capital gains.[90] Dividend income was considered qualified if it came from a taxable domestic corporation and if the recipient had held the corporation's shares upon which the dividend was paid for at least sixty days prior to the ex-dividend date.[91] This relief fell far short of the original proposal to eliminate the second layer of tax altogether. Nonetheless, it was not insubstantial. When coupled with the reduction of the maximum capital gains rate from 20 to 15 percent, the nominal tax rate on dividends was cut by more than half for taxpayers subject to the top individual rates. The problem was that the dividend tax cut was only adopted on a temporary basis.

Under the terms of the legislation, the dividend tax cut was initially set to expire on December 31, 2008.[92] In 2006, this date was extended two years until December 31, 2010 and in 2010 it was extended an additional two years until December 31, 2012. This kind of a sunset provision for tax legislation was developed to get around the so-called "Byrd Rule."[93] During the early 1990s, there was a heightened concern at the growing Federal deficits. Tax legislation was scored for its revenue effects to ensure that any revenue losses would be offset with sufficient revenue gains to be considered deficit-neutral. To minimize the apparent revenue losses associated with tax cuts, legislators would push the losses to future years even as Congress progressively widened the budget windows against which these tax provisions were evaluated. The Byrd Rule was adopted to inhibit the ability of Congress to play games with deficit projections.[94] Under the Rule, senators may object to consideration of

---

[88] *Cong. Rec.*, February 27, 2003, at S2922.
[89] See "Council of Economic Advisers Briefing Paper on Dividend Tax Cut," 2003 *Tax Notes Today* 5–27 (citing a 1992 Treasury study on integration).
[90] IRC § 1(h)(11).   [91] Ibid.   [92] Ibid.
[93] Named after its author Senator Robert Byrd (D–W.Va.).
[94] Elizabeth Garrett, "Accounting for the Federal Budget and its Reform," *Harvard Journal on Legislation* 41 (2004): 187, 194.

reconciliation bills (which include most tax bills) that would increase the deficit in the years outside the budget window.[95] It takes a vote of at least sixty senators to waive the objection and continue with the reconciliation process.[96] Thus, while a bare majority is necessary to pass the tax legislation in the first instance, a supermajority is required to make it permanent. Since Bush did not have the votes to make even the watered-down integration measure permanent, he settled for one that expired within the budget window.

In addition to the budget concerns, which particularly affected several Republican "deficit hawk" congressmen,[97] the reason Bush's proposal fell short of the full and permanent integration it initially sought is a lack of support from business groups. According to Martin Sullivan, politicians were "getting word from a wide variety of business interests that a dividend exclusion is not what they – after being shut out of the big tax cuts enacted in 2001 – had in mind as the long-awaited tax cut for businesses."[98] Although there were "pockets of support" for Bush's proposed dividend exclusion from firms in high dividend-paying industries, members of the high technology industry, where there were many firms that paid no dividends, were "privately vowing to fight the proposal."[99] The *Washington Post* called it "an unwelcome bucket of worms for many major technology companies," reporting that "several industry lobbyists in Washington vowed a congressional fight. They say the measure offers little to stimulate corporate technology spending that is essential for the industry to pull itself out of a deep swoon that is in its third year."[100] Technology companies and their investors preferred entity-level tax breaks. One hedge fund manager who specialized in technology companies penned an opinion piece in the *Wall Street Journal*, titled "I Hate Dividends," where he complained that dividends were a sign of "no-growth companies" and their stocks should be treated as "wearing a scarlet dollar sign."[101] Perhaps to signal this bias against dividends, a proposal to start paying dividends at Cisco was voted down by shareholders at the company's annual meeting and many technology companies announced soon after the introduction of Bush's integration

[95] Ibid.   [96] Ibid.
[97] Shailagh Murray and John D. McKinnon, "Democrats' confidence grows about shrinking Bush tax cut," *Wall Street Journal*, March 3, 2002.
[98] Sullivan, "Dividend Déjà vu," p. 645.   [99] Ibid., pp. 645, 646.
[100] Jonathan Krim, "Tech companies see Bush plan on dividends as troublesome," *Washington Post*, January 8, 2003, p. E1.
[101] Andy Kessler, "I hate dividends," *Wall Street Journal Online*, December 30, 2002.

proposal that they would continue to retain earnings rather than start paying dividends.[102]

Furthermore, although technology companies were the most vocal critics of the push for integration, there were signs that the proposal might be crowded out by other business priorities. For example, the US Chamber of Commerce, which publicly supported the dividend tax relief proposal, conceded that the group thought that cuts in the marginal tax-rate for individuals were a higher priority because of the need for a boost in consumer spending.[103] Similarly, the *Los Angeles Times* reported that "the National Assn. of Manufacturers were sorely disappointed that the Bush tax plan did not include expansion of tax breaks for business investment in plants and other capital equipment."[104] Even apart from the possibility that dividend tax relief would crowd out other legislative priorities, business lobbyists expressed concern that Bush's initial proposal to exempt dividends from tax if the company had paid tax on the underlying income "could diminish the value of popular tax preferences, such as those for capital investments and research-and-development expenses that business has fought hard to protect."[105] The logic behind this objection was that "companies that use other methods to avoid paying federal income taxes would discover that they had also eliminated the right of their shareholders to get tax breaks."[106]

The administration was only able to swing "the fractious business community into line ... or at least drive[] any dissent underground," by "[u]sing a reputation for playing hardball."[107] One senior administration official conceded that in the face of "mounting political problems, Republicans have ratcheted up pressure on business groups to fall in line."[108] As part of that pressure, two technology trade groups – the

---

[102] "Ending double tax trouble," *Wall Street Journal Online*, December 26, 2002; Leonhardt and Deutsch, "Few officials at companies expect surge in dividends."

[103] Brett Ferguson, "US Chamber Favors Consumer Tax Cuts Over Corporate Breaks to Stimulate Growth," *BNA Daily Tax Report*, December 12, 2002, p. G-8.

[104] Janet Hook, "Bush plan to end dividend tax in for changes," *Los Angeles Times*, February 2, 2003, p. A30.

[105] Greg Hitt and John D. McKinnon, "Business fears dividend plan could hurt other tax breaks," *Wall Street Journal Online*, January 17, 2003.

[106] Floyd Norris, "Bush's plan taxes certain dividends, fine print reveals," *New York Times*, January 9, 2003, p. A1.

[107] Jonathan Weisman, "Bush wins business support for growth plan," *Washington Post*, February 20, 2003, at E1.

[108] Jonathan Weisman and Mike Allen, "Bush seeks to enlist economists' support; growth plan has gathered considerable opposition," *Washington Post*, January 22, 2003, p. A7.

American Electronics Association and the Information Technology Association of America – were reportedly "being punished by the Bush White House for public criticism of the Bush plan and for shopping alternatives to the dividend exclusion on Capitol Hill."[109] Business groups were also told that "the Republican Congress would consider additional special-interest tax provisions as long as the groups seeking them were on Bush's team."[110] Grover Norquist, often considered a shadow member of the Bush White House for tax issues, stated this more ominously, threatening opponents that "[i]f what people remember about you is that you are not helpful, you are probably not going to be first in line when we do the next tax bill."[111] This led Representative Robert Matsui, a Democrat from California, to complain that "the White House is basically intimidating [business lobbyists]. It's just very rough tactics being used."[112] As one lobbyist said, "this White House has made it clear that you're either with us on the plan or you're not ... If you're with us, we'll work with you on your concerns. And if it's the opposite, then the message is that you will not be in the tent. There will not be other concerns."[113]

7.3   Convergence?

In light of the growth of multinational corporations and the internationalization of commerce, an inevitable question in any comparative study of corporate law and regulation, including one involving corporate tax law, is whether national differences are breaking down and convergence is imminent. In many respects, the 1997 and 1999 reforms in the UK and the 2003 reform in the USA suggest this could already be occurring. Due to their respective reforms, the two countries each have hybrid systems that offer some partial relief from double taxation, but retain a basic two-tiered tax structure. As described earlier, though, developments in both countries cast doubt on the durability of these reforms. Moreover, it is not clear whether this is real convergence or whether they are merely passing each other temporarily on the way to entirely opposite destinations, with the USA heading toward an integrated system and the UK

---

[109] Sullivan, "Dividend *Déjà vu*," p. 646.
[110] Weisman, "Bush wins business support for growth plan," p. E1.   [111] Ibid.
[112] Patti Mohr and Warren Rojas, "Interest Groups Test Bush Idea of 'Single Tax' on Dividends," *Tax Notes* 98 (March 10, 2003): 1471, 1474.
[113] Ibid.

heading toward a classical double tax system. Nevertheless, the growing importance of the European Court of Justice ("ECJ") to the UK, and indirectly the USA, as well as the general competitive pressure of the global arena, may soon take the issue of direction out of both countries' hands and make convergence inevitable.

Recently, Professor Reuven Avi-Yonah has surveyed the corporate tax schemes in OECD countries and elsewhere and concluded that "a significant degree of convergence" has already emerged.[114] In 1980, according to Avi-Yonah, OECD countries could be divided into three camps:

(1) The classical system of double taxation in place in the USA and a few other countries;
(2) A fully or partially integrated system using the shareholder imputation method; or
(3) A fully or partially integrated system using the dividend exemption method.[115]

The classical system countries, including the USA, have moved toward some measure of integration, while the countries having an integrated system have moved from an imputation approach to a dividend exemption approach. The decision of the USA to tax dividends at the lower capital gains rate is a form of partial dividend exemption. Avi-Yonah explains this convergence as a function of the globalization of the modern economy. "As long as most shareholders are domestic, countries were free to adopt or reject integration for domestic companies with domestic shareholders. However, once portfolio investments became globalized, countries had to deal with their own residents becoming shareholders in foreign corporations and foreign residents becoming shareholders in their corporations."[116] The pure classical system disfavored this cross-border investment by subjecting it to double taxation, while the imputation system was problematic because it required a country either to provide credits to foreign shareholders or to discriminate against them in violation of European Union rules.[117]

Mihir Desai, characterizing this globalization process as the "decentering" of the modern business corporation, has noted that "[t]he archetypal firm with a particularly national identity and a corporate

---

[114] Reuven S. Avi-Yonah, "Tax Convergence and Globalization" (July 8, 2010). U of Michigan Law & Econ, Empirical Legal Studies Center Paper No. 10–019, available at SSRN: http://ssrn.com/abstract=1636299.
[115] Ibid.   [116] Ibid. at 4.   [117] Ibid.

headquarters fixed in one country is becoming obsolete as firms continue to maximize opportunities created by global markets."[118] According to Desai, "[t]he defining characteristics of what made a firm belong to a country – where it was incorporated, where it was listed, the nationality of its investor base, the location of its headquarters functions – are no longer unified nor are they bound to one country."[119]

The breakdown of national affiliation is particularly problematic in the case of global technology companies where the primary asset and source of income is intellectual property that may be easily shifted to tax-friendly locations. This helps explain the rise of Ireland, where the low 12.5 percent corporate income tax rate allowed it to attract major corporations and become a center of high technology jobs in Europe.[120] At the same time, however, the ability to manipulate the legal definition of home, especially in light of differing national standards, plus lax transfer pricing rules, helps explain the rise of the "Double Irish" or "Dutch Sandwich" scheme that helps companies avoid even Ireland's low corporate tax rate.[121] Reportedly used or contemplated by a number of American-identified companies such as Google, Facebook, and Microsoft, the "Double Irish" involves the creation of two Irish companies, one of which has its "effective centre of management" in Bermuda or some other tax haven jurisdiction. The Bermuda-based company pays a relatively low fee to the parent company for a license containing the right to sublicense its intellectual property to the Irish-based subsidiary, which uses it in the sale of products outside the USA. The Bermuda-based company is an Irish company for US purposes, which presumably aids in the approval of the transfer pricing arrangement because of the presence of a USA–Ireland tax treaty, but is a Bermuda company for Irish purposes,[122] which allows it to avoid Irish taxes. This arrangement leaves the American parent with little income in

---

[118] Mihir A. Desai, "The Decentering of the Global Firm," in *The World Economy* (Oxford: Blackwell Publishing, 2009), pp. 1271–2.

[119] Ibid., p. 1272.

[120] Frank Barry, "Tax Policy, FDI and the Irish Economic Boom of the 1990s," *Economic Analysis & Policy* 33 (2003): 221, 222–3.

[121] For a description of the Double Irish scheme, see Jesse Drucker, "Google 2.4% rate shows how $60 billion lost to tax loopholes," *Bloomberg.com*, October 21, 2010; Joseph B. Darby and Kelsey Lemaster, "Double Irish More Than Doubles the Tax Savings," *Practical US/International Tax Strategies* 11 (2007): 2, 12–14.

[122] While the USA uses legal incorporation as the standard, Ireland bases tax residency on where a corporation is managed and controlled. Darby and Lemaster, "Double Irish More Than Doubles the Tax Savings," 13.

the USA because of the low transfer fee, and the Irish-based subsidiary with no net income in Ireland because the royalty payment cancels out its income. To avoid Irish withholding taxes on the payment from the Irish subsidiary to the Bermuda-based Irish subsidiary, the money is funneled through a Dutch firm that qualifies for the exemption available to payments to companies within the European Union. The result is that there is no revenue in Ireland and virtually all of the income is sourced to Bermuda, which has no corporate tax. The parent company is headquartered in the United States, the work is largely performed in Ireland, the license is owned in Bermuda by a company incorporated in Ireland, and the income is taxed nowhere until repatriated to the USA. Effectively, this example demonstrates that the ease in moving corporate assets and the malleability in the definition of legal home, combined with a few tax-friendly jurisdictions, makes it increasingly difficult for countries to maintain the integrity of their separate corporate tax systems except for purely domestic corporations.

This problem of the increasing globalization of business in a world with divergent national corporate tax systems has caused the European Union and other international bodies to respond. Although no treaty provides the EU with authority to interfere with individual Member States' domestic corporate tax schemes, a variety of directives have been advanced "to minimise corporate tax factors as an obstacle to doing business in the Single Market."[123] For example, prompted by the European Community Treaty's guarantee of "free movement of goods, persons, services, and capital," and the provision for nondiscrimination based on nationality,[124] the ECJ prohibited providing domestic individuals and products with more favorable tax treatment than foreign individuals and taxpayers.[125] This same principle was applied in the EU's so-called "Parent/Subsidiary Directive," which focused on outlawing the double taxation of dividends paid by a subsidiary of one member state to its parent company located in another member state.[126] Indeed, the ECJ had decided "more than a hundred cases involving Member States' income tax systems" as of 2007.[127] As a result, Michael Graetz and

[123] Alistair Craig, *EU Law and British Tax: Which Comes First?* (London: The Chameleon Press, 2003), p. 11.
[124] Single European Act Arts. 12–13, February 17, 1986, 1987 OJ (L 169) 1.
[125] Michael J. Graetz and Alvin C. Warren, Jr., "Income Tax Discrimination and the Political and Economic Integration of Europe," *Yale Law Journal* 115 (2006): 1186, 1198–9.
[126] Craig, *EU Law and British Tax*, p. 13.
[127] Michael J. Graetz and Alvin C. Warren, Jr., "Dividend Taxation in Europe: When the ECJ Makes Tax Policy," *Common Market Law Review* 44 (2007): 1577.

Alvin Warren concluded that "the Court has become deeply enmeshed in fashioning the Member States' income tax policies."[128]

In large part, the UK's 1997 and 1999 reforms to the shareholder dividend credit under the imputation system were influenced by the growing influence of the ECJ. The UK had systematically discriminated against foreign individuals through its imputation scheme and had institutionalized that arrangement as far back as the 1975 United Kingdom–United States Double Taxation Convention, in which it agreed to grant the shareholder credit to US investors, less a 15 percent deduction of the dividend and tax credit.[129] Although no specific ruling addressed the UK system, government officials saw the writing on the wall. Within a few years, in *Verkooijen*, the ECJ struck down a Dutch imputation arrangement similar to the one in place in the UK.[130] As Peter Harris and David Oliver observed, "it was the nail in the coffin of the standard European imputation system, which usually provided relief from economic double taxation of domestic dividends, but not foreign dividends."[131]

Some have suggested that the ECJ's formal intervention in Member State corporate tax policies will ultimately lead to the development of a European corporate income tax. In 2003, *The Times* reported that "Britain is losing control of its corporate tax base as tracts of company tax law are overturned by the European Court of Justice" and a study by the Centre for Policy Studies concluded that "Britain, and the other Member States of the EU, have lost effective control over how they set their corporation tax laws."[132] In subsequent years, the ECJ has continued to issue a number of rulings that have resulted in changes or proposals for changes to British corporate tax policy, with little sign of a slowdown.[133]

---

[128] Ibid., 1578.

[129] Malcolm Gammie, "UK Imputation, Past, Present and Future," *Bulletin for International Fiscal Documentation* 52 (1998): 429, 433.

[130] *Staatssecretaris van Financiën* v. *BGM Verkooijen*, 2000 ECR I–4071.

[131] Peter Harris and David Oliver, *International Commercial Tax* (Cambridge University Press, 2010), p. 294.

[132] Gary Duncan, "Chancellor accused of losing control of corporate tax to EU," *The Times* (London), December 5, 2003, p. 41; Craig, *EU Law and British Tax*, p. 11.

[133] See, e.g., Gabriel Rozenberg, "Corporate tax review eyes return of pound," *The Times* (London), June 22, 2007, p. 62 (describing proposal groups with foreign operations in countries with lower corporate tax rates for exemption from a separate dividend tax upon repatriation to Britain).

Beyond the ad hoc ECJ intrusions into British corporate tax policy, in recent years there have been a variety of direct efforts to more formally harmonize European corporate tax systems.[134] Initially, those efforts were focused on rates. After a few attempts to directly legislate corporate tax harmonization, the European Commission issued a draft Directive in 1970 proposing "closer alignment of corporate tax rates across the Member States at levels between 45% and 55%."[135] A similar proposal was made in 1992 when the European Commission's Report of the Committee of Independent Experts on Company Taxation "recommended the harmonization of corporate tax rates between 30% and 40% across the EU."[136]

Although neither effort to harmonize rates was successful, the European Commission has promulgated a number of mechanisms, ostensibly designed to ensure that individual corporate tax systems do not interfere with the smooth functioning of the Single Market, but arguably operating to reduce much of the individual non-rate variation among the Member States. These included the Parent/Subsidiary Directive described above, the Mergers Directive which helped facilitate mergers and reorganizations, and the Arbitration Procedure Convention in which disputes over the taxation of profits earned by related companies in different Member States were settled according to EU arbitration procedures.[137] These measures are relatively modest intrusions on national sovereignty that were widely accepted as helpful to business, but indirectly they help push the Member States closer to a common European corporate tax.

A much more direct harmonization mechanism is the Code of Conduct on Business Taxation, which was first proposed in 1997 and eventually adopted in 2003. Through intensive and prolonged negotiations, the Member States agreed to abolish or limit a number of harmful tax incentives or benefits offered by individual Member States. Although none of the identified tax incentives were present in the UK corporate tax, there is significant potential that the Code will be extended even more broadly in the future. A House of Lords Select Committee Report cited just this risk when it noted "[w]e remain unclear about the implications for the United Kingdom of having agreed to this Code, in particular in relation to national sovereignty and to the principle of unanimity in tax matters ... There remains the risk that the process

---

[134] Charles E. McLure, Jr., "Harmonizing Corporate Income Taxes in the European Community: Rationale and Implications," *Tax Policy & Economics* 22 (2008): 151, 152.
[135] Craig, *EU Law and British Tax*, p. 12.   [136] Ibid., p. 14.   [137] Ibid., pp. 12–13.

could lead to the UK being obliged – in practice if not in law – to adopt tax measures damaging to the interests of the economy or its citizens."[138] One particular concern, expressed by Conservative commentator Alistair Craig, is that the Code could interfere with a British government interested in cutting taxes in a way to induce investment, although there is no precedent for this in other countries.[139]

The European Commission went one step further when it proposed to create a "common consolidated corporate tax base" in Europe. The proposal emerges from concerns that multinational corporations can evade taxes by shifting profits to lower-tax countries and countries are ill-equipped to combat this through transfer-pricing conventions. The common consolidated corporate tax base would use a formulary apportionment system to allocate income from multinational corporations to Member States based on the employees, payroll, sales, and/or assets in the jurisdiction.[140] Such a system is already in place in the USA and Canada to deal with allocating corporate income among the various states and provinces, respectively. The problem, however, is agreeing upon a common corporate tax base for such a system, which would mean each Member State having to relinquish a measure of autonomy over the creation of its corporate tax provisions. This also requires each Member State to agree to such a base under the unanimity principle, which is difficult and has delayed the process considerably. One study warned that British business "would face a higher tax burden, as part of the harmonization of corporate business," costing them as much as £4 billion per year.[141] *The Times* advised that "[i]f Britain really wants to resist a common tax policy, it would need to take an alternative initiative. One might be to encourage EU tax experts to draw up unofficial model rules that evolve with time and that member states can use as a default where they have no different national priority. Otherwise, the Commission's siege engines will roll on."[142]

The European Commission has used several of these mechanisms to pressure Member States when their corporate tax systems deviate too

---

[138] Ibid., p. 16 (quoting House of Lords Select Committee, *Taxes in the EU – Can Coordination and Competition Coexist?*, HMSO July 1999).

[139] Craig, *EU Law and British Tax*, p. 16.

[140] Leon Betterndorf et al., "Corporate Tax Harmonization in Europe," *Economic Policy* (July 2010): 539.

[141] Elizabeth Judge, "Single European tax could cost UK business £4 bn, academics warn," *The Times* (London), May 3, 2007, p. 55.

[142] Graham Searjeant, "EU has company tax in its sights," *The Times* (London), December 16, 2005, p. 61.

substantially from the norm. This is particularly evidenced by the experience with Ireland. The country has a long experience with reducing its corporate tax rate in an attempt to attract foreign direct investment, dating back to the late 1950s.[143] At one point, the country completely exempted from tax income from manufactured exports, but this was phased out starting in 1978 and ultimately replaced in 1980 with a 10 percent rate for the manufacturing industry. This special rate was later extended to cover activities at the International Financial Services Centre in Dublin and in a tax-free zone surrounding Shannon airport, but the prevailing rate for companies not covered by any of those exceptions remained at 32 percent.[144] Eventually, this special rate came under scrutiny by the European Commission, which pressured Ireland to raise it to a rate "much closer to the EU average."[145] Moreover, the EU alleged that the disparate treatment of domestic and foreign manufacturers violated the Code of Conduct on Business Taxation and the OECD's "Guidelines on Harmful Preferential Tax Regimes."[146] In response to this EU pressure both on the level of its rates and on its non-uniform application, Ireland eventually agreed in 1998 to raise its manufacturing rate to 12.5 percent and to extend it to all corporations, effective starting in 2003.[147] The 2010 EU bailout of the Irish government led to renewed calls for an increase in Ireland's corporate tax rate.[148]

Although the USA is not subject to the jurisdiction of the European Commission, this does not mean that its system of business taxation has entirely escaped the scrutiny of international groups. An example of this, albeit one not strictly limited to corporate taxation, is the World Trade Organization's intervention regarding the USA's extraterritorial income exclusion and foreign sales corporation provisions.[149] The foreign sales

---

[143] Barry, "Tax Policy, FDI and the Irish Economic Boom," 221, 223.

[144] Sheila Killian, "Where's the Harm in Tax Competition? Lessons from US Multinationals in Ireland," *Critical Perspectives on Accounting* 17 (2006): 1067, 1075.

[145] Barry, "Tax Policy, FDI and the Irish Economic Boom," 223.

[146] Killian, "Where's the Harm in Tax Competition?," 1075.

[147] Barry, "Tax Policy, FDI and the Irish Economic Boom," 223.

[148] Paul Taylor, "Analysis: Ireland's corporate tax in dispute in EU rescue," *Reuters*, November 19, 2010, available at http://www.reuters.com/article/idUSTRE6AI3HN20101119 (last visited December 18, 2010).

[149] For more description of the background to these provisions and the WTO and preceding interventions, see Testimony of Barbara Angus, International Tax Counsel, United States Department of Treasury before the House Committee on Ways and Means on the WTO Decision Regarding the Extraterritorial Income Exclusion Provisions (February 27, 2002); Charles I. Kingson, "The Great American Jobs Act Caper," *Tax Law Review* 58 (2005): 327, 329–31.

corporation provision, which was enacted in 1984, exempted from US tax part of the income earned on products sold abroad by foreign subsidiaries of US manufacturers. These provisions were enacted to resolve a prior dispute under the General Agreement on Tariffs and Trade (GATT) regarding the European Union's protest of the USA's domestic international sales corporation provisions. A little over a decade later, the EU levied a similar challenge against the foreign sales corporation before a dispute resolution panel of the successor to GATT, the World Trade Organization (WTO), and the WTO upheld the challenge. To respond to this ruling, the USA enacted the FSC Repeal and Extraterritorial Income Exclusion Act in 2000. Adopting the extraterritorial income exclusion as a replacement for the foreign sales corporation, this provision applied to all sales and leases by foreign subsidiaries, regardless of where the products were manufactured, so long as the manufacturer agreed to be subject to the taxing authority of the USA. This was again challenged by the EU in 2001 as an illegal export subsidy, leading the WTO to rule against the USA. After a protracted battle, the USA repealed the exclusion of income for exporters and adopted a deduction for domestic manufacturers under the American Jobs Creation Act of 2004. As "compensation" for the loss of the export subsidy, Congress "slightly reduced the corporate tax rate on *all* goods manufactured in the United States."[150]

Even outside of formal government intervention, there is evidence that the global business community is increasingly pressuring both the UK and the USA to reform their corporate tax systems. This is most apparent in the pressure to reduce corporate tax rates. Although the UK corporate tax rate had dropped two percentage points as part of the late 1990s reforms, there was soon agitation to lower it even further. In 2006, the British Chambers of Commerce cited the fact that the UK's corporate tax rate, which was once the ninth lowest among OECD countries, had dropped to the sixteenth lowest, claiming that "our current rate threatens to harm business competitiveness."[151] The British Institute of Directors "called for the main rate of corporation tax to be cut to 28 per cent," noting that "if we are to remain competitive, we must act now,"[152] while

[150] Kingson, "The Great American Jobs Act Caper," 330.
[151] Gary Duncan, "Chancellor told to cut Corporation Tax," *The Times* (London), March 10, 2006, p. 56.
[152] Ibid.

the CBI claimed that "the present corporation tax rate was 'unsustainable' because it was much higher than those of European competitors" and claimed that "a trickle of companies is relocating and our worry is that it might turn into a flood."[153] Even after the rate was cut to 28 percent, the CBI pushed for an additional drop in rates to 18 percent by 2016.[154] With the change to a Conservative government in 2010, new Chancellor George Osborne announced plans to reduce the Corporation Tax rate to 24 percent as of 2015.[155] This would be the lowest rate since 1965.[156]

Not only has the nominal UK corporate tax rate declined in recent years, but the effective rate has dropped as well. In October 2010, the Trades Union Congress released a report describing several "worrying trends,"[157] including a decline in the effective corporate tax rate from just below 28 percent in 2000 when the statutory rate was 30 percent to 23 percent in 2009 when the statutory rate had only dropped to 28 percent.[158] With the statutory rate dropping from 28 percent to 24 percent by 2015, the TUC predicted that large companies would pay an effective corporate tax rate of only 17 percent by 2014, which would be higher than the rate paid by small companies and the majority of UK households.[159] According to the TUC, this will mean that for the first time there will be "a regressive UK corporation tax system."[160]

There are countervailing trends on the British corporate tax rate, but they may apply throughout Europe. Starting in 2011, a controversial new bank levy will be imposed that negates some of the benefit of the reduction of the corporate tax in that industry.[161] Moreover, outside the context of the Corporation Tax rate itself, the budgetary fallout from the financial crisis led to hikes in income tax rates for individuals that

---

[153] Christine Buckley, "Cut tax or lose more business, says CBI," *The Times* (London), October 10, 2006, p. 52.

[154] Christine Buckley, "Employers and unions lobby over corporate tax rates and non doms," *The Times* (London), March 10, 2008, p. 44.

[155] Suzy Jagger, "Corporation Tax cuts make us global players, say business leaders," *The Times* (London), June 23, 2010, p. 14.

[156] Suzy Jagger, "Corporate tax will be the lowest in G20, Osborne promises CBI," *The Times* (London), May 20, 2010, p. 39.

[157] Richard Murphy, "The Corporate Tax Gap," Trades Union Congress, October 2010, at 2.

[158] Ibid. at 12.   [159] Ibid. at 13–14.   [160] Ibid. at 14.

[161] Jill Treanor, "Bank levy to raise £2.5bn a year, but bigger banks could still gain," *Guardian.co.uk*, October 21, 2010.

spurred a burst of dividend payments prior to the effective date.[162] It is possible that these budgetary pressures will cause the UK to follow suit in the corporate income tax, but such concerns are likely to be at least equally applicable in other debt-laden European nations such as Ireland. That may cause a general reversal of the trend toward corporate-tax rate reductions.

The competitive pressure to harmonize corporate tax rates extends well beyond Europe to include both the USA and Japan. The two countries have the highest corporate tax rate among OECD countries, with the USA's combined federal and state effective rate of 39.2 percent placing it 13.7 percentage points ahead of the OECD average.[163] Japan's effective corporate tax rate of 41 percent is even higher than the American rate, reportedly contributing to the departure of many Japanese manufacturing corporations to lower-tax jurisdictions.[164] Moreover, the gap between these two countries and the rest of the pack has grown with recent rate reductions in Germany, Italy, Spain, and twenty-five other developed nations since 2001.[165] To counter such corporate-tax rate cuts and increase the general competitiveness of business, the Japanese government has already announced plans to reduce its corporate tax rate by five percentage points. Concern about a growing deficit may cause Japan to scale back the size of its proposed rate reduction,[166] but given South Korea's plans to reduce its already very low corporate tax rate to 20 percent,[167] the pressure will continue for further rate cuts in Japan. This could jump-start efforts to mount a similar campaign for a corporate-tax rate reduction in the USA. The effective rate for American corporations is much lower than its statutory rate, but it was still estimated to be 27.9 percent in 2009, which is the third highest among OECD countries.[168] A number of US government reports have been released that have highlighted this problem and even

---

[162] Grainne Gilmore, "Taxman will be deprived of millions of pounds in the great dividend payout," *The Times* (London), February 12, 2010, p. 58.

[163] Peter R. Merrill, "Corporate Tax Policy for the 21st Century," *National Tax Journal* 63 (December 2010): 623, 624.

[164] "Leaving Home; Japanese Manufacturers," *The Economist* online, November 20, 2010.

[165] "We're Number One, alas," *Wall Street Journal*, July 13, 2007, p. A12.

[166] Kyoko Shimodoi, "Japan may scale back 5% point corporate tax cut plan," *Bloomberg Businessweek* online, December 2, 2010.

[167] Cho Jin-seo, "Tax cut initiative to reveal MB's true colors," *Korea Times*, November 16, 2010.

[168] Merrill, "Corporate Tax Policy for the 21st Century," 624.

President Barack Obama signaled some willingness to consider lowering the corporate tax rate.[169]

All of these formal and informal external pressures on both the UK and the USA could call into question whether the three dominant themes in corporate tax reform over the last century – profits, power, and politics – will continue to be relevant. On one hand, many of the most recent developments simply reflect domestic political changes and the ups and downs of each country's underlying economic condition. Moreover, it is not as if multinational corporations and foreign investment are completely new phenomena. The pressure to harmonize has been around for years and yet national differences remain. On the other hand, globalization is a powerful unifying force and has certainly influenced both the state of the global economy and the nature of the corporation. With the growth of dominant regional groups such as the European Commission, domestic politics could also soon succumb to the harmonization movement. It may simply be a matter of time, therefore, before the concept of a developing Anglo-American corporate income tax is taken over by a European corporate income tax or an OECD corporate income tax.

---

[169] Jane G. Gravelle and Thomas L. Hungerford, *Corporate Tax Reform: Issues for Congress* (Congressional Research Service Report for Congress, April 6, 2010); US Department of the Treasury, *Treasury Conference on Business Taxation and Global Competitiveness* (Background Paper, July 23, 2007); Congressional Budget Office, *Corporate Income Tax Rates: International Comparisons* (Comparisons (November 2005); John D. McKinnon, "Obama: corporate tax rate cut could be 'Win-Win'," *Wall Street Journal online*, October 4, 2010.

INDEX